ROLE OF INFORMATION AND COMMUNICATION TECHNOLOGY IN WOMEN EMPOWERMENT

ROLE OF INFORMATION AND COMMUNICATION TECHNOLOGY IN WOMEN EMPOWERMENT

Shikha Mathur Kumar

KALPAZ

ISBN: 978-93-5128-011-8

Price: ₹ 910

First Published, 2014

Published by

Kalpaz Publications
C-30, Satyawati Nagar,
Delhi - 110052
E-mail: kalpaz@hotmail.com

Laser Typesetting: Rajender Vashist, Delhi
Printed at: G. Print Process, Delhi

Cataloging in Publication Data--DK

Courtesy: D.K. Agencies (P) Ltd. <docinfo@dkagencies.com>

Mathur, Shikha.

Role of information and communication technology in women empowerment / Shikha Mathur.

p. cm.

Includes bibliographical references.

ISBN 9789351280118

1. Information technology--Social aspects--India. 2. Women--Effect of technological innovations on--India. 3. Women in development--India. 4. Women--Education--Government policy--India. 5. Literacy programs--India. I. Title.

DDC 306.460820954 23

Contents

Foreword

It gives me immense pleasure, satisfaction and sense of pride seeing the book "Role of Information and Communication in Women Empowerment" by Shikha Mathur Kumar and writing foreword for the same. Fortunately, she is my daughter born and brought up in our progressive and democratic family. As a parent, it is my firm belief that empowerment comes from the roots. This is a commendable work done for this genuine and crucial social cause.

In *yajurveda* it is said, O woman you are a pioneer-resplendent, stable, supporting, nourishing and orderly, cherished like the earth itself a woman is the controller of the family, she is brilliant, she regulates others and observes rules herself. She is an asset as she supports the family. We depend on her for food, strength, prosperity and happiness. (*yajurveda* -14-21, 22)

But it is an ironical and strange fact that in India on one side we say *'yatra naryastu pujyante ramante tatra devata'* on the other side she is ill treated, exploited and suppressed mostly by men and many times surprisingly by women, her own relatives. For his ego, satisfaction and selfish interests, man has established a self-proclaimed supremacy on women. For centuries man has been trying to rule women socially, physically, emotionally and economically taking advantage of her soft but superior qualities. To satisfy his false ego he is not willing to give way to her 'self to be expressed freely, where as far as in a peaceful happy and ideal situation man and woman both should equally respect, care and give proper space to each other's feelings, sentiments, ideas and requirements.

Fortunately, due to education and social awakening to some extent woman are becoming aware of her own existence. Some social organisations are working for their betterment.

Government is also trying to improve the condition of women and empower them by making rules to stop crimes and evils like molestation, dowry etc. Recently, anti-rape Bill (Criminal Law Act 2013) has also been passed. But making rules is not enough unless they are implemented properly. This is possible only when people have respect and fear of them and above all, if men are willing to change their attitude towards women. It requires a strong will power and mental courage but if all (there are already exceptions) men really become progressive, broad-minded and supportive towards women without complexes, the situation will definitely change. In *Markandya puran*, all *Devas* shared their respective weapons and powers with *Devi*; like Lord Shiva gave a *trishul*, Lord Vishnu a *chakra* and so on ..... For destroying Mahishasur and other devils, to bring peace and justice in the world. Undoubtedly, an empowered woman can bring a tremendous positive change by making a happy family, peaceful society and a progressive nation. She can also be a source of inspiration and motivation for man. It is rightly said "There is always a woman behind every successful man". Frankly, speaking interdependence of both on each other cannot be denied. If it is truly, happily and gracefully accepted by both man and woman, the world will be a much better place to live. We can always hope and pray for that!

Science and technology have come to the woman's rescue by making tedious household jobs easy for her. Mobile phones and information technology have brought a revolution in the society and women empowerment is evident from these changes.

It reflects that the book has been written after thorough study of the subject and closely watching the pitiable situation of the women especially from the lower strata of the society. The miraculous positive change the, ICT has brought in empowering the women is certainly a ray of hope for us. The author deserves a lot of appreciation for the book. I, heartily wish her all the success now and always in life.

Prabha Mathur
M.A. Sangeet Prabhakar

Preface

Bill Gates has said "As we look ahead into the future, leaders will be those who empower others". India, after independence, with its Constitution and open democracy has been empowering its people by various economic, social, cultural and legislative measures. Information and Communication Technology, like Radio, Television, and Mobile phones has been playing a very vital role in empowering the citizen of India. The battle against poverty, ignorance, illiteracy and disease is, above all, a fight for the people of India. Even after more than six decades of freedom, democracy and economic planning, India still lives in different centuries. On the one hand, it is the India of the affluent, educated and materially empowered people, and, on the other hand, it is the *Bharat* of those who live under conditions of poverty deprivation, squalor, illiteracy, ignorance, intolerance prejudices, exploration, and almost starvation. Nobel laureate, Professor Amartya Sen has opined "Preventable diseases are prevalent, illiteracy is unceasing, needless hunger and premature mortality does exist, as does social exclusion and economic insecurity. Social barriers, under nourishment, ill-health, illiteracy make it hard to participate in the expanding process of the market mechanism (especially in a world of globalised trade). Historically, under the garb of socio-cultural and religious structures, women have not been treated fairly, leave aside equally.

India as a secular democracy has established its credibility among the nations of the world by enacting the various laws which have opened the doors for empowerment of women and weaker sections of the society including minorities. The Hindu Marriage Act 1955 outlawed polygamy and introduced the concept of divorce in Hindu Community. Equally significant has been the Hindu Succession Act 1956, which conferred full ownership of women for their share of the family property. The Panchayati Raj law demonstrated the efficiency of reserving one third of the constituencies for women, thus empowering rural Indian woman. The National Rural Employment Guarantee Act (NREGA) 2005, recently renamed after Mahatma Gandhi, has guaranteed employment for 100 days in a year to every rural household, volunteering to do unskilled manual work and has thus empowered the rural people, including women. The Protection of Girl Right Act, 1955 protected the Scheduled Castes and Scheduled Tribes against caste prejudices and discrimination. The Scheduled Castes and Scheduled Tribes (Prevention of Atrocities) Act 1989, provided protection from more violent caste-driven offences. The Right to Information Act 2005, acknowledged as one of the most progressive transparency laws in the world, enables citizens to get information from the government.

Information and Communication Technology (ICT) has played a very vital role in empowering people of different walks of life. ICT has registered phenomenal growth in the past twenty years. The increasing use of technology has led to a win-win situation for women, farmers, business people and financial services. The financial services, industry, consumers, students, senior citizens and common man and woman have been greatly benefitted from ICT. The mobile phone is turning out to be the perfect tool for speeding up development and empowerment of people, ensuring efficiencies in governance, farming, business and industry. In 2003, 61 per cent of the world's population was using Mobile Cell signals and in 2010, 90 per cent of the world population is benefitting from mobile telephones. In 2000, 71 per cent people of developing countries were having mobile telephones while by 2012, mobile phone subscribers were sending messages, 26 per cent look pictures on video with a mobile and 10 per cent use mobile internet according to World Bank figures (*Economic Times* 20th August, 2012).

This work closely looks at the life of women in India specially those from marginalised sections of society. A case study of the embroidery sector which is a rich tradition of the country with wide varieties and variations. The *Phulkari* from Punjab, *Kantha* work from Gujarat, *Kutchi* and *Sindhi* work from Gujarat and *Chicken Kari* from Uttar Pradesh to name a few. Every bridal trousseau had a collection of beautifully crafted costumes for the new bride which was treasured generation to generation. This tradition needs to be preserved and revived. ICT can play a vital role in enabling master craftsmen to preserve various designs and patterns coming down the ages. The mobile phone became a potent weapon to break the barriers of domesticity and seclusion specially for the women in *"pardah"* or *"hoonghat"*. It gave her an identity by assigning her a number on which she could communicate and which was truly reachable. Even the house where she lived did not have her name on the name plate in most patriarchal societies, where she could be contacted. The mobile no. has therefore, given her an address an identity. It was an 'interesting journey' of self-discovery and peep into the world where change is difficult due to fixed mindset, biases and belief. Can technology can bring change is a million dollar question for which answers are yet to be found. May be the reader will join my search during the course of this book.

During the course of my research, I met many women from sections who said that mobile phone had certainly broken the walls around them and they could access the world. The internet benefitted the women entrepreneurs, designers and business women due to *e*-commerce where they could get their orders on the internet and reach out to the artisans and workers on the mobile phone. The present study covers a wide canvass and successfully tries to grapple with the many problems, faced by women particularly belonging to Schedule Castes, Schedule Tribes and Minority in empowering themselves socially, economically and politically.

Information and Communication Technologies have become potent forces in transforming social, economic and political life all over the world. Information and Communication Technologies (ICT) are both enabling as well as contributing factors to globalisation and economic development. Information, according to Information Technology Act 2000, includes data, text, images, sound, voice, codes, computer programmes, software and data bases or micro film or computer generated micro-chip. Communication Technologies (CTs) are a diverse set of technical tools and resources to create, disseminate, store, bring value additions and manage information and Communication Technologies (ICT) comprise a complex and technological sets of techniques, applications and services aimed to produce process, distribute and transform information which consists of segments as diverse as telecommunication (telephone, mobiles etc.) television, radio, broadcasting, computer hardware, software and services like internet and *e*-mail. Radio, telephone, mobile phone, television, internet are capable of empowering people and are one of trust sectors for future growth in national wealth and quality employment. ICT has brought a virtual revolution during the last twenty years. ICT (Information and Communication Technologies) recognise the multiple technologies involved as well as the ubiquitous convergence of Communication with Information technology. Broad band has became the most general purpose technology and enables not only Communication but also connectivity to carry out transactions efficiently. It helps develop new activities, raising telecom network capacity by a order of magnitude. For customers its critical functionality is internet access.

It is proposed to explore the full potentials of ICT in empowering women in India. ICT bring women increased access to resources, which enable them to gain a voice and end isolation.

Dr. Janice Brodman of Education Development Centre (Newtoss MA) and Mohammad Yunus of Grameen Bank have worked on a project on using IT to market women's indigenous knowledge, with the aim of generating income for women and empowering women and made a presentation under title — "Once and Future Network Meeting on Gender and its in a Global Economy" on 1st May 2001, at Harvard University. In India, according to India's National Association of Software and Services Companies (NASSCOM) 2004, the number of software professional increased from 2003-2004. in 1998, 18 per cent of the IT workforce was women. In 2003, the proportion increased to 21 per cent and 35 per cent in 2005. Women are employed in IT companies located mainly in cities as Bangalore, Poona, Chennai, Hyderabad, Mumbai and Delhi. SEWA (Self Employed Women Association) use ICT for women empowerment and promote income generating opportunities for women. SMILE (Savitri Marketing Institutions for Ladies Empowerment) is a voluntary organisation in Pune and has helped them market their various products like soft toys, candles, bags and other utility household items. Women have a great deal to contribute to knowledge for development, and information technology can bring much to accelerate the development and empowerment of women. Information Technology could strengthen civic education, guarantee equal access to information and tie individuals and institutions into networks that will make real participatory discussion and debate across great distance! Telephones, Cellular phones, Television and other means of ICT (Internet, radio, film, newspapers, magazine, books) can bring social awareness and empowerment of people both in rural and urban areas in India. Tele-medicine, *e*-Learning, *e*-Governance, *e*-Business, telecommuting, entertainment are some of the main uses of ICT. Each use has its own social benefits. Telecommuting offers saving in travel, congestion and pollution costs. As far tele-medicine, some key functionaries are tele-diagnosis, tele-urltrasound, tele-sonography, tele-monitoring, tele-consultation and tele-radiology. Accroding to Professor Sumit Kumar Majumdar, or University of Texas, U.S., Broad band can transform health care in many unimagined ways. Clearly, the general purpose technology have a phenomenal capacity to transform societies. India's telecom revolution means Indian no longer have to remain silent, nationally and globally. Third and fourth generation wireless broadband functionalities are at its door-step. ICT has great transformational possibilities for Indian economy and particularly for women empowerment. It is only through ICT that people get to know "the compression of the world and the intensification of the world as a whole".[2] India online survey 2007 finds out the usage of internet from homes at 59 per cent place of work (office, school, colleges) remain the single largest place for accessing internet at 78 per cent and Internet usage from cybercafes has remained flat, reaching 47 per cent. The internet usage continues to grow at a steady pace, reaching 30.32 million — a growth of 28 per cent from April 2006 to April 2007. We are today in the midst of this "third wave" transition from an industrial society to an information society T.V. and Radio lead to dissemination of information, entertainment and education bringing social awareness and consciousness related to modem life demands and challenge. There is a classic example of SEWA (Self Employed Women Association) which successfully integrates a complex myriad of lives, occupations and issues into one union. SEWA is an ideal organisation for women to join and make life better by empowerment. There has been recent growth of IT enabled service businesses in India as call centres, medical transcription, technical support and back office processing, engineering and design, geographical information services, insurance claim processing, legal data bases. Business Process Out sourcing has tremendous potential for growth. "The IT sector has not only created a large number of jobs but has also resulted in new types of challenging careers. Workforce trends show that a large number of women are joining ICT sector."

A series of factors including literacy and education language, time, cost, geographical location of facilities, social and cultural norms, users skills constrain women access to information technology. There are great opportunities in employment, particularly in the area of IT enabled services and in entrepreneurship, both in applying IT to existing business and in starting new businesses based on technology services. There are many good examples in India of the use of ICTs for women empowerment. According to Suman Jain, India shop, an *e*-commerce website (2005) in Tamil Nadu, has been designed to sell products made by rural women cooperatives and NGos. The Dhan Foundation (2004) and *Swayam Krishi Sangam* (2004) are using ICTs such as hand held device and smart cards, to improve micro-finance projects to empower poor women. The Self-Employed Women Association (SEWA 2004) has several ICT projects for women including community learning centres, a school of science and technology for self-employed women and the telephone project which provides mobile phone to women in unorganised informal sector. The SEWA has established and ICT programme, aiming to increase the efficiency of micro-enterprise activities. A survey in eight Indian cities has shown that non-working women access the net 63 per cent from cybercafes and 32 per cent from home. The lack of correlation of women in internet use with expected indicators supports the hypothesis that most women internet users in India are not representative of women in the country as a whole but rather are presently part of a small educated urban elite. Studies indicate that — women organisations in India have little access to communication, media between radio and T.V. They are unlikely to have tape recorders, VCRS and standby computers, let alone Internet access. In U.S.A., 46 per cent of homes have internet access and women have become as connected as men and make their lives easier by getting all needed information. ICTs can provide useful health and education informations. ICT can be a very powerful tool for poverty alleviation, economic empowerment of women and education of both men and women. Bill Gates, former chairman and Chief Software Architect, Microsoft Corporation however says: "Poor people need good health, not computers". However, women in India need education to take advantage of the new global communication opportunities. Beyond access to basic education, women have to be equipped with skills to prepare them for range of roles in information and communication technology as users, creators, designers and managers. IT can offer invaluable tools for women empowerment through education, particularly literacy education, continuing education, non-formal education and life-long education through distance learning Delhi, Mumbai, Kolkata and Chennai have crossed 100 per cent teledensity mark. This implies, the number of mobile phone connections in these cities are higher then the number of residents. Delhi has now joined the global league of cities withover 100 per cent mobile penetration such as London, New York, Paris, Tokyo, Hong Kong and Singapore. According to (DOT) Department of Telecom, Chennai lead with a 143 per cent penetrations, followed by Delhi at 138 per cent, Mumbai 112 per cent and Kolkata at 102.4 per cent. the telecom penetration in these cities would be much higher if landline figures are also taken into account."

ICT Being Gender Neutral How can it Empower Women in Embroidery Sector

ICT is a powerful tool for economic empowerment by utilising the women in the service industries for information processing, banking, insurance, printing and publishing. Within the service sector, the major employment for women is in information processing jobs, particularly data entry. The new information economy offers may possibilities for new IT-enabled businesses that women could establish or in which they could work.

Software programming GIS (Geographical Information Systems) and system analysis jobs in several developing countries are targets of highly educated and skilled ITI trained women. Most women internet users in almost all developing countries are presently part of small, educated urban elite women who came from higher strata of the society. In India, all electronic media ranging from satellite television to *e*-mail and the internet, are accessible only to privileged classes and cater almost exclusively to the predominantly information and entertainment needs of the rich urban elite. Empowerment is a cross-cutting issue, from education to health-care to governance and economic policy, activities that seek to empower poor people are expected to increase development opportunities, enhance development outcomes and improve people's quality of life. It is a multi-dimensional, political, socio-psychological and economic process that helps people gain control and autonomy over their own lives. Psychological empowerment is also called self-efficacy and it relates to the development of ability to trust in one's abilities in order to act with confidence.[5]

The main process that could lead to women's empowerment are as under:

1. Changes in women's mobility and social interactions;
2. Changes in women's labour patterns;
3. Changes in women's access and control over resources;
4. Change in women's control over decision-making in social political and economic life of the nation;
5. Raising of educational and politico social awareness in order and politico social awareness in order to build self confidence and self-esteem;
6. Raising of women's income and nutrition level;
7. Strengthening legal systems aimed at elimination of all forms of discrimination against women;
8. Political empowerment by getting some status in politico-social activities;
9. Changing social attitudes and community practices by active participation and involvement of both men and women;
10. The *de jure* and *de facto* enjoyment of all political, social, economic, cultural and civil human rights and fundamental freedom by women on equal basis with men.

In Andhra Pradesh, Nellore area women's organised and fought against liquor barons and contractors. They pressurised the state government to get licenses of these vendors cancelled. They could thus achieve domestic peace and harmony. Money so saved, by both husband and wife, could contribute to the education, health and development of their children. This women empowerment movement was highlighted by the mass media, television, radio, local newspapers and ultimately had remarkable impact on village women of other districts. This "mission-mode-approach" with participatory flourish, in time-target goals, can help women at the macro-level. ICT playa great role in disseminating such news/event all over the country. The concept of empowerment— Andre Beteille points out that empowerment means different things to different people. Empowerment, in his view, involves a radical social transformation encompassing means and ends, human rights, basic needs, economic security, capacity building, skill formation, conditions of dignified social existence, redistribution of power and change from hierarchical to egalitarian system."

Justice V.R. Krishna Iyer, former Judge of the Supreme Court says:

"Empowerment, egalite and dignity of women are the desiderate of a contemporary womanhood, long subject to undeservedly humiliating inferiority of status, discrimination in civil and political rights and subordination in developmental activities.?" There are many problems faced by illiterate ignorant and poor women of India. Even though women are eulogised as *'Shakti'* (which stands of power) the irony of the situation in that *Shakti* symbolises the ideal of women in traditional India society – being an all sacrificing, all-giving, benevolent, sexualised, dehumanised, female image. "The toiling women of India are trapped by the mythic ideal of *Shakti*— an empowerment based on deprivation. The traditional socio-cultural construction of gender, based on *Shakti* (female power) has accentuated an "empowered powerlessnessr."

This is the crux and till socio-economic attitudes are addressed there can be little meaningful empowerment for gender parity. There exists a wide-gap between the professed goal enshrined in the Constitution and the Government and the situational ground reality of the exploitation, oppression and discrimination of the women in India. The common problems faced by all women are:

1. Inequality of power sharing with men and in particular in the decision-making at all levels;
2. Lack of awareness and commitment to internationally and nationally recognised women's rights, even amongst the elite;

3. Insufficient machinery at all levels to promote advancement of women;
4. Poverty discrimination and marginalisation of women from "cradle to grave";
5. Inequality in women's access to and participation in the definitions of economic structures and policies and the productive process itself; unequal access to education, health, employment, credit facilities and other means of maximising awareness of women's right and the use of their capacities;
6. Violence against women, (It is ever on rise);
7. Efforts on women of continuing local, national, international armed or other kinds of conflict. (Indian women are the worst sufferers of the cross-border terrorism);
8. Marginalisation in the decision-making process, with women generally remaining invisible at most levels in public structures. For example, India, considering its vastness, has less than minimum female representation both in Parliament and in Legislatures;
9. Lack of on the job training to elected women members of the Panchayat, Legislatures and Parliament;
10. Patriarchy interfering and eroding the work of the women Sarpanchas and Panchas;
11. In spite of the strong women's movement in the country, the NGOs are too dispersed and isolated in deciding the national and local priorities inaction;
12. Inactive executive and monitoring mechanisms to oversee the implementation of national/state plans and programmes. (There is near total lack of feedback mechanism amongst them);

Being a multi-dimensional process empowerment has four stages in building powerful communities. These are its four R's i.e., Relief, Resistance, Reconstruction and Rectification.[10] Relief ensures survival, reduces further pauperisations and prepares the community to remove towards sustenance. Resistance involves taking back the control over its resources base through political means. Reconstruction involves building platforms of strength such as improving the skills and tightening the resource base. Rectification means reducing the internal injustices and inequalities through conscious acts of restitution and creation of spaces.

Empowerment has to be done at the following five levels:

1. Individual—control over their lives;
2. Social—freedom in social relationship and educational awareness;
3. Economic—capacity to learn and becoming economically self-dependent;
4. Psychological—self-confidence, self-esteem, self-reliance and self awareness;
5. Physical—taking control over their bodies, nutrition and health;

Infanticide, child marriages, dowry, girl trafficking, domestic violence, bonded labour, unequal wages for women and men, malnutrition of girl child, are the social ills that create bottleneck in empowering women. Even in families, a male child and a female child are treated unequally in terms of nutrition education and health. The vision of empowerment of Indian women has been given by National Commission for Women. Empowerment thus: "Indian women of today, culturally rooted, globally oriented, healthy, educated, self-reliant, secure in her home and safe outside with access to all the rights of a citizen with opportunities to contribute in all walks of life."[11] Vision is a bouquet of flowers which will ensure fulfillment of national and regional aspirations to impart a quality of life for the women of India, wherein the women and menfolk are equally participating in social, economic and political terms.

ICT can play a very important and enabling role in disseminating this vision through the medium of mass media, television, radio and even films. DNA of women empowerment metaphorically speaking demands a unique coordination at all levels of democratic policy—the legislature, the executive, the judicial self-help women as groups themselves and the mass media—we have to go for holistic approach. There is a case study of local washer women of district Dharmapuri, Tamil Nadu. In this case of self-help groups, the local washer women raised funds collectively from amongst other women and they then bought a van. They further learnt driving and drove to Banglore and collected work of washing uniforms for the commercial houses. In a matter of six months they earned what they could not earn before in four and five years time. Besides their economic progress, they learnt and practiced community participation and sharing of each other's joys and sorrows besides social defence for all women.

ICT has minimise potential and can empower women through codification and dissemination of their indigenous knowledge of local plants, crops, uncodified history of the community. Fixed-time telephone, fax, mobile phone, *e*-mail, internet access and web site are all useful ICT which can bring information about agricultural prices and information about community assets. Internet can empower women with information on how to access credit and start profitable enterprises. In the process, the women will be able to generate resources to help them acquire property and further their economic base, thus reducing their dependence on men.

Notes

1. Barber, B.R. Strong Democracy Participatory Politics for a New Age, Berkeley University of California Press, 1984, p. 274.
2. Robertson, Roland, Globalisation Social Theory and Global Culture London, Sage, 1992, p. 8.
3. Agarwal, R.,—Educated Women in the Urban Labour Market — A study of career mobility patterns of women professionals in Information Technology, mu, New, 2000.
4 Jogi Termomas Penlip—Metros now have mcre mobiles than citizens Economic Times, Chennai, 2 November, 2009.
5. Also see Bandura, A. (ed.) 1995, Self-efficacy in changing societies, Cambridge, New York, quoted by Anil S. Navale and Mona Sharma, Empowerment: Concept, evolution and strategies—in empowerment of the weaker sections in India, Edited by R.B.S. Verma, H.S. Verma, Raj Kumar Singh, Serial Publications, New Delhi, 2006, p. 69.
6. Beteille, Andre, "Empowerment" Economic and Political Weekly, 34, 1999, pp. 589-597.
7. V.R. Krishna lyer, A Vibrant Vission and Militant mission—in Search for a vision on women empowerment vis-a-vis legislation and judicial decision. The National Commission for Women, New Delhi, p. VII.
8. Bagchi. Tashodhara, Women's Empowerment: Paradigm and Paradoxes—From Myth to Market, (eds.) Kum Kum Sagari and Uma Chakarvarti, IAS, 1999, p. 377.

9. Search for a vision statement on women empowerment vis-a-vis legislations and judicial decision—National Commission for Women, New Delhi, pp. 2-3.
10. Verma, H.S., Empowering of the OBCs in India: Emerging tasks and response from the leading segments of the civil society in empowerment of the weaker sections in India, Serial Publications, New Delhi, 2006, p. 289.
11. Search for a Vision on Women Empowerment vis-a-vis legislations and judicial decisions—National Commission for Women, New Delhi, p. 8.

Shikha Mathur Kumar

Acknowledgements

Dedicated to the women of India whose strength and courage knows no boundaries when taking on the vagaries of life in a land which worships them on one hand and has reduced them to the 'lesser half', nameless, faceless 'behind' the men under shackles of tradition, poverty, repression and caste even in the 21st century. They may be patronised in the name of being protected or brutalised in face of men, who turn demons of lust but the women remain just as strong and resilient that they rise from the ashes like 'Nirbhaya'. Clutching the straw to cross the stream—real or imaginary that divides them. They tread their way through the morass of social and moral obligations and financial and economic challenges of daily chores to get what they deserve-empowerment.

I would like to express my gratitude to the people, who have supported me throughout the writing of my book. It began as an experience sharing episode with my colleagues who felt digital divide has widened, rather than narrowed the gaps between the 'have's' and the 'have nots', made differences more sharp between those who have access to ICT and others who do not. The most potent instrument of change was information and communication technology. It aroused my interest to go on a fact finding exercise. Life has its own ways that it set me on a sabbatical during which this work was undertaken for which I am extremely thankful the department of Telecom for granting me leave. Ms. Sadhana Dikshit, Member (Finance) Telecom Commission was extremely kind and encouraging.

I am grateful to Centre for Dalit and Minority Studies Jamia Milia Islamia headed by Prof Mujtaba Khan who guided me on my endeavour to study the change that let had brought to the women of India. He gave me continuous support for the project from initial advice in early stages of conceptual inception till successful completion of my research for doctoral thesis.

A special thanks goes to Sri Badar Tasleem and Sri Mishra who helped me in typing and formatting this book.

I am thankful to Kalpaz publications.

I wish to thank my father Dr. Krishna Mohan Mathur and mother Mrs. Prabha Mathur for their unstinted support and inspiration to complete the project.

I have no words to express my heartiest gratitude for my life partner Mr. Niraj Kumar, who stood by me during this mission like an anchor. He facilitated my research work and field visits. His ideas and thoughts made this project possible. His parents were kind enough to take care at home and free me from all the domestic responsibilities to take up my work. I thank them from the bottom of my heart. My two sons Samvit and Shashwat gave me the biggest empowering feeling by filling my world with untold joy and sublime bliss. I thank the Gods of Mount Abu where my moorings lie and my strength is recharged by mere thought of Arbudachal and Somnath. My spiritual *'guru Swami Ishwaranandji Giri'* helped me to tide through most trying times with equanimity.

I thank my colleagues, friends and so many new acquaintances I made during this journey for motivating me and appreciating my work. I thank God and pay obeisance for making this possible.

If this book could be even a little more than just a drop in the ocean in making lives of women better than what is, my purpose is fulfilled.

Shikha Mathur Kumar

A National Perspective on Role of ICT in Empowering Women

"I find the great thing in this world is not so much where we stand as to what direction we are moving." —Goethe.

Thus brilliant thought of Goethe reflects the thrust, contents and substance of this research work, what is important is not so much the present status of empowerment of women and the role of Information and Communication Technology (ICT) but whether the Indian nation is moving in the right direction towards its goal and vision. Information and Communication Technology (ICT) has emerged as a key driver of socio-economic development in an increasingly knowledge intensive global scenario, in which Indian nation needs to play a leadership role. Swami Vivekananda once said, *"The best thermometer to the progress of a nation is its treatment to its women."*[1] The National Policy of Education (1986, 1992) has recognised the need for women and has clearly spelt out the parameters of empowerment as follows:

1. Enhancing the self-esteem and self-confidence of women;
2. Building a positive image of women by recognising their contribution to the society, polity and economy;
3. Developing the ability to think critically;
4. Fostering decision-making and action through collective processes;
5. Enabling women to make informed choices in areas like education, employment and health, especially reproductive health;
6. Ensuring equal participation in development processes;
7. Providing the information, knowledge and skill required for economic independence;

8. Enhancing access to legal literacy and information relating to their rights and entitlement in society, with a view to enhancing their participation on equal footing in all areas.

Strormquist (1993) has identified four dimension of empowerment. They are cognitive, psychological, economic and political.[2] The UNDP Human Development Report of 1995 says "Investing in Women's Capabilities and empowering them to exercise their choice is not only valuable in it but is also the surest way to contribute to economic growth and overall development." Dr. Manmohan Singh, Prime Minister of India in his speech before the National Development Council (NDC) meeting at New Delhi on 26th December 2012 said: "women and girls represent half the population and our society has not been fair to this half........."

The resurgence of women in public spaces which is an absolute essential part of social emancipation, is accompanied by growing threats to their safety."[3] Chief Ministers were urged to take on these remarks as their priority to give women an enabling environment in all senses of the word. Women represent half of mankind and 48 per cent of India's population. The important contribution that ICT can make in bridging the gender divide and empowering women has been recognized by the International Telecommunication Union (ITU) of which India is a member. "Equal right for women and men is a fundamental human right. Ending gender discrimination by 2015 is one of the Millennium Development goals...... Information and Communication Technologies (ICTs) can be used to close the gender gap by creating new jobs for impoverished women. Women for example, have been at the forefront of the village phone movement, selling airtime to rural people too poor to own their own phones. ICTs can also be used to promote basic literacy and education for women and girls, provide job training and prepare women for careers in the ICT sector as well as to ensure health and safety".

Information and Communication Technologies: Brief History and its Role

In 1958, Leavitt and Whisler in an article published in the *Harvard Business Review* described ICT as the new technology that was emerging involving the use of Computers and Software to manage information. Information Technology not only deals with the storage, retrieval, transmission and manipulation of data but for other technologies that are used to distribute information such as telephony, television and telecommunication in general. The period between 1840 to 1940 is generally called as the electro mechanical age of I.T. because it witnessed the beginnings of tele-communications with the invention of telegraph, Morse Code, telephone and radio. In 1937, John Vincent Atanasoff and Clifford Berry conceived the first electronic digital computing device. In 1946 John Manchly and J. Presper Eekert conceived and designed ENIAC, the first electronic general purpose computer capable of solving a full range of computing problems. Gradually the huge computers, baring a machine as big as a room and weighing 30 tonnes were replaced by smaller and faster models in the period 1940's to 1950's by making several advanccs and refinements.

The first electro mechanical computer called Mark-1 was built at Harvard University using punch cards and was two metres high, 15 metres long and weighing five tonnes. In 1948, the first electronic digital stored – programme computer was the Manchester Small – Scale Experimental Machine called SSEM. Computer first appeared in 1977 and was Apple 11. Today more than 10,000 application programmes are available for use on personal computers. The hard disc drive was first introduced by IBM and is used for storing and retrieving digital information today because it provides a wide variety of benefits and advantage to its users. After the economic reforms of 1991-92 Government. of India provided major incentives enabling IT to flourish and acquire a dominant position in the worlds IT scenario. The growth of the ICT Sector in India in the past twenty years has had a transformational effect on the Indian economy. Information Technology and Telecommunications are the twin sectors that best epitomise what modern resurgent and democratic India is capable of accomplishing. From under four per cent in 2001, tele–density has reached 77.04 per cent in September 2012, leading to substantial economic and social benefits for the country. While urban voice penetration has reached 161.03 per cent, rural voice penetration is at 40.36 per cent. With about 70 per cent of the country's population living in rural areas, bridging the rural-urban divide is critical for India's inclusive economic growth agenda. India currently has only about 22.5 million broadband connections, of which 15.08 million are provided through, fixed line while the rest are through wireless data cards. India is amongst the high growth mobile markets in the world and contributed more than 142 million new connections in 2011. Over the past decade, Mobile operator revenue alone contributed for 2.4 per cent of India GDP for the year 2012, coupled with an estimated 2.3 million jobs. Empowerment is a socio-economic process which requires dialogue and reflection, awakening of the social consciousness, and a social conscience to the conditions of women in India particularly belonging to the Scheduled Castes, Scheduled Tribes, Muslims and the weaker sections of the society. By and large, women have been accorded an inferior social status coupled with retrograde social customs like *sati*, child marriage, dowry, social boycott of widows etc., women experience several disadvantages. They face not only gender discrimination of various degrees and types at different levels, but also suffer sexual harassment, atrocities and crime.[5] Empowerment has resulted in economic development and social relationships, creating many challenges in the newly developed situation.

Jo Row Lauds (1998), reviews the literature of empowerment, dividing it into three overlapping categories, viz. personal empowerment (developing industrial consciousness and confidence to confront oppression), relational empowerment (an increased ability to negotiate and influence relational decisions) and collective empowerment (collective action at the local or higher level to change offensive social structure).[6] Paolo Freres has emphasised "consciensisation and radical social action as essential pre-requisite for bringing about women empowerment.[7] Empowerment is bound to have an impact on social change. Empowerment is a political-socio-economic process by which individual, organisations and communities gain control and mastery over social and economic conditions, over democratic participation in their communities.[8] The key goal of empowerment is at the individual, community and national level. Information and Communication Technology has become a source of empowerment in the social-politics-economic context in India. Information and Communication Technology will have an important role in the process of empowerment of marginalised individual, group and organisation of women. This calls for grassroots organising and communicative social action on part of the women, the poor, minorities, dalits and others who have been consistently and increasingly marginalised during the last many decades in India.

The recent 16th December 2012 gang rape case in Delhi is symptomatic of a larger vicious circle. The cliché "Justice delayed is justice denied" tends to cloud the better truism, "Justice denied is injustice perpetrated". In the Indian criminal justice system, major crimes against women are likely to remain unreported: if reported, frequently not registered, if registered, the true perpetrator not found, if found, not prosecuted, if prosecuted, not charged, if charged, usually not convicted, if convicted, frequently not adequately punished.

Atrocities and Crime against Women in India – In India, it is easy to get insured to the raw deal that women get, female foeticide, neglect of infant girl leading to higher mortality and stunted bodies and brains, girls being withdrawn from school on reaching puberty, child marriages, privileging of sexuality, when it comes to women, over all other attributes as a human being, demands for dowry after leading to violence, frequently fatal, in the marital home, a wide spread notion that male hands have the license to wander over the women's body in crowded public spaces—these are unpleasant but common facts of the Indian reality.[9]

India is the most dangerous place in the world for a baby girl as can be seen from the Table given below.[10]

Gender Bias

Ratio of Male to Female Mortality (per 100 females)

Country	*Infant (0-1)*	*Child (1-5)*
India	76	56
Pakistan	120	97
Sri Lanka	125	111
Less Developed Region	122	111
World	122	116

Information and Communication Technology will have an important role in the process of empowerment of marginalised individuals, groups and organisations of women. This calls for grassroots organising and communicative social action on part of the women, the poor, minorities, dalits and others who have been consistently and increasingly marginalised during the last many decades in India.[11] India is expected to miss the crucial U.N. Millennium Development Goals (MDG) including those related to reduction in poverty, hunger and infant mortality.[12] The poverty in India is likely to be 26.7 per cent by 2015 as against the target of 23.9 per cent while Infant Mortality Rate (IMR) would be 43 per 1000 live birth against the millstone of bringing it down to 27. The proportion of underweight children has declined from 43 per cent during 1989-99 to 40 per cent in 2005-06. At the historical rate of decline, the proportion is expected to come down only about 33 per cent by 2015 vis-a-vis the target of 26 per cent. Malnutrition of children particularly girl and girl babies continue to be a major hurdle. The process of empowerment has unleashed the great Indian women. There exists a gender bias in a patriarchal society and it leads to unequal opportunities for women, particularly belonging to the poorer and weaker sections of the society. In India, one half of our human resource is relegated to the back benches. Certain men (I am trying to avoid generalisation) assume it is their right to abuse and inflict sexual violence on the opposite sex.[13] The recent heinous and horrifying gang rape of a young woman (in New Delhi on 16th December, 2012) seems to have shaken the silent conscience of every Indian, especially women, who, after decades of suffering in silence, have finally decided enough is enough and have taken to street to demand justice and protection.[14]

Crimes against women are increasing constantly over the years. The table 1, given in the next page indicates how rape, molestation, sexual harassment, cruelty by relatives, abduction, dowry deaths and all other crimes have increased over the years.[15] It is matter of concern that juveniles are being found involved in such heinous crimes as rape. More alarming is the fact that they are found to be part of gangs that indulge in such crimes.[16] Agne Kharshing, secretary of civil society women's organisation, a Shillong-based NGO, blames the system when there are dozens of wine shops even near schools and religious institutions, when there are more wine shops than medicine shops and book stores, what else can we expect from our young people? Meghalaya, a small state with a population of 20.64 lakh saw 21 juveniles arrested for rape under IPC Section 376 during 2011. Juveniles apprehended for crimes against women in 2011 are shown in Table 1 given below:-

Table 1: State-wise Juveniles Apprehended for Crimes Against Women in 2011

State	*Rape*	*Molestation*	*Abduction*	*Harassment*
MP	281	173	109	25
UP	152	19	76	0
Maharashtra	142	124	41	33
Rajasthan	92	47	67	0
Chhattisgarh	80	66	14	14
West Bengal	76	20	60	0
Delhi	56	10	25	3
Orissa	48	10	10	0
Assam	36	4	34	0
Meghalaya	21	1	0	0

(*Source:* National Crime Records Bureau).

ICT has a very important role to play in preventions, control and prosecution of crimes against women all over the world, particularly in an advance, dynamic and transitional democratic society like India. For the average world generation person, brought up on a staple of internet technologies and tools, ICT has a very vital role to play. "ICT tools for local situations such as the traffic jam at the next signal, details of personal traffic violations, pollution on the street, progress of a local infrastructure project or even the coordination for the local councillor or authorities" can be very vital.[17] For example, the Bangalore Transport Information System, built in collaboration with the traffic police and transport authorities, integrates information with 160 traffic cameras, cellular service providers and public transport GPS system to provide real-time feedback on the traffic and crime situation.[18]

ICT has already accelerated the attainment of the societal goal of women empowerment by providing them:

1. Education, information and knowledge
2. Training
3. Occupational opportunities
4. Markets
5. Financial Services
6. Information about appropriate government programmes
7. Information about health agencies and works
8. Feedback mechanism
9. Support system and net working.

[19]ICT by its nature and capabilities, can address many challenges that rural women face. ICT has the potential to help women access information for the following:

1. From the comfort and safety of their environment and address challenges of lack of women's mobility. Within the culturally accepted boundaries thus helping women to focus on access to knowledge without much opposition and constraints.
2. By transcending literacy and language barriers.[20]

Empowerment of Muslim women

On the occasion of the Independence Day 2005, Prime Minister of India announced 15-point programme for the empowerment of Muslim minority and enhancing opportunities for education, ensuring an equitable share of minorities in economic activities, improving the conditions of luring and prevention and control of communal disharmony. The new 15-point programme as amended in October 2009, is as under:

1. Equitable availability of Integrated Child Development Services (ICDS).
2. Improving access to school education.
3. Greater resources for teaching Urdu.
4. Modernizing Madarsa education.
5. Scholarship for meritorious students.
6. Improving educational infrastructure through the Maulana Azad Education Foundation.
7. Self-employment and wage employment for the poor.
8. Up gradation of skills through technical training.
9. Enhanced credit support for economic actuaries.
10. Recruitment to State and Central Services.
11. Equitable share in rural housing scheme.
12. Improving conditions of areas inhabited by minority communities.
13. Preventions of communal incidents.
14. Prosecution for communal offences.
15. Rehabilitation of victims of communal riots.

At the Central level the progress of implementation is being monitored once in six months. This has provided the desired benefits to the Muslim community. Zoya Hassan and Ritu Menon, after a research survey have found that despite triple talaq system, less than two per cent of Muslim women are divorced or deserted. They further found that Muslim women have a slightly greater say in the areas of decision-making within the family than their counterparts in other communities. Growth in the education of Muslim girls in India as can be seen from the chart below:

Table 2: Share Among 17-29 Years Old Continuing Education

Social Groups	*2004-05*	*2009-10*	*Change 2004-2005 to 2009-10*
Hindu-SC	3.5	5.3	1.8
Hindu-ST	3.5	4.3	0.8
Hindu-OBS	5.0	10.2	5.2
Hindu-UC	11.5	20.9	9.4
Muslim OBC	3.8	5.4	1.6
Muslim Others	4.0	4.8	0.8

(*Source :* NSSO-Turns of India New Delhi 14th January, 2013).

In a unique exercise, Member-Secretary of the Sachar Committee Abusalah Sharif has calculated that providing education to Muslim and SC/ST communities' in the world on its own can boost the GDP growth rate. At present Muslims contribute only 11.2 per cent to GDP, while Dalits and Adivasis contribute 16.5 per cent.[22] Muslims were given bank loan per account in minority concentration districts to the tune of Rs. 10.6 lakhs in the year 2008 and Rs. 1.24 in the year 2011 as part of empowerment programme.

Empowerment of Dalit Women and their Present Miserable Lot. Dr. B.R. Ambedkar recognised the social construct of Indian villages about six decades ago and said: "The love of the intellectual Indian for the village community is of course infinite if not pathetic...... What is the village but a sink of localism, a den of ignorance, narrow mindedness and communalism?"[23] Although gradually things are improving in cities and a few other areas of the country but India's Dalit population suffers from two key forms of disadvantages - social indignity and material poverty- which emerge from - the intentioned social and economic inequality, resulting in visible signs of social inequality, such as servility, humiliation and lack of self-respect. They experience sexual and physical violence, discrimination and social exclusion.

Dalit women constitute half of the Dalit population and 16.3 per cent of the total Indian female population. They are discriminated and humiliated not only by people of higher caste but also within their community by the male population. Indian Dalit women have been selected to cultural biases, social exclusion and atrocities and patriarchal controls over women since time immemorial and unfortunately it still continues. Congress President Smt. Sonia Gandhi has said: "Atrocities on women, both in urban and rural India, are a blot on our collective conscience and a matter of great shame."[24] During the last sixty years gradually the scenario is changing for the better with a number of hic-cups due to the mind-set of the people. A study conducted by the Tamil Nadu Dalit Panchayat Presidents Forum (TNDPPF) said: "150 Panchayat presidents were attacked by Non-Dalits while they were performing their duties and two were killed since 2006. What is ironical is that 15 per cent of Dalit panchayat presidents never occupy their official chair fearing reprisals.[25] Dalit chiefs were killed since 2006 by the Upper Caste People. In fact nearly 80 per cent of Dalit Panchayat presidents were elected only birth the approval of non-dalits. Dalit candidate are usually selected or sponsored by upper caste people and the upper caste members choose their servants as candidates in many places. But after their victory they are forced to continue doing home chores and other menial work and never fulfill their functions as Panchayat Presidents" said D. Dayalan, District Adviser of TNDPPP (Tamil Nadu Dalit Panchayat Presidents Forum).

However, in Uttar Pradesh, the things have really changed after Mayawati became the Chief Minister.[26] Illiteracy is the real hurdle in the way of Dalit empowerment. Further 18.1 per cent of the Dalits are engaged in their own land for farming. The Dalits engaged in livestock and dairying and non-farm employment is only 1.9 per cent and 2.6 per cent respectively in Karnataka State. The private sector employment for Dalits is around 5.6 per cent and round 2.7 per cent in government/related sectors for employment. Nearly 78.9 per cent of the total Dalit working population is working in agriculture and related activities in Karnataka. Nearly 60 per cent of Dalit workers do not have subsidiary occupation, according to a study by Centre for Study of Social Exclusion and Inclusive Policy (CSEIP), Mangalore University.[27] Elaborate systems of patriarchy, caste and social and sexual inequality flourish in Indian society and particularly against Dalit women and the weaker sections of the society the law has to provide real penalties for rapists and protection for victims.[28]

In spite of clear orders from the Government of India that 15 per cent quota for SC, 7.5 per cent quota for ST and 27 per cent quota for Others Backward Communities need to be reserved, there is in reality a large gap. The data given by the Government of India is as shown in Table 3: [29]

Table 3: Reservation in All Categories

<table>
<tr><th></th><th>SCs</th><th>STs</th><th>Top Level</th><th>Secy</th><th>Addl Secy</th><th>Joint Secy</th><th>Director</th></tr>
<tr><td>Group A</td><td>11.1</td><td>4.6</td><td>Total Officers</td><td>149</td><td>108</td><td>477</td><td>590</td></tr>
<tr><td>Group B</td><td>14.3</td><td>5.5</td><td>SCs (%)</td><td>- (0%)</td><td>2 (1.9%)</td><td>31 (6.5%)</td><td>17 (2.9%)</td></tr>
<tr><td>Group C</td><td>16.0</td><td>7.8</td><td>STs (%)</td><td>4 (2.7%)</td><td>2 (1.9%)</td><td>15 (3.1)</td><td>7 (1.2)</td></tr>
<tr><td>Group D*</td><td>19.3</td><td>7.0</td><td colspan="5" rowspan="4">As on 14-3-2011</td></tr>
<tr><td>*Safai Karamcharis*</td><td>39.3</td><td>6.2</td></tr>
<tr><td>Total</td><td>17.0</td><td>7.4</td></tr>
<tr><td colspan="3">As on 1.1.2011</td></tr>
</table>

At the very top level of the government bureaucracy, out of total of 149 secretary level officers there were no SC officers while there were only four ST officers as on March 2011. At the level of the Additional Secretary, out of 108 officers, there were only just two each from SC and ST. Out of 477 Joint Secretaries, 31 belonged to SC that is 6.5 per cent and 15 belonged to ST that is 3.1 per cent. Out of 590 Directors, 17 belong to SC (2.9 per cent) while seven belongs to ST (1.2 per cent). These figures include both male and females since there is no reservation for these posts. If one sees all Central Government employees, 17 per cent of them were SC while 7.4 per cent were from S.T. Dalit women in U.P. took a pledge to snatch their rights from the oppressive social structure, the self-appointed guardians of the society. In Haryana, U.P. and some other states Dalit women have risen against the castiest and patriarchal society. The biggest road block faced by Dalits is the considerable disadvantages in food programmes like PDS (Public, Distribution System and Integrated Child Development Scheme) ICDS and MDS (Mid-Day Meals) which has finally resulted in poor nutritional indicators of the majority of the SC/ST communities.[30]

Dalit women are extremely poor and it is necessary to implement (Millennium Development Goals) enthrall rights.[31] The National Federation of Dalit Women (NFDW) was launched by Dalit women themselves to fight for their rights.

Employment of Manual Scavengers and Construction of Dry Latrines (Pro) Act, 1993 took 19 years for the states to ratify. The Central government has assured the bench of Justice Death and Ranjan Gogar that the centre was fully committed to the early passage of the bill for getting "Prohibition of Employment of Manual Scavengers and their Rehabilitation Bill 2012. The bench was hearing appeal on death of manual scavengers while cleaning manholes and sewer lines. It was alleged that these people are hired on daily wages and on their death; the families get no compensation.[32] This problem is directly related in Article 21 of the Constitution. Although things are gradually improving in the years since 1950" certain kinds of violence are traditionally reserved for Dalit women being forced to drink urine and eat faeces, branding, pulling out teeth, tongue and nails. The violence including murder after proclaiming craft, are only experienced by Dalit women. Dalit women are threatened by rape as part of collective violence by higher caste. However, sexual assault and rape of Dalit women and girls also occur within their own communities.[33] During the last twenty years, things have improved tremendously thanks to the ICT and mass media coupled with democratic governments with more enlightened leadership. On the other hand, Dowry Prohibition Act is perhaps the most misused and often, parents and relatives of the husband's side are harassed and exploited in many cases.

Role of ICT Expanding

World Wide Web has drastically changed our lives, and youth today, including educated girls and women spend a large amount of time surfing the information super highway to get required information and knowledge needed by them. The internet has dramatically increased access to information and this in turn has greatly enhanced their capacity to absorb knowledge, consequently increasing their thinking skills.[34] Recognising the vital role that ICT can play in the empowerment of women, the gender budget and the USO Funds of DOT have launched a programme of Pilot. Projects aimed at facilitating SHG's (Self-Help Groups) access to ICT enabled services. Salient Features of the Mobile Value Added Services (VAS) are as under:

1. Focus on SHGs
2. Focus on livelihood
3. Focus in ICT
4. Relevant Value Added Services (VAS) messages
5. Training of SHGs

The activities under the project are as under:

(a) Provision of mobile VAS Subscription to SHGs with a service validity/warranty of at least one year.
(b) Setting up of SHGs seen mobile repair centers in rural areas.
(c) Setting up of SHGs run modem repair centers in rural areas.
(d) Setting of SHGs run solar-based mobiles CDMAFWT charging centers.[35] NABARD, NGOs mobile service provides handset. Modem manufacturers and application service providers are the stakeholders with their identified roles and responsibilities, so far the beneficiaries of the projects and SHG activities are as shown in Table 4:

Table 4: Beneficiaries of SHG Projects

SHG Activity	*States/Districts*	*No of Beneficiaries*
1. Textile handicraft workers	Uttar Pradesh (Gautam Budha Nagar)	2250
2. Beekeeping, Banana products, handicraft	Tamil Nadu (Kanya-Kumarri Coimbatore, Kerala (Thrissur)	3000
3. Agriculture, Tarboring, Pace -making, animal produce, vegetable vending, NREGS etc.	Andhra Pradesh (Krishna and Rangareddy)	2250
4. Agriculture, animal husbandry, sericulture	Maharashtra, (Pune) Uttarakhand, (Almora, Tehri, Banheshvar, Uttar Kashi, Chamoli.	2200 2200
5. Agriculture, handicrafts, farming, fish products, bio-fertilizers	Tamil Nadu (Cuddalore, Teranjavur, Padukkotai, Pondicherry, Dindigul	1130
6. Agiculture, fisheries, beekeeping, atta-chakki, dairy farming, ICT entrepreneurs	Tamil Nadu (Vellore, Thirruvanamalai	2000

Underscoring the urgent need to respond to the more aspirational and more impatient youth and young population of the Indian democratic society, ICT needed to be pragmatic in bridging the gulf between the rich, middle class and weaker sections of the society. The greatest danger India is facing is the divide in ICT access that parallels the other divide in accessing infrastructure, capital and information that exist between India's rich and poor, educated and illiterate or semi-literate and urban vs. rural people. Community radios and televisions for example can be invaluable in building complementary technologies that give information to the people. A kiosk is another mechanism that is proving quite effective in rural India.

The National e-Governance Plan (NGP) launched in 2005 planned 100000 such kiosks to provide a variety of state services across India and thus empower the rural masses. ICT has been playing a vital role for the rural farming class. These efforts constitute a few step forward in the empowerment processes in the long and difficult journey. India has always seemed to be defined by many contradictions, to the extent that our contrasts are clichés: Asia's second largest slum is here, in the world's fastest growing democracy. A nation that is burgeoning knowledge power also has the largest number of school drop outs in the world.[36] In order to make India an IT superpower, India must move from today's paper ridden: red tape driven governance to electronic governance.[37] ICT and the mobile phone are turning out to be perfect tools for speeding up development, ensuring efficiency in governance, farming and business and reduce the digital divide." The digital divide deprives population to access and use ICT, furthering social economic and educational inequalities.[38] The 1999 Human Development Report issued by the United Nations has asserted that Information Technology is actually widening the gap between the world's have and have not instead of narrowing it. [39]. While the percentage of the world's population with mobile cell signal was 61 per cent in 2003, it has grown up to 90 per cent in 2010. In 2000, high income countries added 71 per cent more mobiles as compared to 29 per cent in developing countries. In 2012, the figure was roughly 23 per cent for the high income countries, whereas the developing countries added 77 per cent.[40] The internet has created a digital divide with some poor nations watching from a far as the World Wide Web (www) transforms commence and creates vast new source of wealth in the developinmg countries.[41]

India as a secular democracy has established its credibility among the nations of the world by enacting the various laws which have opened the doors for empowerment of women and weaker sections of the society including minorities. The Hindu Marriage Act 1955, outlawed polygamy and introduced the concept of divorce in Hindu Community. Equally significant has been the Hindu Succession Act 1956 which conferred full ownership of women for their share of the family property. The Muslim Women (Protection of Right on Divorce) Act, 1986 gave the man the option of making a one-time provision within three months for her life time depending on his economic status.

The Gandhian dream of *Gram Swaraj* (village self-governance) was realised in 1992 when the Government of India passed the 73rd Constitutional amendment followed by the 74th Constitutional Amendment to institutionalise Nagar Palikas in urban areas. The Panchayati Raj law demonstrated the efficiency of reserving one third of the constituencies for women, thus empowering rural Indian woman. The National Rural Employment Guarantee Act (NREGA) 2005, recently renamed after Mahatma Gandhi, has guaranteed employment for 100 days in a year to every rural household, volunteering to do unskilled manual work and has thus empowered the rural people, including women. The protection of Girl Right Act 1955 protected the Scheduled Castes and Scheduled Tribes against caste prejudices and discrimination. The Schedules Castes and Scheduled Tribes (Prevention of Atrocities) Act 1989, provided protection from more violent caste driven offences. The Right to Information Act 2005, acknowledged one of the most progressive transparency laws in the world, enables citizens to get information from the government.

India is a young democracy, saddled with problems of inexperience and that has endured ineffective, populist governments...... India's biggest weakness in fact may have come from too little democracy, rather than too much of it.[42] Problems of women particularly from the Scheduled Castes/Scheduled Tribes, Other Backward Classes and the Muslim minority are still being subjected to injustice, atrocities crimes and economic poverty. According to Vaughan- the priority of the scientific community and government should be empowering citizens, developing the tools and approaches to bridge the gap.[43] India stands at the crossroads of being a "state society"- a polity- quo and rejects change or "a dynamic society", one that is open to change.... It is about a mindset that refuses to accept change of any kind.[44] India is expected to miss the crucial UN Millennium Development Goals (MDG) including those relating to reduction in poverty, hunger and infant mortality. The poverty ratio is likely to be 26.7 per cent by 2015 as against the target of 23.9 per cent, while the Infant of Mortality Rate (IMR) would be 43 per 1000 live birth against the milestone of bringing it down to 27 per cent. The 21st century belongs to the Information and Communication Technology. Technology has given a voice to the young of the world. They are speaking out loud about issues that concern them, causes that they believe in things they stand for, all thanks to their constant companion technology.[45] In the present age Internet, smart phones, Tabs or what have you everything has fallen in place for the Gen Next to work their world magic on to keep themselves updated with stuff and are ready to launch their opinion in the online world without any hesitation.

Right from politics to prices of essential commodities, from Presidents election to rights of students, illogical comments made by some public figures about burning issues, the young blood, when it boils, lets out the steam by screaming out their views online by just using their smart devices.[46] India has to build a National Information Infrastructure with a strong political will to empower its people by providing them education, training, economic social and political impetus to build a dynamic society having all inclusive policy with due emphasis to the following:

1. Increasing awareness of ICT.
2. Increasing availability of computers at affordable rates.
3. Making effective cyber laws and making important amendments to the existing laws.
4. Making computer-learning a pre-requisite at various appointment levels.
5. Computerisation of personnel management system in the state and Central Government.

6. Constituting of the National Task Force for information Technology, Software and Training.
7. Adopting various appointment strategies to boost learning and use of I.T. in Indian Languages.

The enactment of the Information Technology Act, 2000 is a major step in promoting the use of Info-Tech in government and Industry.[47] Bill Gates has said: "As we look ahead into the future, leaders will be those who empower others" Dr. B.R. Ambedkar once said "I measure the progress of a community by the degree of progress which women have achieved." The UNDP Human Development Report of 1995 says "Human Development is impossible without gender equality. As long as women are excluded from the development process, development will remain weak and lopsided.

Sustainable human development implies engendering the development paradigm." Empowerment of Indian women is gathering momentum at least in metropolitan cities and some states. The contours of women participation have changed somewhat since the Lok Sabha Elections in 2009. This is evident in the most recent round of assembly elections in states like Bihar and Punjab in which women voters outnumbered men voters.[48]

In Gujarat Assembly Elections of 2012, the women voters outnumbered men in almost 50 per cent constituencies. This shows the political empowerment of Gujarat women and role of ICT in making them active participants in the political process of the country. Television has been able to play an important role in the changing nature of India's democracy by creating awareness about fundamental rights, Right to Information Act and the role of NGOs in bringing civil consciousness. Television we making people conscious of what life is like outside the walls of their villages.[49] The telecom sector, which has emerged as the India Infrastructure poster boy, has seen quite a transformation during the last two decades and has highlighted the role of ICT, in inclusive growth efforts. Role of ICT in bringing inclusive growth of the country can be assessed by the case study of MTNL, as discussed in the following paragraphs.

Case Study of MTNL

MTNL was set up on 1st April 1986 by the Government of India to upgrade the quality of telecom services, expand the telecom network, introduce new services and to raise the revenue for telecom development needs of India's key metros of Delhi and Mumbai with a stated vision to:

"Become a total solution provider company and to provide world class telecom services at affordable prices.

Become a global telecom company and to find a place among the Fortune 500 companies.

Become the largest provider of private networks and leased lines.

Venture into other areas in India and abroad on the strength of our core competency."

MTNL is the largest provider of fixed services in Delhi and Mumbai with its 567 digital exchanges and CDMA 2000 1X based fixed wireless service covering every corner of the two metros. It provides ISDN and centers facilities to customers on demand. It provides various free of cost phone plus facilities like: (a) Call alert, (b) Call Transfer/Forward, (c) abbreviated Dialing, (d) Hot Line Facility, (e) Dynamic Locking, (f) Three-Party Conference, (g) Wake up/Reminder Call, (h) Call Hunting Facility' and (i) Calling Line Identification Presentation (CLIP).

MTNL offers India's 3G Mobile services christened MTNL 3G *Jadoo* with network capacity of 5.05 million. The service provider high-speed mobile application like "Video Streaming" Live T.V., movie downloads, high-speed data download up to 3.56 mbps etc.

The service enables customer to make video calls and VOIP Calls to more than 100 countries. 3G data card is available with 3G Sims for high speed broadband upto 3.6 MBPs on a move. It provides its postpaid GSM mobile under the brand name Dolphin. Its mobile services come with a bouquet of value added services like location based services, Mobile Cricket and Radio, Play Tunes, Express Alerts, WAP/Gprs (176 kbps). Mobile T.V etc. It provides its Pre-paid services under the brand name of Trump. It comes with a package value added services like locationbased service, Mobile Cricket and Radio Play tunes, Express Alerts, WAP/GPRs (176 Kbps), Mobile T.V. etc. MTNL CDMA-based mobile service is provided under the brand name Garuda Mobile. The service is available to customer in both post-paid and pre-paid options. MTNL offers broadband services under the brand name Triband based on latest ADSL 2+ technology capable of data download speeds up to 26 MBPS. For entertainment MTNL offers India's first IPTV service, a television viewing experience with high quality digital signals and single point delivery of voice, video and data along with time -. T.V., Video on demand and gaming etc. MTNL provides other service like Wi-Fi services, Voice Over Internet Protocol (VOIP), MG MTNL Data card, intelligent network services and conexus mobile alliance. These services are providing customer care with the help of its 40500 highly trained work force as on 31.08.2012.

Concluding Remarks and Recommendation

Currently India is ranked 100th in terms of women representation in the Lok Sabha (Chief Legislature).

The per cent women reorientation is a mere 11 per cent which is much below the averages of most nations across the world including certain developing African nations. March 9, 2012 incidentally a day after International Women's Day, witnessed the historic sanction of the Women's Reservation Bill in the Rajya Sabha. The Bill answers 33 per cent reservation for women in Parliament as well as other state legislative bodies.[50] The move will not only help women their concerns addressed more effectively, it will hopefully enable Indian women the shackles of cultural stereotypes.

In a recent judgment of a division of Madras High Court bench/ comprising Justice Elintra Venkataraman and R. Karuppiah, on the petition of A Jothhimain said: "A Dalit women married to a Christian can retain status. We do not understand how visiting Church would result in the conversion from one religion to another.... The Constitutions recognises the freedom to practice any religion visiting places of worship is a matter of individual choice."[51] India is gradually making long strides in socio-economic development. There are anecdotes that marvel at the *pan wallah's* daughter with an I.T. degree, the farmer's daughter with an MBBS certificate, a three-wheeler driver of Bombay has a daughter who topped Indian Chartered Accountant final examination. Dalit women from U.P. becomes Chief Minister of U.P. four times in last twenty years. In the last decade, nearly two women have become literate to every man. More women are joining the workforce (though still too few).

Public participation of women in politics and in the media has increased. However, gender equality (like caste equality) is still a long way. The last decades have seen visible Dalit empowerment in politics and in wealth. We can witness the demographic din. India is growing younger, more urban, more middle class and with more women in Public roles.[52] With rapid urbanisation it is a journey millions are making as Ashish Nandy calls "an ambiguous journey to the city. In Uttar Pradesh and some other modern cities, the plight of Dalits has undergone a change. A research team consisting of Davesh Kapur, Chandra Bhan Prasad, Laut Pritchett and D. Shyam Babu, drew on a unique survey designed and implemented by members of the Dalit community to capture social practices and household conditions of two blocks of Uttar Pradesh in 1990.

They noticed the following three changes. "First, there have been major changes in the grooming, eating and ceremonial consumption patterns of Dalits, and signaling higher social status through adoption of higher status consumption patterns. Second, respondents report changes in the accepted behaviours between castes, with rapid erosion in discriminatory processes that stigmatised Dalits and non-Dalits increasingly accept hospitality in Dalit homes. Third, there have been shifts in the pattern of economic life, both away from and within the villages with increase in circular migration to distant cities to work and their shift into profession, as tailors, masons and drivers and into businesses as grocers and *paan* shop owners.[53] The survey reveals very substantial shift in Dalits lives, consistent with a growing sense of empowerment and opportunities and declaiming ability of others to impose social inequalities. Democratisation increasing levels of literacy, reforms carried out in response to empowerment policies of the government and important role of ICT, particularly television, have brought tremendous changes in the contours of women's political participation since 2009 Lok Sabha elections. The AIADMK in Tamil Nadu and BSP under leadership of Mayawati, have changed the outlook of voters and their levels in other socio-economic activities.

However, empowerment of women is a pre-requisite to transform a developing country and ICT particularly will have to play a very vital and dynamic role. Material prosperity, enlightened and better levels of professionalism, political participation and social emancipation will all be able to build a progressive India where women will be empowered into the following five components: Sense of self-worth, right to have power to contrast their own lives, both within and outside home, and their ability to change to create just social and economic order in India.

Mahatma Gandhi National Rural Employment Guarantee Scheme (MGNREGS) and Empowerment of the Poor

On 2nd February 2013, MGNREGS completed its seven years and it is the world's largest scheme for the empowerment of the poor people including SC/ST women and other rural peasants. Dr. Man Mohan Singh waxed eloquently on the success of the scheme and called it a key instrument for "Financial inclusion "at a Sarkari conference held at Vigyan Bhawan in New Delhi. Maharashtra, Tamil Nadu, Kerala, Haryana. Chhattisgarh and J and K have shown on increase in the jobs created under the scheme. Some other states have shown major decline in jobs over the period 2009-10 to 2011-12 from 284 crore person days to 211 crore person days. There is a dip of about 25 per cent in the first three years of UPA government. One person day is one person working for a day. In major decline in jobs over the period are Karnataka (65 per cent decline), Rajasthan (53 per cent), Assam (52 per cent), Gujarat (47 per cent), Bihar (45 per cent) and Madhya Pradesh (40 per cent). In most of these states, jobs for Dalits have declined by 70 per cent or more.

Latest data reveals a picture of declined employment generation under the scheme. Even more startling is the fact that the marginalised sections - Dalits and Adivasis have suffered the biggest decline as can be seen in Table 5 below:

Table 5: MGNREGS Work (Crore Person Days)

Year	*Total*	*SC*	*ST*	*Women*
2009-10	284	86	59	136
2010-11	257	79	54	123
2011-12	211	47	38	102
2012-13 (as of Feb. 2)	146	33	23	78
Decline over four years (%)	-48	-62	-61	-43

Source: Ministry of Rural Development and Report of *Sunday Times*, New Delhi February 3, 2013.

In three states, Tamil Nadu, Maharashtra and Chhattisgarh, this increase hides a bitter reality-work given to Dalits actually declimed while work given to "others" that is Uppar Caste poor, increased. According to Subodh Varma, in the case of Dalit households, work created under MGNREGS came down by 46 per cent over the first three years of UPA-II, from about Rs. 86 crore to Rs. 47 crore person, days. Average households too seem to be getting increasingly excluded from this lifetime of employment as work given to them declined by 35 per cent from Rs. 59 crore to 38 crore person, days.

Congress President Sonia Gandhi stressed to check graft in MNREGA and while addressing a meeting to mark the Seventh Anniversary of the launch of scheme said: "We frequently hear complaints of corruption and mis-utilisation of funds in this scheme. It is very essential to put a check on this". This scheme has brought momentum in the financial inclusions of the rural population. More than four crore bank accounts (of beneficiaries) have been opened and even more accounts have been opened in the post offices. This scheme can be used to provide irrigation facilities to small and marginalised farmers, for developing land and promoting farming among other things. Sonia Gandhi stressed the importance of timely conduct of Social audit and suggested using the modern I.T. Technologies to plug the deficiencies in the implementation of this scheme.

Criminal Law (Amendment) Ordinance 2013

President of India, Pranab Mukharjee on 3rd February 2013, gave his assent to the Ordinance sharpening laws against sexual assault, mandating harsher punishments like death penalty for offenders in cases where the victim dies or is pushed into a persistent death within six months. This Ordinance is a big leap towards empowerment of women and harsher punishment for crimes against women. The Ordinance goes beyond the recommendation of the Justice Verma Committee. The Ordinance prescribes a minimum in rarest of the rare rape cases and sentence of 20 years for serious offence. The Ordinance changes various clauses in existing criminal law by amending the Indian Penal Code, Code of Criminal Procedure and the Evidence Act. However, change in the mindset of police, proseution and judges is needed to make if really effective. The Supreme Court of India has recently in a division bench comprising of Justice Desai and Aftab Alam on January 3rd, 2013 said: "There is a phemomenal rise in crime against women and protection granted to the women by the Constitution of India and other laws can be meaningful only if those entrusted with the job of doing justice are sensitised towards women's problems". "The Supreme Court further added: In this case we will be failing in our duty if we ignore the insensitivity shown by the learned session judge to a serious crime committed against a hopeless women."

Less than Equal Status for Indian Women

Being equal to their male counterparts is still a far cry for Indian women. Not only are they marginal as public figures, an average Indian women can hardly call the shots at home or outside. In 2012, women occupied only eight out of 74 ministerial positions in the union council of ministers. There were only two women judges out of 26 judges in the Supreme Court and there were only 54 women judges out of 634 judges in various high courts, women can't even decide whether they can go to a doctor or pop a pill. Married women living in rural areas take 26 per cent of the decisions regarding obtaining health care for themselves and 7.6 per cent for purchasing major household items. Only 10 per cent decisions are taken by females regarding visiting their family and friends. The situation is no better for urban women, who take 29.7 per cent decisions regarding access to health care and 10.4 per cent for purchase of major household items; 12.2 per cent can decide whether to visit family and friends. Forty Six per cent of women (15-19 years) are not involved in any kind of decision-making. Around 40 per cent women have no access to money. Cruelty by husband and relatives continues to occupy the highest share (43.4 per cent) among the crimes committed against women in 2011, followed by molestation (18.8 per cent).

Only 10.4 per cent cases of cruelty committed by husband and relatives—underwent trial in 2011 and conviction was done in a paltry 8.3 per cent cases. The highest conviction rate of 16.5 per cent was observed by crime, importation of girls and the lowest at four per cent for indecent representation of women.[61] These statistics serve to underline the well-known fact that the overwhelming majority of women in India are severely disempowered. At a time, when "inclusive growth" is a popular *mantra*, it is sad-that as much as half of the population starts off with a disadvantage merely because of its gender. As urban Indian women seek more control over their lives and socio-economic empowerment, they face greater violence, more assaults and harassment by their own family members.

Women in India face systematic discrimination, patriarchal control and systematic disempowerment in almost all the parts of the country. However, there are some very powerful women in India today. It is not just Mrs. Sonia Gandhi, Jayalalitha, Mamta Banerjee, Mayawati and Meera Kumar who have proved that they are no less capable of doing anything. Sudha Murthy, wife of Infosys co-founder Narayan Murthy, Yasmeen Premji and Rohini Nilekani wife of UIDAI chairman, are the most empowered women in Corporate India. Nowadays there are some other women business leaders who have proved their merit and capabilities in the corporate world.

While women continue to makeup a small percentage of the senior leadership in organisations globally, Indian companies are doing much worse in terms of advancing female professionals to top leadership roles, says an unreleased report by a global HR consulting firm. Women leaders hold only five per cent of the top 100 senior roles in half on the Indian companies surveyed by Mercer where only 11 per cent organisation say they have more than 30 per cent women in the top deck. The survey covered 55 companies operating in India and 663 in Asia-Pacific. On a positive note, the report which was shared exclusively with TOI, also pointed out that 64 per cent of Indian firms say they have no barriers preventing women from advancing senior roles.

Around 14 per cent of companies blamed women's leadership styles and their unwillingness to promote themselves as one of the causes for their stagnation in the company hierarchy. India even when compared to the rest of Asia and numbers dip further when we consider only the boardrooms. "While the issue has been long established, what remains to be seen is a discernible impact of all the gender inclusivity initiatives and policies on the ground," says Nishchae Suri, MD, Mercer India.

But executive search firms say the change is being seen largely in the pipeline of potential CEOs which is strengthening gradually. "Today a global engineering major asked us to get a woman CEO for their India centre. These are new sectors opening up to women. So attitudes are changing. Judging women by the number of hours that they spend at work, that is an incorrect barometer and that's where companies go wrong", says R Suresh, CEO, Station Chase, an executive search firm.

Things are changing gradually. Vodafone India has started an executive committee level mentorship programme for high potential women in the middle management to propel them to the top spot. Additionally, it is mandatory for everyone in the senior leadership teams to have one female among their direct reports, what the Telco call the Plus One Target programme. Similarly, IT firm Mahindra Satyam kicked off a programme "Starting Over" last year aimed at getting senior women associates who are between 35 and 40 years back to work."We continue to engage in these programmes but things have not altered dramatically. We also recruit from the outside at senior roles with the aim of having at least 10 per cent women in leadership roles," says Hari T, Mahindra Satyam's Chief People Officers.

However, the green realities of injustice to women are a well-established fact in India. Even after six years of implementation of Rajinder Sachar Committee Report, there is little improvement in the socio-economic conditions of Muslim women. In Delhi and other capitals there are schemes galore but women are still unsafe and subjected to all types of harassment, cruelties and sexual assaults. It is actually about the mind-set that refuses to accept change of any kind. A complete overhaul of the criminal justice system particularly police enquiring agencies and courts is the need of the day. Supreme Court bench has said that there should be zero tolerance for anti-women crime after the following figures were seen by them.[62] The mind-set of the judiciary can be assessed by the following statistics in Table 6:

Table 6: Trials, Convictions and Acquittals Completed in 2011

1 of 6 Rape Trials Completed, 3 Acquittals for every conviction 15,423 of 95,065 trials completed in 2011	*4,072 Convictions Against 11,351 Acquittals*		
Trial Over	*Total Cases*	*Convicted*	*Acquitted*
MAHARASHTRA		205	807
1,012	13,819		
WEST BENGAL			
686	13,718	79	607
MADHYA PRADESH			
3,507	11,337	826	2,681
ASSAM			
769	5,777	179	590
UTTAR PRADESH			
1,447	5,725	816	631
ORISSA			
639	5,176	148	491
CHHATTISGARH			
886	4,687	217	669
KERALA			
201	4,521	31	170
BIHAR			
847	4,101	210	637
RAJASTHAN			
785	3,949	205	580
ANDHRA PRADESH			
1,007	3,794	111	896
GUJARAT			
211	3,151	31	180
TAMIL NADU			
353	1,973	72	281
DELHI			
448	1,887	186	262
KARNATAKA			
374	1,864	74	300
HARYANA			
578	1,555	135	443

1 of 6 Rape Trials Completed, 3 Acquittals for every conviction 15,423 of 95,065 trials completed in 2011	*4,072 Convictions Against 11,351 Acquittals*		
Trial Over	*Total Cases*	*Convicted*	*Acquitted*
PUNJAB			
427	883	155	272
MIZORAM			
57	165	46	11
SIKKIM			
20	98	11	9
CHANDIGARH			
21	67	9	12

In last eight years, one killer rapist was hanged and 25 were spared the gallows. India cannot build a 21st century progressive economy and democratic country with old age patriarchal, tradition ridden, conservative society – insular homes, fearful parents, shackled women, a gender-biased police and judiciary and a soft non-governing state apparatus." Inequality is a gender issue. It is time India began to address it. There is no turning back.[63] A festering sense of injustice and anarchy. To readdress the problems we need to carry out some fundamental reforms. Do we have the will, the political consensus and the dynamism to implement them?[64]

Suggestions and Recommendations

1. The role of ICT must be clearly identified in a comprehensive manner with a view to provide a positive role in empowerment of women in India. New web technologies ensure that you are only a broadband connection away from all your data your Google ID gets you five GB of free online storage and works with all the Google's web apps. All new ICTs can be effectively employed for empowerment of both urban and rural women provided they learn to utilise it.
2. The national knowledge network provides a huge potential for sharing knowledge and learning resources and it can help knit the education system in the country together says Dinesh Singh, Vice Chancellor Delhi University. The National Innovation Council, Constituted by the Prime Minister, under the chairmanship of Sam Pitroda, has been Committed to boost

innovation performance in the country, with a focus on inclusive growth.[65]

3. Digital democracy should be built-up in India for inclusive growth of the poor for their empowerment. According to Mahesh, former NASA Scientist, "We have a model in which we identify problems that we think can be solved using technology and we just build those platforms for their solutions and in the process a whole branch of other things starts to happen. You became public faces; you begin to impact government itself. We can usher digital democracy via social technology.
4. Researchers from the Centre for Energy Efficient Telecommunications and Bell Labs explain that the ICT industry, which delivers internet, video, voice and other loud services, produces about two per cent of the global CO_2 emissions. Internet emits 830 m tones of CO_2 per year. All efforts should be made to reduce the radiation effect. Controlling these harmful effects require new scientific researchers and efforts to find alternative systems.
5. Programme undertaken by the Central and State governments for empowerment of both rural and urban women should have regular quarterly social audit and also with the help of ICT, regular monitoring of these schemes must be carried out and findings with recommendation must be made public.
6. Illiteracy is the bane of empowerment of women particularly Dalits, minorities and weaker sections of the society. All efforts should be made at all levels to educate women at least up to 8th standard by granting them monetary and other incentives.
7. Access to employment is also an important aspect for empowerment of women. MGNREGS and other government schemes should target unemployment of women.
8. Malnutrition particularly of girl babies is also a great impediment in women empowerment. Nation should put greater efforts to reduce maternal mortality rate (MMR) by providing them hygienic and nutritional food during pregnancy period and after delivering at least for three months with proper medical facilities for delivering and at pre-natal stages.

9. The enactment of an Ordinance promulgated recently on the recommendations of Justice Varma Committee report is a very big leap in empowerment of women in India. The Ordinance needs to be publicised in all newspapers so that police, investigating officers and judiciary become sensitive for the strict enforcement of the Ordinance.
10. Indian women have been participating in genocide against female foetuses only because the patriarchal mindset sanctions it. Both men and women should be educated on gender equity and thus mindset needs to be changed.
11. Laws that need to be changed for gender parity should be properly identified and gender parity laws should be made on priority basis. A committee of legal; experts and social workers should be constituted to indentify gender-based laws and necessary amendments in the laws of the country should be made on priority basis.
12. Traffickers sell North East women, particularly girls for earning lot of profit by selling them, for work as bonded-labourers: as wives to men around the country too old or infirm to get one or as prostitutes in the brothels of the country.[66] The largest markets for trafficked women are metros like Delhi and Mumbai and States like Bengal, Goa, Kerala, Maharashtra and Haryana. Assam has become the hotbed for human traffickers from all over the country. Police and intelligence agencies should identify these traffickers and take legal action against such crime. Judiciary must be also sensitised to these inhuman criminal acts and they must grant them justice and freedom.
13. To stop crime and violence against women, it is imperative that the new generation is sensitised. The need of the hour is to sensitise the new generation about gender justice and gender equality, so that they develop a more balanced outlook towards women and girls. Sensitisation to women's rights and respect for the fairer sex has to be included first at home and then at school and universities. ICT can play a very vital and educative role in empowering women and to provide gender sensitivity. In Himachal Pradesh during recent state elections out of 29 women in fray, only three won and most women

candidates lost their deposits. Women must vote for their sisters and mothers and must empower them politically by voting for them and thus building-up their political empowerment. We need to change the mindset of our people, political bureaucrats and public at large.

14. ICT and education are two major tools in the hands of the government to focus on the total development and empowerment of women for better gender equity. Education for women should aim at the following: (a) All-round development of women, (b) Vocational development, (c) Communication skills, (d) Organisational skills, (e) Physical development including education on physical health and sex, (f) Social development including awareness about social issues, (g) General competence.[67] Women's study centers in various universities and colleges are already working on this and these institutes need better finance, better staff and a conducive environment to carry out women training for empowerment. What is required is the political will to implement and institutionalise the mechanism which will ensure that gender sensitivity is selected in the implementation of education programmes.
15. Gender sensitisation programmes for leaders, teachers, educators, administrators should be regularly organised and conducted in all sincerity and effort at their best. The entire educational syllabus at primary, secondary and higher levels should incorporate women-related issues with emphasis on women empowerment.

References

1. Collected works of Swami Vivekananda Volume 8 : Notes of class talks and lectures: Women of the East (p. 198) Quoted by "Awakening India" by Swami Vivekananda Publisher Ramkrishnan Mission, New Delhi 2011, p. 137.
2. Stromquist N.P (1993 "The Theoretical Basis for Empowerment" Paper presented at International Seminar on Women's Education and Empowerment (Hamburg: UNESCO Institute of Education).
3. Sydeda Hameed, Nations Conscience Finally Churned, NDC puts women and children at the Centre of Development. *The Times of India,* New Delhi Saturday, December 29, 2012.

4. http://wwwitu/ITU/D/SIS/gender/Index.html Mobile Connectivity and ICT Related Livelihood Skills for Women's SHGS-Adding Value to Lives of Rural Women, Gender Budget Cell, DOT, Govt. of India, New Delhi, workshop on gender Budgeting – March 18, 19, 2010 – Ministry of Women and Child Development and Indian Institute of Public Administration.
5. Jaya Indiresan, Education for Women's Empowerment, gender positive initiatives in pace-setting women's colleges. Konark Publishers Pvt. Ltd. 2002, pp. 4-5.
6. Rowlands J. (1998), Questioning Empowerment working with women in Honduras, London.
7. Freire P. (1970), Pedagogy of the Oppressed – New York the Seabury Press – 1973, Education for critical consciousness New York. The Seabury Press. p. 47.
8. Zimmerman M.A and Rappeport J.A (1988), "Citizen Participation, perceived control and psychological empowerment" *American Journal of Community Psychology* (16/5) pp. 725-50.
9. T.K. Arun, Democracy includes Women, too, *Times of India,* Chennai edition Eight February, 2011.
10. Edition Eight February 2011, *Times of India* – Rukmini Shrinivasan – India worst place in the world for girl child, *Times of India,* 5th August 2012.
11. Abhishek Singhvi – The Denial of Justice – To redress the problem, there are some fundamental reforms we need to carry out". *The Times of India,* New Delhi, Friday December 28, 2012.
12. Mahendra Kumar Singh, India to miss UN goals for poverty, hunger and infant mortality, *Times of India,* New Delhi 2nd January, 2013.
13. Harrimrat Kaur Badal (Lok Sabha M.P) – Apathetic at Raisina Hill – Photo – op accurse and empty platitudes rule the day. "*Indian Express,* New Delhi 25th December, 2012 p. 11.
14. Gul Panag, "Made by Patriarchy – while women's lack of safety is a societal problem, the state makes its worse." *Indian Express,* New Delhi December 25, 2012 p. 11.
15. (Source, NCBR reports (2002-11) Census Report 2001-2011. *Indian Express,* New Delhi 26.12.2012.
16. Sumudra Gupta Kashyap, when café by juveniles becomes a trend. *Indian Express*, New Delhi January 11, 2013.
17. Johnson T.A., To Digital Democracy via Social Technology, *Indian Express* New Delhi 21st January 2013, p. I.
18. Sanchar Shakti, Universal Service Obligations Fund – Department of Telecommunication, Department of Telecommunication, Govt. of India – p. 11.
19. Sumegha Gulati, Want women in crucial post Delhi Police, *Indian Express*.
20. Sanchar Shakti, Govt. of India p. 11.

21. Naazreena Bhaura, Empowerment of the Indian Muslim Women. The Multi-gazette September 26, 2006.
22. Subodh Varma, Have Govt. schemes failed Muslims.
23. These remarks were made at the Constitutent Assembly debates in 1948. (Ambedkar 1994), Ambedkar B.R. Writings and speeches Vol. I, Bombay 1979.
24. *Indian Express,* New Delhi, Sonia to Congress: Respect to demanding, changing India 19th January 2013. From the upper caste, mostly in caste-sensitive southern parts.
25. Casticism rules roast in Panchayat Mahalingam Ponnuswami, *Sunday Times of India*, Chennai, October 16, 2011.
26. Mayavati (born 15th January 1956) is an Indian Women Politician of U.P. who has been Chief Minister of U.P. for three short terms and one full term of five years.
27. Illiteracy bane for Dalit employment TNN Oct., 30, 2012. 05:39 AM IST.
28. Sohaila Abdulali, Because it is not about honour, The Indian Express New Delhi. 09/01/13 (She is the author of the famous novel "Year of the Tiger".
29. Subodh Varma, SC/ST fail to break the Caste Eailing, *Times of India,* Chennai, September 6, 2012.
30. Mohammed Ali, Dalit women pledge to snatch their rights, *The Hindu,* Dec. 5. 2012.
31. Ruth Manorama, Background information on Dalit women in India.
32. Dhananjay Mahapatra, Anti manual scavenging law soon: Govt. to SC, Times of India New Delhi 9th January 2013.
33. Ruth Manorama, Background information on Dalit women in India. Ibid
34. *Times of India*, View- the internet enables innovation Times of India 29th Decemebr 2012.
35. *Ibid*, Sanchar Shakti – Department of Telecommunication, Govt. of India, New Delhi, p. 16.
36. Nandan Nilekani, Imagining India, Ideas for the new country Penguin Books India, 2008.
37. Vittal Nand, Dr. S. Mahalingam, Information Technology, India Tomorrow, Manas Publications 2001, p. 97.
38. National Telecommunications and Information Administration (NTIA), US Department of Commerce 2002. A nation on line, How American are expanding their use of the internet Washington DC, also falling through the net, towards digital inclusion, Washington DC, NTIA.
39. Kanwar B. Mathur, Communications Indian Perspectives and Prospects, Mohit Publications, New Delhi, 2001. p. 149.
40. Mobile phone, Dial M for development, *Economic Times,* 2nd August 2012.
41. Mathur K.B., *Ibid.* p. 150 adopted the constitutions which declares India as a democratic socialist Republic.

42. Nandan Nilekani, Imaging India, Ideas for the new Country, Penguin Allen. 2008 p. 27.
43. Vaughan Hague 2007, Citizen Science as a catalyst in bridging the gap between source and decision-making proceedings of the citizen science toolkit conference, New York, June 2007.
44. Jug Suraiya, for a change, India at the crossroads of a static society and a dynamic society. *Times of India,* New Delhi 16/01/2013. To the report the poverty is likely to be 26.7 per cent compared to MDG target of 23.9 per cent by 2015. It was 29.8 per cent in 2009-10.
45. Anu Bhambhani, Crack the T-Quotient *Times of India,* 25th January 2013. p. 15.
46. Mahendra Kumar Singh, India to miss UN goals for poverty, hunger, infant mortality, *Times of India,* 2nd January 2013.
47. NN. Vittal and Dr. S. Mahalingam, Information Technology, India's Tomorrow, Manas Publications New Delhi, p. 162.
48. Rajeshwari Deshpande, No women constituency, *The Indian Express,* 18th January 2013, p. 13.
49. Nandan Nilekani, *Ibid* p. 169.
50. Nandita Sharma, The status of Dalit women in India from Depravity to Supremacy – An international literary Journal – Vol II Issue, spring (ISSN-2249-4529).
51. A Subramanium, "Dalit women married to a Christian to retain status". *Times of India,* New Delhi 31/12/12.
52. Vinay Sitapati, No escape from freedom, *India Express,* New Delhi 4th January 2013. p. 11.
53. Dawesh Kapur, Chandra Bhan Prasad and others, Rethinking inequality – Dalits is Uttar Pradesh is the Market Reform Era, *Economic and Political Weekly,* August 28, 2010 Vol XLV No. 35.
54. *Sunday Times*, New Delhi, February 3, 2013, MGNREGS records a sharp slide in job generation. pp. 1 and 16.
55. Need to check graft in MNGREGA Scheme can learn second green resolution, *Indian Express,* 3rd February, 2013.
56. Swati Deshpande, Judges must be sensitive to women's problems: S.C. *Sunday Times on India,* New Delhi, February 3, 2013. p. 15.
57. Data Source, "Men and women in India 2012". Ministry of statistics and programme implementation. Also Kounteya Sinha TNN, *Times of India,* New Delhi, December 4, 2012 for full report log on to www.times of india.com.
58. Zero Tolerance for anti-women crimes–says SC, *Times of India,* New Delhi 5th January, 2013.
59. Lord Maghnad Desai, The women question–out of my Mind, *The Sunday Express,* New Delhi 6th January 2013.

60. Abhishek Singh, Congress M.P. – The Denial of Justice, *Times of India*, New Delhi, Friday December 28, 2013.
61. 500 Institutes link-up DU for knowledge network take off Indian Express, New Delhi 24/1/13.
62. *Times of India,* New Delhi 24th December 2012. Women under Attack-Traffickers sell NE Women like cattle.
63. Jya Indresen, Education for women's empowerment. Konark Publishers Pvt. Ltd. 2002, pp. 43-44.

1

Introduction

Pandit Jawaharlal Nehru –

"to awaken the people, it is women (or the woman) who must be awakened' once she is on the move, the family moves, the village moves and the nation moves."

Shabana Azmi – *"Change towards empowerment can only come through drastic changes in mindsets."*

Brinda Karat – *"No amount of legislation will be ineffective as long as the political will to promote gender equity is absent."*

The Information and Communication Technology (ICT), comprises a complex and technological sets of goods, applications and services used to produce, process, distribute and transform information which consists of segments as diverse as telecommunication, television, radio broadcasting, computer hardware, software and services, like internet and *e*-mail. The term ICT has been used to encompass technological innovation, economic and business practices, education, occupation, health, leisure and entertainment. Over the past decade, ICT has become a powerful instrument for advancing economic development including empowerment through creation of new types of:

(i) educational advancement through computer-based education, on-line education, internet educational expansion and higher education with emphasis on research and specialisation;

(ii) economic activities;

(iii) new employment opportunities and avenues;

(iv) social networking and participations;

(v) Interaction between government; various organisation and people;

(vi) Transparency and accountability in government

The Twenty First century is the age of mass communication through satellites in outer-space. Information Technology (IT) has become a potent force in transforming social, economic and political life globally. A series of factors, including literacy and education, language, time, cost, geographical location of facilities, social and cultural norms and women's computer information, search and dissemination skills constrain women's access to information technology in India and other third world countries. Information and Communication Technologies are both enabling and contributing factors to globalisation, political governance and expansion of business.

Communication Technologies (CTS) are a diverse set of technological tools and resources to create, disseminate, store, bring value-addition and manage information. They are for everyone and women have to be an equal beneficiary to the advantages offered by the technology, and the products and processes which emerge from their use. The benefits accrued from the synergy of knowledge and CTs need not be restricted to the upper strata of the society but have to freely flow to all segments of the women population.[1] The gamut of areas in which ICTs can put a greater control in the hands of women is wide and continuously expanding, from managing water distribution at the village level to standing for local elections and having access to life-long learning opportunities. In low literary societies, non-print mass media – i.e., radio and television – are a more important source of entertainment and information than print media, especially for women[2]. During the last 20 years, there has been a dramatic expansion of television in different parts of the country.[3] Information and Communication Technology affect the quality of work and careers, skill enhancement and autonomy at work. Telephone, mobile telephone, television are gender neutral and are capable of empowering people. The growing share of knowledge-based production at the global level warrants economies to develop a degree of technological capability that would equip them to compete in the global market better given a perceived ability to create decent employment opportunities. Government perceives the promotion of ICTs to be critical to employment generation and thereby reduce or aggregate inequities across segments. Diffusion of ICTs has increased, the ability of firms to link distant markets, economise on inputs and increase speed of product design, development and production. The government has identified ICTs to be a thrust sector for future growth in national wealth and quality employment. The application of IT in India was characterised by the Population Census Compilation in the 60s, Airlines reservation in the 70s, Railway reservation in the 80s and Stock Exchange Trading in the 90s. The growth of the IT/IT enabled services has been impressive jumping from $4.8b and 1.2 per cent of GDP in 1998 to $37.4b and 4.7 per cent of GDP in 2006. Some 1.3 m people are directly employed in the sector with many more in the subsidiary and supporting industries.[4] The Department of Information and Technology is encouraging investment in this sector by promoting all infrastructure growth, fiscal incentives, and tax exemptions to reap benefits of growth in service sector, exports, and employment generation.

Empowerment of Women – Main Components and Indicators

Noted economist, Amartya Sen has opined that "India's population problem has only one remedy; social development in a gender-sensitive way. What is required to check the growth in fertility rate is education, social awareness and emancipation of women." In 2001, 63.24 per cent of the male population has been returned as literate compared to 45.15 per cent of the female population nationally. The analysis of literacy levels of the 'worker' population for 2001 reveals a disturbing contrast between male and female workers. While 70.50 per cent of the male workers are literate, only 35.70 per cent female workers are literate. In India, gender inequities are structural in nature. It is, therefore, proposed to study how women could be empowered in India. In 1990s, when terms like 'participation', consultation and partnership began to enter the development thinking, importance given by development agencies was shifted to enabling approach i.e., enabling people to identify and express their needs and priorities. It is in this context the notion of empowerment has arisen.[5] The use of the concept of empowerment has greater relevance and applications to third world countries (including India) which are characterised by high levels of poverty, feminisation of poverty, low female literacy, invisibility of women and strong patriarchal and community values.[6] The components of empowerment are (i) women and men's sense of internal strength and confidence to face life; (ii) the right to make choices; (iii) the power to control their lives within and outside the home; (iv) the ability to influence the direction of social change towards the creation of a more just social and economic order nationally and internationally. Empowerment therefore has multiple dimensions. These are education, economic development, consciousness raising and organisational skills and political participation[7]. The following indicators broadly formed the premise for women empowerment:

(1) Increase in age of marriage.

(2) Becoming beneficiaries of development programmes.

(3) Visible changes in physical status/nutritional status.

(4) Improvement in literacy level.

(5) Becoming members of a political party or local self-government.[8]

Empowering implies increasing women's self-reliance, internal strength and choices through enhancing their ability to gain control over material as well as non-material resources including access to credit, right to own land and property, political equality and adequate protection against male violence etc., which have been defined as strategic gender need.[9] Empowerment is an activity which aims to reduce the powerlessness that has been created by negative valuation-based on membership in stigmatised group. Empowerment is a holistic approach for achieving women's socio-economic development. To help women to attain economic independence is the first priority.

It simply means the idea that giving women powers over their economic, social and reproductive choices which will raise their status, promote development and reduce population growth. Women empowerment has to be viewed as a continuum of several inter-related and mutually reinforcing components:

1. Awareness building about present status, discriminations and rights and opportunities as a step towards gender equality. Awareness has to be individual as well as collective.

2. Capacity building and skills development in the present age of computers and communication technology.
3. Participation and greater control and even decision-making power in the home, community and society.
4. Developing appropriate mind-sets and attitudes towards life, society and family.
5. Education and vocational training to bring confidence and competence.
6. Action to bring greater equality between men and women.
7. Willingness to challenge and fight inequalities, gender bias and even domestic violence.

According to the National Policy of Education, Government of India (1986), "Women become empowered through collective reflection and decision-making". Its parameters are building a positive self-image and self-confidence, developing the ability to think critically, building up group cohesion and fostering decision-making and action, ensuing equal participation in the process of bringing about social change, encouraging group action in order to bring about change in the society providing the wherewithal for economic independence. Women's empowerment implies individual as well as collective empowerment. Empowerment may merely aim at improving women's income, health or eradication of social evils like dowry, child marriage etc, or it may deal with questioning gender relations and power equations."[10] Individual empowerment is building positive self-image and self-confidence, developing the ability to think critically, cultivating decision-making power etc. Collective empowerment means enabling women collectively to take control of their own lives, to set their own agendas, to organise to help each other and make demands on the state for support and on society itself for change. Empowerment is access to and control over productive resources, knowledge and awareness of one's self and society and personal needs, health issues, legal rights, technological innovations and the availability of social and economic resources, how to take advantage of them, self-image, i.e., realisation of one's capabilities and the potential and confidence to take action in one's life are the components of empowerment. According to Naila Kabeer, "Women empowerment is a process whereby women are able to organise themselves to increase their own self-reliance, to assert their independent rights, to make choices and to control resources which will assist in challenging and eliminating their own subordination."[11] It is the right to determine the choices in life and to influence the direction of change, through the ability to gain control over material and non-material resources. In Indian context, the empowerment process is both strategic and practical. It is more strategic i.e., changing patriarchal norms, gender division of labour, gaining equality and changing the attitudes of society towards women. It is more practical to meet the basic needs, increase in income, educating and giving training in skill – development to meet the basic needs of daily life – food, housing, health-care, and welfare measures to the women. Encouraging self-employment of women is one of the ways of empowering women who are in unorganised sector. Going further the embroidery sector is a creative pursuit of woman who finds means to express her world and also earn a living. Since it is an unorganised informal sector, the IT revolution which 'networks' the world makes her a 'part' of the 'whole' from which she can benefit in manifold ways.

According to UNICEF findings, "One of the most understudied areas in informal sector activities in developing countries are that of home-based manufacturing activities.

(S Mehrotra, M Biggeri - World Development, 2005 – Elsevier. http://scholar.google.co.in/scholar?hl=en&lr=&q=related:dqfyul9_LZoJ:scholar.google.com/&um=1&ie=UTF-8&ei=jvNrS5bqGY7o7APZi-l2&sa= X&oi=science_links&resnum=1&ct=sl-related&ved=0CAkQzwIwAA)

Embroidery fits into this requirement perfectly, so it becomes an area of wide interest for research. For analysing empowerment of women in India during (2000-2005), an important question relates to how equal women are vis-à-vis men. The Constitution of India adopted in 1950 is progressive not only in granting equality to women but also in empowering the state to adopt measures of affirmative discrimination in favour of women.

Constitution of India and Women Inclusion

The Indian Constitution shows the way in which the Founding Fathers visualised the erection of modern India where everyone will have liberty and equality of opportunity. Did they foresee the future of women as equally provided and privileged is a question that weighs on the researcher's mind.

One of the crucial functions of Indian Constitution is to safeguard the interest of the minority. In India, Muslims are the largest minority. In 1991, there were 110 million, Muslims making up 12.6 per cent of the population. There are five states in which the Muslim population is higher than the national averages: Assam (28.43 per cent), Kerala (23 per cent), West Bengal (23.16 per cent), Uttar Pradesh (17.3 per cent) and Bihar (16 per cent), Karnataka has 11.6 per cent. Professor Neera Chandoke in her book Beyond Secularism – The Rights of Religious Minorities has made the following basic assumptions:[12] (1) Individuals are embedded to specific traditions and historical contexts and they acquire their substantive conceptions of the good from their affiliative community. (2) Communities have the capacity to mould and shape individual perceptions of the good therefore they are of value. (3) The value of the affiliative community should be granted recognition in the sense of being respected and given regard. (4) Different communities have different notions of the good. (5) Since communities are good for the individual, communities that are vulnerable to majoritarionism should be granted special protection through special rights. (6) Minorities cannot abuse their rights as far as other communities are concerned. There are a number of popular myths that Muslims have to constantly negotiate which are as follows:

(i) Successive governments have pampered and appeased the Muslim Community.
(ii) Muslims are polygamous and therefore their numbers are increasing.
(iii) Muslims are opposed to family planning methods, their fertility rates are higher because of which they will soon outnumber the Hindus.
(iv) Muslims are anti-national and have deep emotional ties with Pakistan.
(v) Muslims have been given special privilege through Article 370 of the Indian Constitution.[13]

All these myths are baseless and are floated out of media and prejudices against minorities for political advantages. There is absolutely no truth in these myths.[14] Actually, Muslim women are victims of overt and covert discrimination. Their social indices are very close to those of Dalits who in more ways than one have been the most discriminated lot of Indian Society.

A national survey covering about 10,000 Muslim and Hindu women has made the following findings: The low socio-economic status of Muslim women is now well-known; like the Scheduled Castes, they are disproportionately represented among the poor and have the lowest per capita income indicators. This is ascribed not only to lack of access to asset ownership, but also to poor educational attainment and occupational patterns, which show clustering in low-paid activities, as well as the concentrations of the Muslim population in the economically backward regions of the country. In the survey, 59 per cent had never attended school and less than 10 per cent had completed school. Financial constraints and gender bias dominated over other factors in determining levels of education. The study found that 26 per cent of the educated Muslim women had illiterate husbands.[15] The low age of marriage is a major inhibiting factor. At the national level, the mean age of marriage of Muslim girls is very low at 15.6 years and in the rural north it falls to an appalling 13.9 years. Low marriage age is usually associated with high early fertility, which affects women's nutrition and health status. By sheer strength of their numbers, Muslims constitute the second largest segment of the country's population. Muslim women's early marriage and fertility tend to reduce women's autonomy and create conditions of patriarchal subservience that gets perpetuated through life and it thereby often reduces self worth. The work participation rate of women across Muslim communities tends to be low in certain regions, especially in the north and the east. Seventy per cent of the women in the survey reported that they need permission from their husbands to work outside the home and they have relatively less autonomy of decision-making within the household.[16] Muslim women are also victims of domestic violence and they come third (after SC/ST and Other Backward Castes) at 18 per cent and husbands were identified as the primary perpetrators in more than 80 per cent of cases.

The Government of India is committed for implementing the National Policy for Empowerment of Women (2001) into action through: (a) creating an enabling environment for women to realise their full potential; (b) *de jure* and *de facto* enjoyment of all human rights and fundamental freedom in political, economic, social, cultural and civil spheres; (c) providing equal access to participation and decision-making in national building and to health care, quality education, career and to health-care, and vocational guidance, employment, equal wages, occupational health and safety, social security and public office etc; (d) strengthening the legal system aimed at eliminating of all forms of discrimination and violence against women and (the girl child); (e) changing societal attitudes by involving Community participation – both men and women; (f) mainstreaming gender perspective in development process; and (g) building and strengthening partnership with Civil Society (particularly women's organisation and the corporate and private sectors).

Empowerment–Theoretical Thrust

A review of available literature reflects considerable diversity in the terminology, emphasis and agenda used to discuss women's empowerment. The concept of empowerment is process (Kabeer 2001; Oxaal and Baden 1997; Rowlands 1995)[17]. "Empowerment is a process of change – towards greater freedom of choice and action or greater equality, or gender equality or female autonomy or women's status in family or society. Women themselves must act as agents of change or agency of change in the form of significant actors. Empowerment is the expansion in the people's ability to make strategic life choices in a context where this ability was previously denied to them. Education and Employment are the enabling factors, resources or sources of empowerment. Information and Communication Technology is a powerful means and end for both education and employment therefore greatly instrumental in empowerment process". Mass media like television, radio, and internet are vital and visible instruments for education and information dissemination (Kishor 2000).[18] Economic, social and political resources are often critical in ensuring that women are empowered but they are not by themselves sufficient. The word "Empowerment" is a comprehensive process of empowering both individual and collective capacity. At a workshop of Pacific Women entitled "Women Development and Empowerment", Vannessa Griffen spoke about what empowerment means to her. According to her power means:

(1) Having control or gaining further control;

(2) Having a say and being listened to;

(3) Being able to define and create from a women's perspective;

(4) Being able to influence social choices and decisions affecting the whole society (not just areas of society accepted as women's place);

(5) Being recognised and respected as equal citizens and human beings with a contribution to make;

(6) Power means being able to make a contribution at all levels of society and not just in the home. Power also means having women's contribution recognised and valued.

In India, empowering marginalised groups such as Scheduled Tribes, Scheduled Castes and Muslims is a great challenge to the policy-makers and economic planners. In India, social exclusion essentially involves "the process through which individuals or groups are wholly or partially excluded from full participation in the society within which they live-in this sense it is opposite of social integration."[19] The Scheduled Castes (SCs) constitute the largest social group [accounting for about 17 per cent (equivalent to 167 million of India's population. The Scheduled Tribes (STs) or Adivasis constitute second largest social group, accounting for about 8 per cent of India's population and are closer to the SCs in terms of exclusion, deprivation, discrimination and violation. These two social groups have suffered from immense backwardness and deprivation. Muslims belonging to minority community also present a dismal scenario in education and employment, greater economic deprivation and lower levels of consumption. Women of above mentioned groups face survival inequality, natal inequality, unequal facilities, ownership inequality, unequal burden of household chores, domestic violence and physical victimisation in India and need empowerment.

The paradigm shift from women as recipients of state bonanza to agency is the approach where women are considered equal to men and capable of contributing to the economic development in the recent occurrence in India. Women self-help groups have often been considered as a strategic way to organise the poor women into homogenous groups and make way for channelising services like micro-finance, micro-enterprise and micro-insurance with necessary linkages to technology, market support and other needed inputs. Women constitute one-half of the segment of population in India. The 2001 Census counted 495.7 million females against a total population of 1027.01 million in which 207.8 million women live in the rural areas and 27 per cent of the rural women live below the poverty line. Empowerment of women is a complex and deeply meaningful word. Empowerment – a big word – isn't some weighty, abstract notion, but a pulsating idea that evokes both hope and frustration, engenders consensus as well as debate and holds a great promise and much greater challenge for every one. Empowerment means different things to different people. Aruna Roy says, "Democracy theoretically offers every individual an equal voice in deciding our collective future. This is empowerment. But it is a long voyage from theory to practice." Empowerment has to be seen through the eyes of the dis-empowered. The battle against poverty, ignorance, illiteracy and disease is, above all, a fight for the empowerment. It is a continuous fight against conditions of poverty, deprivation, squalor, illiteracy, ignorance, intolerance and prejudices. The women who constitute almost 50 per cent of our population are yet to have an effective share in the political decision-making processes, especially in our representative institutions only through universalisation of education, laying special stress on vocational training and on the higher education of the girl child; we can achieve true empowerment of our women. It is through well-designed and career-oriented education that can equip the women to make their own contributions to the productive processes in the society. Empowerment implies participation in the decision-making process at all levels. Empowerment implies freedom to live free from fear, freedom to study and to work, freedom of have choice and freedom to choose. Empowerment cannot be truly meaningful without a minimum level of high quality education, basic health services and adequate child nutrition. Empowerment would be meaningful only when women electorate, weaker sections like Scheduled Castes and Scheduled Tribes and Minorities are provided equal opportunities of free participation in the electoral process without any fear of malpractices or guns and there is level-playing field for all women. Professor Amartya Sen has opined, "The ability of the poor to participate in economic growth depends on a variety of enabling social conditions. It is hard to participate in the expansionary process of the market mechanism (especially in the world of globalised trade), if one is illiterate or unschooled, or if one is bothered by under-nourishment and ill-health or if social barriers (such as discrimination related to race and gender), excludes substantial parts of humanity from fair economic participation." It is important to attend to those - "unfreedoms" – a term used by Professor Amartya Sen, which refer to preventable diseases, illiteracy, needless hunger, premature mortality, social exclusion and economic insecurity.

Vasundhara Raje has said, "Historically, under the garb of socio-cultural and religious structures, women in India have not been treated fairly, leave aside equally. I hang my head in shame when I hear about conscious female foeticide; is the girl child still so unwelcome". For empowerment of women, organising women to be economically productive citizens is both a challenge and a fulfillment.

Pranab Mukerjee has said, "Empowerment to me means internalisation and implementation of normative values of democracy, freedom, equality, education and equitable socio-economic development, as enshrined in our Constitutional network that subsumes the organs of both state and society". Empowerment to women will come when they would have complete freedom and ability to make "informed judgement" about their destiny. Empowerment is about the ability to make "choices".

Kapil Sibal says, "Empowerment means the use of science and technology to resolve issues of everyday life". Empowerment is about providing opportunities to achieve its potential, through education, health care, nutrition, shelter and employment.

This exercise aims to examine and refer the role of ICT in creating the "enabling environment". These can be powerful source of sensitising the poor and rural women who have been denied access to formal education. The television has achieved this, though in a small way, as proved by many research studies conducted in several states in India.

However, the labour impacts of ICT have received little research attention in the content of developing economies even though they seek to provide highly productive, efficient and quality employment in the economy.[20]

A very revolutionary and successful experiment has been carried out by putting ICTs in the hands of the 'Chikan Embroidery' workers of Kanpur and Lucknow. The Data Mation Foundation and Info-Dev Designed multi-dimensional, multi-stake holder information and communication technology (ICT) in the hands of embroidery workers in twelve poor communities in the Lucknow, Kanpur area to impart training in I.T., handicrafts and other traditional vocations in addition to providing information on health, education and women empowerment. In each CMC, computers with internet access, high-speed printers and scanners have been provided to enhance both the vocational and basic ICT skill to the disadvantaged and marginalised women by assigning them to Self-Help Groups (SHGs) and these groups were trained using the Micro-soft unlimited potential curriculum in addition to ICT-based vocational and skill-based modules. Results of this experiment have been mentioned in subsequent chapters. For example, Rail Bazaar CMC Kanpur was established in September 2004 and has trained 525 participants through the Microsoft unlimited potential curriculum, four women have been trained to use 'chikankari' and 585 participants have been trained in ICT-led vocation courses and soft skills such as tailoring, embroidery, stitching, painting, hennamaking, ceramics and tailoring. Participants and trainees were motivated to complete their higher education through distance learning programmes through the National Institute of Open Schooling (NIOS) and Indira Gandhi National Open University (IGNOU). Muslim women of Basmandi CMC Kanpur, took advantage of this project. And 82 women completed their Microsoft Untapped Potential Courses.[21] – Empirical studies upon empowerment have been made from a range of disciplines – political science, anthropology, sociology, demography and economics. Empowerment of women is not an issue to "Women" alone, it is an issue creating a more human, equitable and democratic society where every human being can live a life of dignity and fulfillment. Women have the primary role of home-makers and national builders by rearing children in all societies since time immemorial. There are numerous studies on empowerment but only a few selective studies are being reviewed here. A.K. Sinha in his book "*Panchayati Raj and Empowerment of Women* (2004)", gives a detailed account of the empowerment of women in villages of Haryana State-based on his field work.[22] Brinda Karat has grouped her book into six section each around distinct theme, such as strategies adopted by AIDWA over time; globalisation and survival issues; political participations; women's interface with communalism and violence against women.[23] Similarly, *Micro-credit, Poverty and*

Empowerment-Linking the Triad (2005), edited by Burra Neera is a collection of six case studies of governmental and quasi-governmental organisations initiated by NUDP and ICICI Bank to assess the impact of micro-finance activities on women's empowerment and poverty reduction in India. "Women's Empowerment through capacity building – Enduring efforts in Bangladesh" by Ashutosh Bose (2004) with a foreword by Ela Bhatt is a pioneering work. It is a brilliant study of capacity building of the rural women of Bangladesh through the organisation of Ganosasthya Kendra. Important elements of the Ganosasthya Kendra strategy include the following:

1. Capacity building not charity (every member has to pay an initial fee);
2. Skill formation is essential and everybody can be trained;
3. What men can do, women can also do;
4. No gender discrimination at work;
5. Vital role of para-medics;
6. Pervading spirit of idealism, patriotism and solidarity.

Sujit Kumar Dutta and Dilip Kumar Ghosh analyse several interesting aspects of women empowerment issues in their book "*Empowering Rural Women* (2002). The major discussion of the empowerment process pertains mainly to the profile of women workforce, status of female-headed households, policies and programmes related to women, empowerment of women through literacy and women in Panchayat. The book is broadly divided into six chapters and it adopts both macro and micro considerations.[24] The women empowerment has to be understood through various dimensions conjointly rather than in isolation. Micro Finance for Women (2005) by S.N. Dhar deals with the concept of Micro-finance and its development implication as well as its impact on women's empowerment. Sadhna Arya in her book "*Women, Gender, Equality and the State*" (2000), writes about the various measures for empowering women. The various approaches to women's issues that have been adopted are as follows:

1. Poverty alleviation and income generation through programmes like IRDP, DWCRA and TRYSEM;
2. Education and employment received much attention in the decade 1975-85 and this is called development approach;

3. Participation and Empowerment approach stressed that empowerment can be achieved through groups, raising awareness and providing economic and social support services.

Neeta Tapan in her book, "*Need for Women's Empowerment*" (1998), Rawat Publication, Jaipur, notes that women are still not empowered and gender equality and justice are yet to be achieved. Women have to make an effort to change their attitude and liberate themselves from the socio-cultural quagmire. Rita Bakshi, M.S. Rathore, Meena Agarwal and Manjula Tyagi (eds) brought out *Economic Empowerment of Rural Women in India* (2003). The Issue of economic empowerment of women is of paramount importance to political thinkers, social scientists and reformers, women activists, politician, academicians and administrators. The book covers the following major aspects pertaining to the economic empowerment of women in India:[25]

1. Role, status and contribution of rural women;
2. Problems of rural women;
3. Efforts made by the Government for betterment of women's economic condition and status in society;
4. Remedial measures and alternative strategies required for accepting and enhancing the contribution of women in socio-economic and other spheres of life.

Mondal Sheikh Rahim in his book: *Rural Muslim Women – Role and Status* (2005) is a study of women of North Bengal. Muslim women in his sample are not economically independent. Illiteracy and low education are quite rampant although some positive changes are taking place due to modernisation and younger generation getting education. Muslim women play an invisible role in their society but have concealed power and position in functioning of the society. They are respected for their domestic role but are also exploited in many ways. V Mohini Giri (1998) in her book: "*Emancipation and Empowerment of Women*"[26] with her intimate knowledge and incisive analysis, presented an authentic account of the multiple concerns of social-political and economic facts, such as empowerment of women, gender justice, women's rights, social legislation, custodial justice, gender equality with social justice, role of media, democracy and governance and other related subjects. It contains fourteen chapters. *Conditioning and Empowerment of Women: A Multi-dimensional*

Approach (2003) has been edited by Mukerjee and Bhattacharya. The issue of empowerment is viewed from different dimensions by well-known feminist writers. It deals equally with the theoretical issues relating to empowerment as well as issues involved in practice. Male cooperation is essential to really empower women. *Education and Socio-economic Perspectives of Women Development and Empowerment*, is written by Aruna Goel (2003). She highlighted the discrimination women face in employment and in the economy especially in this age of liberalisation, privatisation and globalisation. Government should impart excellent educational and vocational training to women so that they can compete with men. She enumerates various rural development schemes which are meant to empower women but have not been able to do so to the full extent due to poor implementation. Promila Kapur in her book "*Empowering the Indian Women*" (2001), Delhi Publications Division, Delhi has recognised the empowerment of women as a central issue in determining the situational reality of their status. The book contains articles by experts and scholars dedicated to the cause of women empowerment. Although the Government of India declared the year 2001 as Women's Empowerment year, yet women continue to be exploited, abused, discriminated and victims of crimes and violence. This publication is a unique collection of data covering comprehensively the analysis of the concept, multifarious facets and the obstacles that come in the way of women's real empowerment. There are eighteen articles regarding various aspects of empowerment such as education, poverty, health-care, combating violence of women victims, women's political participation, and family for women's empowerment and positive values and attitudes for women's empowerment.[27] Goldstein study *Indian Women in Transition* (1972) is an empirical study and has a purely sociological perspective. It seeks to probe how the new values created by higher education among women are creating conflicts with the traditional family-centered values.[28] Srivastava in her study, "Employment of Educated Married Women – Its causes and consequences with reference to Chandigarh" (1972) has proved that at each socio-economic level wives are working in occupation which are consistent or only slightly lower in prestige from that of their husbands occupations. An important finding of her study is that working women harbour a sense of guilt due to realisation of fact that constant attention of the mother and her presence are needed for the development of a child's personality.[29] Another book "*The Women, Gender and Development Reader*" *edited by Nalini Visvanathan*, Lym Duggan, Laurie Nisonoff and Nan Eiegerma, (1997) is a useful collection of 35 articles written by various scholars. The book examines the key theoretical debates and discourses surrounding women and development from historical perspective. The book contains one article "*SEWA – Women in Movement*" written by Rose Kalima, based in Ahmedabad (Gujarat) SEWA (the Self-Employed Women's Association) successfully integrates a complex myriad of lives, occupations and issues into one union. SEWA has four main functions, Cooperatives, Unions, Bank and Services. SEWA has three cooperatives: Artisan Cooperatives, Vendor Cooperatives and Service Cooperatives. Embroiderers are members of the artisan cooperatives in Gujarat. The SEWA bank deals with savings, credits, life insurance, mortgage recovery and asset titles. The SEWA services cover video SEWA, child-care, training communication, legalaid, community health service, SEWA polytechnic and maternity protection scheme. SEWA Unions have trade groups covering garment stitchers, *bidi*-rollers, used garments dealers, vendors, domestic workers, scrape collectors, construction workers, *papad* waferrollers, carpenters, smiths, agricultural labourers, tobacco processors, full trades. SEWA has more than 30,000 members in its fold. SEWA is an ideal organisation for women to join and make life better by empowerment.

Neerja Desai's (1957) book "*Women in Modern India*" has attempted to describe the actual position of women in their varied role from the past to the present. She has asserted that women themselves must throw away the crushing burden of the past and for their purpose they must launch concerted action.[30] Social empowerment of women is about freedom of thought and speech, freedom to participate in decision-making and freedom to work without social bondage. It also demands equality of opportunity that is, equal access to economic, social, political and cultural opportunities to all citizens. V.S. Naipaul in his book "*India – Million Mutinies Now*" (1990) observes: "The processes quickened with the economic development that came after independence. The liberation of spirit that has come to India could not come as release alone. In India with its layer below layer of distress and cruelty it has to come as disturbance. It had to come as a rage and revolt. India was now a country of a million little mutinies."[31] People both men and women are now caught in wave of change where they are prepared to commit any upheaval. Empowerment of women of minority and Scheduled Castes/Tribes are bound to stir many mutinies in Indian families. The sleeping women folk are gradually awakening up with various socio-political developments.

In the same view on other work such as *Women Empowerment – Issues, Challenges and Strategies* (2005) by Kumar H. and Varghese J.; Empowerment of Women (2002) by Grover and Grover; *Empowering Rural Women – Issues, Opportunities and Approaches* (2205) edited by Samanta R.K. and *Empowerment – Sustainable Human Development Strategy for Poverty Alleviation* (2004) by Puthen Kalam J.J. dealt with various faces of women's empowerment and various strategies to achieve them. Games S. Jaquette[32] seeks to catalyse innovative thinking and practice within the field of women and gender in development. They have brought together scholars, policy-makers and development workers to reflect on where the field is today and where it is headed. From the analysis of changing institution to the control of resources, political participation, gender mainstreaming and many other relevant themes the book makes an excellent contribution to the historical analysis of the field and its current developments and tensions. In USA, in the 1990s the development paradigm also included women. This shift meant that resources began to flow to women in villages and slums and supported the elite women who organised them. Women broke out of their patriarchal shackles and began to accumulate power, status and ultimately empowerment. According to Irene Tinker, development programmes not only encouraged women in U.S. to organise but also provided them with funding, training and a broader world-view. Danish economist Ester Boserup in her research in India in the 1950s convinced her that the prevailing theories about agricultural development were inaccurate and failed to measure women's economic activity on or off the farm. Khulsam, a Muslim tea-seller in Ahmedabad, had been a SEWA worker for fifteen years. She received 35 rupees a day for trying to recruit more SEWA workers. This case has been reported in this book.

Ranade and Ramchandran's study Women and Employment (1970) is based on reports of two studies – one conducted by the

Delhi School of Social Work and the other, on behalf of the Ministry of Education, Govt. of India. The main purpose of these studies was to find out the attitude of women towards employment particularly part-time employment. The survey concluded that a large majority of women did not favour part-time jobs because of insufficient remuneration.[33] "*Sociology of Globalisation – Perspectives from India*"[34] edited by Sakarama Soamayaji's and Gandsha Soamayaji (2006) has been published by Rawat Publications, Jaipur. It contains articles contributed by 23 scholars dealing with diversity of themes and offering context. As a concept and an empirical process, globalisation has been attracting much social scientific attention in recent years, so much so that the word has attained the notoriety of being a buzzword. Sabir Ali has given a sociological perspective of the globalisation and the urban poor being enumerating lessons from Delhi Slums.

Devki Jain (1975) in her book "*The Indian Women*" has analysed various problems that confront women of various categories and belonging to different regions of the country. The author maintains that this is a need for formulating a carefully thought-out ideology which should suggest alternative paths of progress for women and also provide an alternative vision of future.[35] *India – Social Development Report by Council for Social Development* (2006), Oxford University Press, New Delhi, contains contributions from some of India's leading scholars and policy planners. The report deals with the social problems of India and analyses the complex nexus between the factors of exclusion and inclusion in history, value and cultural ethos. The various topics discussed including;

(i) Poverty, unemployment and the role and importance of public intervention;

(ii) Challenges in the health sector;

(iii) Achievements and failures in education;

(iv) Challenges in urban governance;

(v) The role and locations of women in social development;

(vi) Inequality and population policy;

(vii) Decentralisation and empowering local government;

(viii) Social security, and

(ix) Communal relations as an important factor in attaining social integration.

Kala Rani in her study "*Role Conflict in Working Women*" (1976) has highlighted the different areas of role conflict among working women and the nature of their adjustment with jobs and with traditional female roles in the family. It is largely a psychological exploration. She stated that strong emotional support from the husbands who take the employment of their wives as a source of women empowerment gives inner-strength and psychological boost up to the working women.[36]

Zenab Banu's work "*Tribal Women Empowerment and Gender Issues*" (2001) has analysed the status of tribal women in the light of the 73rd Constitutional Amendment which has empowered women in Panchayati Raj institutions.[37] By and large the scholarly discussion of empowerment on third amendment of the Constitution has given reservation to women at grassroots level democratic institutions. This study is restricted to four districts of Rajasthan-Udaipur, Dungarpur, Banswara and Chittorgarh. The empowerment of women in the Panchayati Raj has the basic objective to involve women in development action. Mangala Subramanian's book titled "*The Power of Women's Organising – Gender, Caste and Class in India* (2007). This work addresses the mobilising and organising of the India Women's movement in the larger context of globalization and the national social fabric. It provides a case study of Dalit women's challenges and the tension resulting from the representation of varied interests. The recent body of literature emphasizes the significance of intangible social resources – internal strength and confidence, collective organisation, reflection and analytical skills, information, political participations and knowledge. One recent publication "*Women in India – Issue, Perspectives and Solutions*" edited by Ramesh Wari Pandya (2007), contains informative research studies on women empowerment. In one of the papers, Shakuntala C. Shettar and Shanta Bangari highlight the following eight problems of widows namely:

1. Loss of love and affection,
2. Lack of social security,
3. Loss of Self-image,

4. Loneliness,
5. Loss of weight,
6. Sleeplessness,
7. Shock of the loss, and
8. Mental disorder.

Through Articles 14 and 21, the Supreme Court has conferred on widows the right to life property, health-care and livelihood. Through self-employment, women's income generating activities should be increased to augment widow's economic autonomy and to enhance self-confidence in them.[38] Achala Gakkhar has advocated information empowerment among women related to marriage, sexuality, and pregnancy, STD, HIV and Aids besides knowledge about nutrition, child-care, reproductive health, population policy and family planning. Research papers of Sarjoo Patel and Veena Gandotra on Rameshwari Pandya and Varsha Parikh's Paper on Women Empowerment through educations" are very informative.

R.M. Sethi in her book "*Attitudes of Educated Working Women in India and Turkey: Modernization of working women in two developing societies*" (1976) has examined the factors like urbanisation, education and employment etc. and their impact upon several changes, both qualitative and quantitative in the life of women.[39] According to the author, the cultural conditions in both the societies had deep effect on the process of modernisation as a result of which even the urban educated working women were still tradition bound rather than modern. Ambitious and highly-talented women feel that their dual role proves a hindrance to attaining excellence in their careers and by and large the dominant male is unable to adjust himself to the fact that working women have rights and privileges of their own. Empowerment of women is closely linked to level of education. The levels of literacy and schooling in India according to castes and religions are shown in Table 1 and literacy levels of various social groups are given in Table 2. These two tables provide us a close insight into the levels of illiteracy in India. Since this research study deals with Dalit minority women workers doing embroidery work, these two tables will provide the readers with a national perspective of literacy in India.

Table 1: Level of Literacy and Schooling According to Caste and Religion

	Scheduled Tribes	*Scheduled Castes*	*Hindus*	*Muslims*	*All*
Literacy rate 7+ age					
Total	39.3	41.5	53.3	49.9	53.5
Male	51.4	53.4	65.9	59.5	65.6
Female	26.0	28.2	39.2	38.0	40.1
Enrollment rate					
Total	60.3	62.5	72.0	61.6	71.4
Male	67.6	69.6	78.1	66.2	77.1
Female	51.5	54.7	65.1	56.6	64.8
Discontinuation rate (Average for 6-14 years)					
Total	7.2	7.0	5.9	6.9	6.0
Male	6.6	5.7	—	6.4	4.8
Female	8.0	8.8	—	7.7	7.6
Per cent matriculates 15+ years					
Total	4.9	4.9	8.5	5.9	8.6
Per cent students aged 6-14 years in private schools					
Total	3.2	5.8	9.3	13.3	9.8
Male	3.8	6.9	10.4	14.4	10.8
Female	2.3	4.2	7.7	11.9	8.3
Annual household expenditure on schooling					
Government Schools	397	450	531	515	539
Aided schools	664	544	671	542	665

Source: Shariff (1999).

Table 2: Literacy (7+) and Percentage of those who Completed at least the Relevant Higher Levels of Education

	Literacy Rate 7+	*Percentage who Completed at least*					
		Primary	*Middle*	*Secondary*	*Higher Secondary*	*Technical Diploma*	*Graduate*
All religions	64.8	52.3	32.9	21.0	10.5	5.5	5.0
Muslim	59.1	44.4	24.2	13.6	6.0	2.7	2.5
Hindu (Including SCs/STs)	65.1	52.7	33.4	21.4	10.9	5.7	5.2
Hindu (Excluding SCs/STs)	70.5	59.1	38.9	25.8	13.4	7.2	6.6
SCs	54.7	40.2	22.1	11.7	5.1	2.2	2.0
STs	47.1	30.8	16.2	8.5	3.6	1.5	1.3

Source: Census 2001.

The book "*Empowerment of Weaker Section in India*", edited by R.B.S. Verma, H.S. Verma and Raj Kumar Singh (2006) contains 20 informative and well-researched papers. This is perhaps one of the most outstanding recent publications on the theme of empowerment of the weaker sections in India. It contains proceedings and papers of the three-day National Seminar on Empowerment of the Weaker Sections held at Lucknow in 2004. The Seminar primarily aimed at:

(a) Understanding the concept, evaluations and strategies of empowerment, and
(b) Formulating strategies and action plan for empowerment of the weaker sections of the country.

The process of empowerment begins in the mind, from women's consciousness. It starts:

1. From the change in her attitude and approach to understanding life and her very beliefs about herself and her rights, capacities and potential;
2. From transformation of her self-image and an emerging consciousness of how gender as well as other socio-economic and political forces are acting against her;

3. From breaking free of the inferiority complex imprinted on her since early childhood;
4. From gaining an ability to recognise her strengths in terms of knowledge, intelligence and skills and above all;
5. From her growing belief in her innate right to live a dignified life of freedom and justice.[40]

Dr. Nirula has written on *Dalits – A Bruised Dignity* in two Volumes (2009). These volumes present a study on the historical and contemporary responses of caste groups to oppression, prejudice, modern socio-political environment and development. There is an epistemologically gender-specific leaning towards Dalit Women, polarisation and inequality have increased among various strata of the Scheduled Caste and SCs are mainly landless (69.6 per cent) with little control over resources like land forest and water.[41]

Empowerment is very closely related to education and the various levels of literacy. Higher education brings social empowerment of women particularly in Muslims, Scheduled Tribes/Castes.

According to N.R. Narayan Murthy, Empowerment is about providing opportunities to individuals to achieve their aspirations and achieve their full potential, through education, health-care, nutrition shelter and employment. Empowerment implies the right to education and employment, the right to embrace new frontiers and unleash their true capabilities. Bharat Nirman is an ambitious yet pragmatic effort towards empowerment. Handicrafts and other cottage industries are being recognised to create an export strategy that would benefit the craftsman. Ministry of Commerce and Industry commissioned a study on employment – oriented export strategy. The report submitted by Research and Information System for developing countries in June, 2005 showed that the 26 per cent increase in export in 2004-05 (from 63 billion dollar to 80 billion dollar) created 1 million additional jobs. However, Patnaik has given the case-study of two Orissa girls who represented the whole of India at an international forum on child's development in Beijing. The twelve-year old daughter of a daily wage earner and the ten years old daughter of a village school teacher, both as child reporters, presented papers covering gender and children's issues, tribal culture and the economic development in their areas. Padmashree Tulsi Munda, pioneered the phenomenon of the growing strength of women by setting up a school in Orissa's mining areas and who could free hundreds of tribal children from a future as exploited daily labourers by providing them education. In Orissa, self-help groups have empowered two million women who have banked over one billion rupees in five years and with the initial investment of only ten million rupees from the government According to K.R. Narayanan, former President of India, Empowerment has meaning and significance only when the dispossessed and the disinherited have access to the basic necessities of life and are given opportunities to play their rightful role as the citizens of country. Empowerment means uplifting the unprivileged and making them partners and beneficiaries of nation-building activities. According to K.R. Narayanan, Empowerment means improving the status of women and treating them with care and concern. Empowerment of women becomes an empty slogan when we check up the figures for female foeticide and infanticide. In some parts of our country there are areas where almost 70 out of 1000 girls fail to see the light of the day. Economic empowerment is a process and an outcome that results from women organising and then working to address the economic, socio-cultural and policy constrains they encounter in trying to achieve sustainable livelihoods for themselves and their family.[42]

Purpose of Research Study

How far can Information and Communication Technologies be relevant to the empowerment of women in India? Do poor women in developing countries like India need information technology? While Bill Gates and others believe that providing basic needs must come first, many economists and others feel that IT can help meet basic needs and can provide access to resources to exit from poverty. The present research focusses on the role of Information and Communication Technologies in the empowerment of women – a case study of embroidery sector with reference to Dalits and Muslim women. This is a micro-study of women empowerment and aims to provide useful findings about women's conditions conducted through intimate dialogue with them. It will add to the knowledge about the role of Information and Communications technology for entrepreneurs and workers in Embroidery sector. The study has been undertaken in view of recent attention to India world over in the field of ICT. India has seen a revolution in Information and Communication technology in the last ten years. From a very low density of telephones there has been a rapid expansion in mobile telephony and internet. The Y2K (year Two thousand) issue gave tremendous boost to software activity. IT sector revenues went up by 9 times from 1994-95 to 2000 as per NASSCOM report. Year 2001, saw the National Policy on Women Empowerment. The idea was to focus on the benefits that accrued to women in this revolution.

India became a focal point of fashion and beauty pageants with many Miss World and Miss Universe from India. Fashion and Textile went together to bring focus on Indian culture, design and dress. Embroidery is an integral part of Indian costume. Curiosity led the researcher to study the impact of ICT on embroidery sector where we have the finest designers who have carved a niche and name for themselves. Their creations are a culmination of finest tradition of Indian dress and design. Their designs are actually made by master craftsmen who are still marginal workers of informal sector. Have both gained from this revolution and how has it especially affected women who are from low caste and minority communities. Did the two worlds meet, share the benefits or it made the digital divide starker?

References

1. Stephen Anita, *Communication Technologies and Women Empowerment*, New Delhi, Rajat, 2006.
2. Zoya Hasan and Ritu Menon, *Unequal Citizens – A Study of Muslim Women in India,* Oxford Press, New Delhi, 2004, p. 24.
3. Purnima Mankekar, *Screening,* Culture, Viewing Politics: Television Womanhood and Nation in Modern India, Oxford University Press, New Delhi, 2001, p. 6.
4. Hutchinson, Francis and P Vigneswara, Ilavarasan in *Economic and Political Weekly*. Nov. 15, 2008, p. 65.
5. Jo Roland, *Questioning Empowerment*, OX fam, Oxford, 1997.
6. Banerjee N.K., *Grassroots – Empowerment* (1975-1990) Occasional Paper No. 22 CWDS, New Delhi, 1995.
7. *Ibid.*
8. Hemalatha H.M., '*Empowerment of Women – A perspective' in Empowerment of People, grassroots strategies and issues*. (Eds.) R. Venkat Ravi, N. Narejan Reddy and M.Venkataraman, New Delhi, p. 19.
9. Moser C – 'Gender Planning in the Third World: Meeting practical and

strategic needs', in R. Grant and K. Nweland (Eds.) *Gender and International Relations*, Miltor Keynes: Open University Press, 1991, pp. 106-107.

10. Srilatha Batliwala, *Empowerment of Women in South Asia*, 1995. p. 3.
11. Naila Kabeer – *Reversed Realities, Kali for women*, New Delhi 1996.
12. Neera Chandoke, *Beyond Secularism – The Rights of Religions Minorities*, Oxford University Press, New Delhi 1999, pp. 22-24.
13. Hasan, Mushirul, *Legacy of a Divided Nation. India's Muslims since Independence*, Oxford, New Delhi, 1997.
14. Ram P. R., Hindutva and the *Exploited – oppressed sections of society in Fascism of the Sangh Parivar*. Ekta Committee for Communal Amity. Also India-Social Development Report – Council for Social Development, 1999.
15. Zoya Hasan and Ritu Menon, 2004, *op. cit.*
16. *Ibid.*
17. (i) Kabeer Naila Reflections on the measurement of women empowerment in discussion women's empowerment; Theory and Practice, SIDA Studies 3, Stockholm: Swedish International Development Cooperation Agency; 2001. (ii) Oxaal, Ioe, with Sally Baden, 1997, Gender and Empowerment; Definitions, Approaches and Implications for Policy, Bridge Report 40, Revised edition Institute of Development Studies, University of Sussex, Brighton, UK; and (iii) Rowlands, JO 1995 Empowerment Examined, Development in Practice 5(2); pp. 101-7.
18. Kishor, Sunita, Empowerment of Women in Egypt and Links to the Survival and Health of their infants, in *Women's empowerment and demographic processes; Moving Beyond Cairo*, (Eds.) Harrut Presser and Gita Sen, New York, Oxford University Press.
19. Haan, Arjan, 'Poverty and Social Exclusion; A comparison of Debate on Deprivation' working Paper No. 2, Poverty Research Unit, Sussex University – Brighton, 1997.
20. Vijaybhaskar M. and Parthasarthy, Balaji, Diffusion of Information and Communication Technology in India: Labour market implications for developing countries: Final Report, Indian Institute of Information Technology, Banglore.
21. Berra, Ranadiv, Murthy (Ed.) Micro Credit Poverty and Empowerment, 2005, Sage Publication. Boise Ashish, Empowerment through Capacity Building, Sanskriti Publication, 2004.
22. Sinha, A.K., *Panchayati Raj and Empowerment of Women*, Northern Book Centre, New Delhi, 2004.
23. Karat Brinda, *Survival and Emancipation, Three Essays*, 2005.
24. Dutta Sujit Kumar and Ghosh, Dilip Kumar, *Empowering Rural Women*, Akansha Publications, New Delhi, 2002, p. 112.
25. Bakshi, Rita, Rathor, M.S., Agarwal, Meena and Tyagi, Manjula, Editor, *Economic Empowerment of Rural Women in India*, RBSA Publications, Jaipur, p. 166.

26. Giri, V. Mohini, *Emancipation and Empowerment of Women*, 1998, p. 354.
27. Kapur, Promila, *Empowering the India Women*, Publications Division, New Delhi, 2001, p. 440.
28. Goldstein, Rodha L., *Indian Women in Transition*, Meuthen the Scarecrow Press, 1972.
29. Srivastava V., *Employment of Educated Married Women: Its Causes and Consequences with reference to Chandigarh*, National Publishing House, New Delhi, 1972, p. 104.
30. Desai, N., *Women in Modern India*, N.K. Vohra Publishers, Bombay, 1957, pp. 13-23.
31. Naipaul V.S., *Indian a Million Mutinies Now*, Rupa and Co., New Delhi, 1999, p. 517.
32. Games S. Jaquette and Gale Summerfield, Women and Gender equity in *Development Theory and Practice Institution, Resources and Mobilisation*, Duke University Press, London, 2006.
33. Ranade S.H. and Ramachandran, *Women and Employment*, Tata Institute of Social Science, Bombay, 1970.
34. Sakarama Soamayaji's and Gandsha Somayaji, *Sociology of Globalisation – Perspectives from India*, Rawat Publications, Jaipur, 2006.
35. Devki Jain, *The Indian Women, Publications Division*, Government of India, New Delhi, 1975.
36. Rani, Kala, *Role Conflict in Working Women*, Chetna Publications, New Delhi, 1976, pp. 19-20.
37. Banu, Zenab, *Tribal Women and Empowerment and Gender Issues*, Kanishka Publisher and Distributors, New Delhi, 2001.
38. Rameshwari Pandya (Ed.), *Women in India – Issues, Perspectives and Solutions*, New Century Publications, New Delhi, 2007, pp. 110, 111.
39. Sethi R.M., *Attitudes of Working Women in India and Turkey*, National Publishing House, New Delhi, 1976.
40. Verma, R.B.S., Verma, H.S. and Singh, *Raj Kumar, Empowerment of the Weaker Sections in India*, (Eds.) Serial Publications, New Delhi, 2006, p.329.
41. Nirula, *Dalits–A Bruised Dignity Recasting Caste*, APH Publishing Corporation, New Delhi, 2009, pp. 1-5.
42. Regional Policy Seminar, Women workers in the informal sector in South Asia: creating an enabling environment, Kathmandu – 18-20, October 2000, p. 4.

2

Information and Communication Technology: A Means and an End

"The illiterate of the 21st Century will not be those who can not read and write, but those who cannot learn, unlearn and relearn." *–Alvin Toffler*

There is no chance for the welfare of the world, unless the condition of women is improved, it is not possible for a bird to fly on one wing. *–Swami Vivekananda*

We live today in a well-connected globalised world with unparalleled access to information and communication technologies. The internet and other information tools like the television are having ever more control in our lives – we chat, blog, *e*-mail and *e*-shop, leaving behind our foot prints in this version of public space. In addition, we are constantly bombarded with different kinds of informations that seek to mould our thinking, our attitudes and our desires and demand of material things in subtle ways. Information and Communication Technology is an unprecedented mega phenomenon which has enabled the transmission of information of any event taking place in any part of the world to any person, any where any time. ICT has revolutionised human life across the globe. Computer and Communication technology have converted our society into an information society due to quick and unimaginable speed at which information can be transferred and data can be processed. Since it is an integrated technology which includes within its sphere, computer, telecommunication and broadcasting products and then convergence, it has led to "the compression of the world and the intensification of consciousness of the world as a whole." Information could mean a chunk of data like the stock price of a company, a stream of data elements like a movie or television episodes or a system of interacting elements like application software on your computer. Information can also be in the form of reusable artifacts like music CD, books, technical papers, business information etc. Perhaps the most potent form of information use is as a mechanism for controlling or at least influencing or withholding information.[1] Information as a source of power and influence has certain unique characteristics. The predominant role of Information and Communication Technology (ICT) as a *sine qua non* for achieving rapid social and economic development has been recognised the world over.[2] Information Technology could strengthen civic education, guarantee equal access to information and tie individuals and institutions into networks that will make real participatory discussion and debate across great distances.[3] According to Information Technology Act 2000, "Information includes data, text, images, sound, voice, codes, computer programmes, software and databases or micro film or computer generated micro chip." The Information Technology Act 2000, provides "Legal recognition for transactions carried out by means of electronic data interchange and other means of electronic communication, commonly referred to as 'electronic commerce' which involve use of alternatives to paper-based methods of communication and storage of information to facilitate electronic filing of documents with the government agencies." The IT revolution is sweeping every corner of the globe. USA, UK, China, Hong Kong, Australia and Singapore – all are using this technology in their various projects and schemes. Full potentials of IT can be tapped and harnessed in education, health, banking, water and power supply, transport and public distribution. There is a growing body of evidence on the use of ICT to empower women all over the world. For example, in Kenya, women weavers were trained in using the internet to learn new weaving techniques and access more realistic prices for their products. In Senegal, the multi-media caravan project provided women with the opportunity to develop their own ideas on how ICT can be used to meet their development goals and needs. The African women's network of the Association for Progressive Communications (APC) has conducted training workshops to support electronic networking among women groups. The UNDP telecentre project in Ukraine applies ICTs to agriculture and farm management to support women farmers who identified lack of information and networking tools as the major obstacles in their becoming successful entrepreneurship in a new market economy. N.R. Narayan Murthy, mentor and former CEO, Infosys Technologies Ltd. Banglore, while delineating many uses of IT says: "Every school and college in the country will have the opportunity to listen to the finest teachers and professors and remote process control technologies will make it possible for top surgeons to conduct or assist local surgeons in performing intricate operations or for physicians to provide consulting services to patients in remote areas." The term IT has come into common use since the mid80s with the integration of the computer technology. The main components or sub-systems are:

(i) Information storage, selection and retrieval (database) system;
(ii) Inforamtion consolidation system (data and text processing);
(iii) Information communication system (networking); and
(iv) Information analysis (decision support) system.

Internet and Intranets have opened new frontiers of IT applications. Flow of information within the organisation and from various external sources has become very smooth and instantaneous. The application of IT in India was characterised by the population census compilation in the 60s, Airlines reservation in the 70s, Railway reservation in the 80s and stock exchange trading in the 90s.[4] IT is an integrated technology, which includes within its sphere computer, telecommunication and broadcasting products by recognising the technological convergence of these three fields. Computer is the core of IT world. The internet brought the "anytime, anywhere" paradigm to consumers allowing them to conduct their transactions at their convenience. The internet connects everything and everywhere. Internet is a publicly accessible network connecting many smaller networks from around the world. It began with a US Defense[5] Department program called ARPANET (Advanced Research Projects Agency Network) established in 1969 between computers at the University of California, Angeler Stanford Research Institute, University of California Santa Barbara and the University of UTAH. This network aimed at conducting research in computer networking to provide a secure and survivable communications system in case of war. This network quickly grew as academics and researchers began to use it as well. In 1971, first *e*-mail was sent which was extended to Britain and Norway which led to development and increase in mailing lists, newsgroup and bulletin board systems. As Dr. S. Radhakrishnan aptly observed – "Education must make our people the master of technology and not its slave." Internet is "a self-regulated global network of computer – networks."[6] It is broadly a loose amalgam of hundred of thousands of computer networks connecting a widely diverse community of government departments, other PSOs, universities, commercial establishments and millions of individual citizens all over the world. It can be best described as a "cloud of links and super-links."[7] Internet services handle diverse forms of information, including text, sound, graphics, images, video and multi-media combinations.[8] Internet offers the following basic services:

1. Automatic title search (Archic, Veronica),
2. Automatic content search (WAIS),
3. Bulletin Board (Network News) service,
4. Electronic publishing,
5. Fast global electronic (*e*-mail) multimedia communication,
6. File Transfer Protocol (FTP),
7. Information browsing (gopher),
8. The global digital library,
9. Remote Login (TELNET).

In 1990 only 20 countries of the world were connected by the internet. In 1991, the WORLD WIDE NET was released to public by 1997 there were 10 million hosts on the internet and more than one million registered domain names which was an addressing system. The Business Process Outsourcing (BPO) and the Knowledge Process Outsourcing (KPO) are illustrations of the large bank of Indian technological talent that is being utilised by the so-called hi-tech countries. The Knowledge Process Outsourcing industry is expected to reach US$17 billion, out of which $12 billion (Rs. 52000 crore or 70 per cent) would be outsourced to India in the next five years and generate 2,50,000 high paying jobs.[9] The number of internet users is now in excess of 200 million.[10] In India, the number of internet and broad-band subscribers increased from 69 lakh and 13 lakh respectively as on March 31, 2006 to 86 lakh and 20 lakh respectively as on December 31, 2006.[11] 710 cities have been provided with broad-band connectivity by the public sector undertakings. The Internet offers a wealth of new applications in the following fields of education.

1. On-line access to school prospectus, syllabus, vacancies etc.
2. Electronic handling of scholarships, fee exemptions, loans etc.
3. Edutainment (an interactive combination of education and entertainment) that uses games, simulations etc. for learning.
4. Remote multi-media lectures from experts, specialists and scholars.
5. Schooling on the net – "Schools on-line."
6. Parent teacher interaction on *e*-mail.
7. Networking and collaboration among institutions for exchange of facilities, experience and research purposes.
8. Development of life-long learning centres on the web.[12]

Mass media has a powerful role in empowerment of women as has been depicted in the figure below.[13]

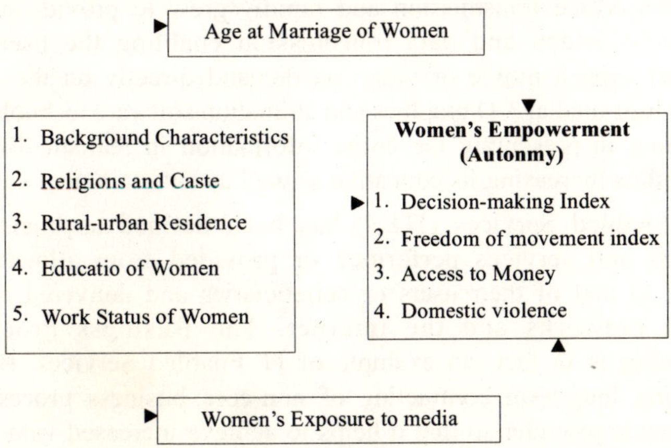

ICT knowledge is light, weightless and intangible. It can easily travel across the world enlightening the lives of the people everywhere.[14] Internet is a development of such vast significance that will affect every aspect of culture and commerce. Over the last decade telecom has been one of the robust growth drivers, which has contributed immensely to the country's impressive economic performance and world leadership in IT. During 2005-06, 27415 lakh new connections 50.9 lakh by BSNL and MTNL and 223.25 lakh by private sector were provided. The total telephone connections as on December 31, 2005 were 1257.88 lakh comprising 571.78 lakh fixed lines and cellular connections were provided by BSNL and MTNL and 686.10 lakh by the private sector. As on December 31, 2005, approximately 585.03 lakh Cellular Mobile Phones (CMPs) and about 5.40 lakh Village Public Telephones (VPTs) were provided by both public and private operators.[15] The growth of rural connectivity has not kept pace with the impressive growth in urban connectivity. Under the *Bharat Nirman Yojna*, a total of 17182 villages have been provided Village Public Telephones (VPTs). More than two lakhs Public Call Offices (PCOs) and 14.18 millions phones have been provided in the rural areas as on December 31, 2005. Village Public Telephones (VPTs) have been provided to 17,182 uncovered villages. The growth in telecom sector on the one hand has resulted in increased rural teledensity (from 0.68 per cent as on March 31, 2000 to 1.79 per cent as on December 31, 2005) but on the other hand, the gap between rural and urban teledensity has widened during this period. Initially cellular mobile phone started as just analog voice transmission and rapidly grew to provide wide band audio, video and data transmission enabling the user to download even a movie of video on demand directly on the cell phone. Multi-media, 3-D graphics and animation software technology are helping in presenting the entire information in realistic–lively fashion, thus increasing its educative as well as entertainment value.

IT Enabled Services (ITES) has been defined as business processes and services performed or provided from allocation different to that of their users or beneficiaries and delivered over telecom networks and the internet. The Business Process Outsourcing is in fact, an example of IT Enabled Services. BPO comprising long-term contracting of non-core business processes to an outside provider so that it helps to achieve increased value of shareholding. Call centre service is a large scale industry by itself. The Call Centre revenue in India in the year 2000 was Rs. 200 crore and is expected to rise to Rs. 6000 crore by 2008.

Internet has given boost to *E*-Commerce and *E*-Finance which is also an IT Enabled Service. Thus, ICT has provided jobs to thousands of young men and women in the country and has brought economic prosperity to the country. Total revenue earnings of BPO industry in the year 2005-06 was US $5.2 million and US $7.2 billion in 2006-07. IT had employed around 2,84,000 persons by the end of 2000 in India. The number increased to 1,28,7000 in 2005-06 within indirect employment of 30 lakh persons. Interestingly, there are more women than men working in BPO sector with a ratio of 69:31. ICT creates simultaneous state in all aspects of human existence. The cell phones device symbolises not just technology but freedom to communicate.

ICT and Labour Market Implication for Developing Countries

ICT sector promises to generate new employment opportunities by creating a demand for fresh skills and new occupational categories. The promotion of ICT based industrialisation leads to:

1. Skill polarisation i.e., skilled workers with better knowledge of use of ICTs have better career and work opportunities, leaving the rest of work force in low paying jobs.
2. Deskilling i.e., ICTs render traditional skills redundant and therefore tend to deskill the work force.
3. Disintermediation i.e., ICTs reduce transactions costs involved in information flows within an organisation and therefore undermine the need for middle management.
4. Gender neutrality i.e., ICTs reduce the need for physical labour and create white collar jobs. Women, therefore find better employment prospects due to diffusion of ICTs.
5. Flexibility i.e., reduce coordination costs, allowing firms to reply on external labour markets and therefore promote great labour market flexibility.
6. Autonomy at work i.e., ICTs ensure greater access to information among employees, therefore helping decentralised decision-making and giving employees greater autonomy at work.[16]

ICT and new technologies provide an opportunity for a more creative engagement with work for labour as well as encourage team-work (Piore and Sabel, 1984). ICT favour women's employment, unlike traditional technologies that denied women access to the domain of paid work. Impacts of ICTs on the organisation of production and employment in industrialised and to a limited extent in less industrialised countries have been extensively discussed by many authors such as Castells 1999; Bryanjolfsson and Hitt 1998; I Lo 2001. ICT and especially IT enabled services like call centers, medical transcription, back office work processing etc. are held to offer considerable employment awareness for women. Use of ICTs make available better quality information to firms and thereby reduce the scope for opportunism. The development of computer-aided software threatens the most glamorous of the technical professional associated with computer technology programme. The impact of the introduction of IT cannot be analysed apart from its immediate context of social relations and the existing organisation of work. ICTs through provision of transparency and easy access to information can enable employees to participate in decision-making and therefore reduce hierarchical authority. In India the growth of IT was dominated by medical transcription in the initial phases, only to be replaced by Call Centers as major type of IT and of late by back office processing work. Medical transcribing audio-medical records of doctors in the U.S. into a written retrievable format and sending it via satellite to the client firm. The last five years have witnessed the mushrooming of call centres. Call centers are relatively flat organisations with few levels in the organisational hierarchy. According to Belt, Richardson and Webster (2000), call centers require the hierarchy of skill requirement in declining order:

(a) Communication skills,

(b) Customer service,

(c) Product knowledge,

(d) IT skills.

Recruitment is largely based on walk-ins that may or may not be backed by advertisements. While most firms insist on a minimum of a Bachelor's Degree, a few firms insist only on completion of 12th standard, knowledge of English language, ability to react to a situation quickly and communication skills along with the IQ, are the requisites for recruitment. Women are generally preferred in ICT jobs as they have personality traits like ability to be pleasant even when confronted by angry and abusive clients. ICT draws more women into paid employment. In house training is also provided to all new entrants in ICT related jobs. However, in IT firms, given the small number of levels in the organisation, prospects of intra-firm mobility are highly limited. ICTs thus offer little scope for vertical mobility within the firm. This scenario is true of both MT and BOP firms as well as of call centres. Indian Labour Laws bar women from being employed in night shifts. On personal interview by the researcher one young woman said: "Only because my mother didn't want me to work in night shifts, I had to quit." ICT is also contributing to the growing socio-economic inequalities. In the IT, ICTs are used to reduce worker autonomy and centralise power in the top elite of the organisation. The ICTs do undermine some of the conditions that are seen to have hitherto excluded women from entering into the labour market like reduced need for physical labour. However, such possibilities do not automatically translate into greater avenues for women's employment unless they are educated, forward looking and qualified in computer application. ICT has the potential to uplift women out of educational backwardness. Dr. A.P.J. Abdul Kalam has said; "Information technology is an area of India's Core Competence within five years time, our software product potential has increased from a few hundred million dollars to a four billion dollars; and more than half of the software products are exported. Some of our software companies have been recognised as equal professionals in various software export houses of the world and if India decides and works for it, India can indeed be a developed nation."[17] Two service providing departments viz., Department of Telecom Services (DTS) and Department of Telecom Operations (DTO) were corporatised w.e.f. October 1, 2000 as Bharat Sanchar Nigam Ltd. (BSNL). BSNL is a 100 per cent Government of India owned Public Sector Undertaking with an authorised capital of Rs 17,500 crore, a paid up capital of Rs 12,500 crore. BSNL is a technology oriented company and provides all types of telecom service namely telephone services on landline, WLL and mobile, leased circuits, Internet and long distance telecom services. The vast switching network for land lines comprises 37,636 exchanges having a capacity of 473.67 lakh lines as on December 31, 2006. out of 6.07 lakh villages in the country 5.45 lakh villages have already been provided telephone facility by BSNL by the end of December 2006, employing a work force of around 3.27 lakh. The mission of BSNL is to provide world class state-of-the-art technology telecom services on demand at affordable price.[18]

ICT and Empowerment

In accordance with the strategic approach of the government to achieve the goals of gender mainstreaming and gender justice laid down in the National Policy for Empowerment of Women, the following steps have been taken towards furthering empowerment of women employees:-

(a) Special care is taken in case of female employees working in night shift and they are provided with rest room and dropping facility after duty hours.

(b) In order to redress and prohibit sexual harassment at work place, sexual Harassment Complaint Committee has been constituted at the unit level as well as in corporate office.

(c) The service conditions are uniform and there is no gender bias.

(d) Crèche facility has also been provided for women employees with infants.

(e) Special grant is being sanctioned on annual basis for MTNL Women Welfare Association which in turn provides vocational training to kith and kin of working as well as retired or deceased employees.

BSNL employs more than 40,000 women at various levels. They are retained on promotion to the extent possible when they are working. Generally, they are posted at the same station where their spouses are working or posted. ITI limited, being a socially conscious Public Sector undertaking, is giving due importance to the welfare of women employees. The Centre for Development of Telematics (C-DOT) has about 33 per cent of staff as women and the organisation is creating a climate/culture reflecting gender equality. Career growth opportunities for women are available to all women employees. During 2005-06 of the total employees promoted to higher grades 37 per cent of them were women. In management cadre, about 24 per cent are women. In Trichy (Kerala State) an NGO created a helpline for women in distress to handle issues such as rape, sexual harassment, battering, dowry harassment and eve-teasing. The complaints disclose information anonymously which is routed to the all women police stations for further action. The service has received a positive response as women can avoid the social stigma of having to go to a local police station. There is an option of *e*-mailing other types of complaints to the police control room. Thus, ICT is empowering the women of Kerala state by helping the victim women.

ICT has a very important role to play in empowerment of both urban and rural women. Telephone, cellular phones, television and other means of ICT bring social awareness among women. Dr. Upendra Baxi has said: "Complimentarity of social consciousness and organisation constitute the quintessence of empowerment." Empowerment of women has a long history of women's struggle against the society and its traditional gender-biased values. It is only through ICT that people got to know "the compression of the world and the intensification of the world as a whole."[19] Though globalisation is a universalising and homogenising process, the actual experiences of the people and communities of globalisation differ from one another. Thanks to ICT, the universe we live-in is in a state of simultaneity. In it, everything is connected to everything. National Informatics Center has designed and developed a portal for National Resource Centre for women as per the Annual Report of the Ministry of Women and Child Development of the Government of India for the year 2005-06. NIC also developed a web-based software to monitor the progress report of various schemes of the ministry like *Swayamsiddha* and *Swawlamban*.[20] *Swayamsiddha* was an integrated project for development and empowerment of women through formation of Self-Help Groups. *Swawlamban* aimed at providing training and skill to poor and needy to get employment on sustained basis. Through *e*-training and *e*-education a great majority of poor women can be empowered as functional literates. The bio-village project of the MS Swaminathan research foundation (MSSRF) in Pondicherry is a brilliant example of reduction of gender divide through *e*-learning in the marginal sector. Networking, research, training, sharing of ideas and information – all these could be made infinitely easier through relatively affordable computer mediated communication such as *e*-mail, internet, hyperlink and hyper media. India is signatory to the CEDAW (Convention of Elimination of Discrimination Against Women) 1995 and NFLS (Nairobi Forward Looking Strategies) in which empowerment through communication is given top priority. Information Technology will play a progressive greater role in globalised world. The future will be marked by the creation of greater state of information presence, storage and decidedly more advanced applications. The fascinating world of information technology is about what it can do by looking at the Micro and Macro at the same time. A village vegetable cultivator who lives 30 kms. away from Delhi can find out the latest rates of vegetables on mobile/phone and sell it to the agents accordingly. Today a lifetime pre-paid card, with all incoming calls free, costs only Rs. 500 and that combined with a Rs. 2,000 Cell phone means disengagement with the middle man.

There is a very interesting case study of Micro credit in Bangladesh. Mohammad Yunus, created the concept of giving cell phones preprogrammed with the numbers of local Legislators, the police and even the Prime Minister's office, to women who run their own Micro-credit organisations. That gives a voice and accountability to a moribund people tied-up in knots of gender inequality, social segregation, lack of education and religious fanaticism – all working with a singular goal to keep the poor in their place. For the first time, there is hope, there is women empowerment for these women in the handheld device that symbolises not just technology but empowerment. Here is a case study of an inspiring successful IT technocrat. A middle class Andhra girl goes to a high-class English medium school in Hyderabad; then goes on to the U.S. where her brother has migrated as an electronic engineer and she enrolls and obtains first class electronics engineering degree and joins an IT company in the U.S. She then returns to Bangalore where the company has subsidiary on a princess's salary of Rs. 1,00,000 (over $2000) per month. Half the day, she is the traditional daughter speaking Telegu to the traditional parents in this AP suburb of cyber city. In the other half, she is the English speaking Project Manager for an American firm supervising 50 technical colleagues working even on night shifts. After her work, she transforms back to the traditional daughter now pampered by the family as the principal bread butter and jam earner.[21] This is the double life-microcosm of a successful IT professional entrepreneur.

India online survey 2007 has some interesting findings. The usage of internet from homes is at 59 per cent. Place of work (office, school, colleges) remains the single largest place of accessing internet at 78 per cent. Internet usage from cyber cafes has remained flat, reaching 47 per cent. Only 1.4 per cent of the regular internet-using population access the net exclusively from a cyber cage with increase in education and greater use of internet this percentage should go up every year. The internet usage continues to grow at a steady pace, with the internet using population in urban India reaching 30.32 millions a growth of 28 per cent from April 2006 to April 2007. Of the 30.32 million urban internet users, 25.17 million (83 per cent) log on at least once a month, the balance of 5.15 million (17 per cent) are occasional users. The penetration of the internet among urban Indian stands at nine per cent now, assuming the total urban population at 336 million. At least three of the four regular internet users (77 per cent) who access the net from home now do so using some form of broadband or superior connection. 56 per cent of internet users undertake social or professional net-working. In actual usage, Google is the front runner with 29 per cent of all internet users preferring to use Google the most among all the websites. Several theories predict a "liberating" effect brought about by information and communication technologies. Inherent in these theories is the understanding that the information age will put an end to hierarchical social systems, liberate both individuals and societies from ignorance and by implications, repressive policies. Further it will break down bureaucratic structure and bring transparency in the working of organisations. Not only that, the information age would also create a "global free market" making free trade possible across national borders.[22] ICT is not only a means to attain certain information and social objectives it is also an end in itself. ICT can be a very useful tool for empowering women and poorer sections of the society including Dalits and Muslims. To extricate women from vicious circle, ICT should aim at:

(i) Bringing services closer to the women;

(ii) Involve women in formulation of policy and its management and its implementation;

(iii) Make women the point of contact in order to deliver services directly to the beneficiary and receivers.

Dr. Amartya Sen has said: "Nothing arguably, is as important today in the political economy of development as an adequate recognition of political economic and social participation of women".

Recent advances in ICT have introduced fundamental changes in human behaviour patterns leading to new and unexpected changes in our life style, societies, organisations and economies.[23] We are today in the midst of this "third wave" transition from an industrial society to an information society. The third wave may contain new and hitherto inconceivable opportunities and threats like telemedicine. Information can flow efficiently across geographical boundaries and Business Process Outsourcing (BPO) are the best example of it.

Datamation Foundation started a project in 2003 in Delhi for Muslim Women empowerment by localising appropriate communication and information networks by setting up an ICT centre at the madarsa. Datamation Foundation actively champions deployment of innovative ICT tools and capacity building solutions for vocational skills enhancement targeted towards sustainable livelihoods for the socially and economically disadvantaged women and youth most vulnerable to poverty and exploitation. Besides ensuring the creation of mass-scale employment generation in the organised sector of the economy, the Foundation has been working actively towards creating livelihoods for the women and youth engaged in the vast, unregulated and hazardous informal sector of the economy. As part of the organisational philosophy, the Foundation has been successful in putting ICTs in the hands of the women of the predominantly minority ghetto of the Seelampur-Zaffarabad in North East Delhi. The Project is one of selected chosen South-Asian UNESCO ICT for Poverty Reduction (ICTPR) sites. The project aims at training Muslim women in the application of ICTs for their income and vocational skills enhancement. The project envisions assessing social and economic impact of ICTs in improving the quality of their lives. The ICT centre has created self-confidence in Muslim women and created awareness, helping them to take collective decisions.

ICT – A Sociological Perspective

Technology is a potent instrument for eradication of hazardous monotonous and stigmatised work. However, technology can not delete the boundary between the prestigious and non-prestigious work. Those who can afford avoid the unpleasant work, and their time and energy is invested in work appropriate to their competence and inclination while others face the drudgery though they have to drag themselves against their will and wish. Gender disparity was supposed to be reduced through abolition of sexual division of labour but it is observed that only the mode of functioning has changed. Unpleasant work shifted to machines (washing) or market (dry cleaning). Similarly, cooking at home is being greatly substituted by tiffin systems or eating out in restaurants and food courts/ *dhabas*. Who will do the difficult and dirty work in societies of equals is an emerging problem.[24] Technology solutions are being imagined as much as homes with programmed refrigerators and vacuum cleaners and microwave. The inmates of home will still need to programme and put reminders. The work will again be given to the 'weaker sex'.

In case of embroidery sector, strange facts came to light. The traditional hand embroidery was being done by women. Once it was done it formed a part of the bridal trousseau. Today, solution comes from importing migrant workers which creates new social boundaries. The television, internet and radio has created new boundaries where face to face conventional interactions have been eliminated. It has created a unity in mutual avoidance and silence providing to individual and households ample private space. In T.V. and radio there is one-sided communication. Interaction is one-sided and non-dialectical, controlled by performer and not susceptible of mutual development. Therefore, new boundaries emerge between privileged and deprived. In numerous ways, T.V. and radio lead to dissemination of information, entertainment and education, thereby those who do not have the means to use them, move into further abyss. Many women, despite having access to T.V. are unable to gain the benefits due to lack of time to sit and watch T.V. compelled load of household work and earning a livelihood.

The Beijing Platform of Action (BPFA) therefore spelt out two strategies objectives:

1. Increase the participation and decision-making through media and new technologies of communication.
2. Promote a balanced and non-stereotyped portrayal of women in media.

Communication and empowerment have been regarded as effective strategies as more equitable access to the means of mass communication will lead to higher levels of self-determination. Although throughout the world, communication is fundamental to human behaviour and a means of voicing their experiences, feelings and emotions. Indian women have long been schooled into a "culture of silence" thus depriving them of the opportunity to express their life-situations and engage in unraveling the complex web of cultural, social, political, economic and family factors that enmesh their lives and thereby make them totally disempowered. The disempowerment of women in India is, in a very large measure, about the voiceless and powerlessness of their subjective experiences, deprivations and sufferings. Empowerment of women has to build and sustain the ability of the women to think critically and frankly about oppressive ideology, practices, traditions and prejudices and encourage them to firmly resist the oppressive forces that desire to isolate and silence them and thus expose the oppressive elements of the modern India society. Awareness has to be the starting point of women's empowerment where information and communication technology can play an important role.

As technology advances, unskilled hands are replaced by machine, if women do not acquire the new skills, they will lose their jobs on which they depend to feed themselves and their children. With changing times, the women need to equip themselves. If they fall into self-deprecation which is characteristic of the unprivileged, gradually they become convinced of their own unfitness. To change this dismal situation and bring transformation in a woman's condition, the ground for acquisition of vocational, entrepreneurial and managerial skills has to be prepared. Training of women for management is one of the most effective approaches to set in motion a process of personal development. In order to transform, one needs to address "the values that society attaches to various skills". Axel Homels theory of mutual recognition helps to realise that it is not enough to grant people material goods. It is important to grant them recognition in the sense of valuing the importance of acquiring new skills. There is an intricate and reciprocal relationship between experiences, translation of these experiences into articulated formulation and the corresponding impact of these formulations on the way these experiences are interpreted.[25] With globalisation due to computerisation and its network, people all over the world are in a position to derive the benefits of the system and contribute their share in all contexts and levels to the running of the system. Women in developing countries are gradually gaining access to the use of information technology. They are using IT at work. Users at work are generally divided into two categories:

1. Who use IT as a tool of jobs programming i.e., software generation.
2. Those who use it as tool of communication like office work, data entry, manufacturing computer industry jobs like Business Process Outsourcing, Call Centres and related works. As a tool of communication, women have used IT to promote their business interests and sometimes political advocacy. *E*-mail is major IT application.

The women are producers of IT whether as internet content providers, programmers, designers, inventors and fixers of computers. Women are conspicuously absent from decision-making strictures in IT from developing countries. They are mostly concentrated in end user low skilled IT jobs, related to word processing and data entry. A very small percentage of managerial maintenance and design personnel are women. In India, very few girls make it to the IITs and engineering colleges for full computer science course but large numbers enroll in NIITs and computer courses to get a reasonable job of receptionist or a data feeder. Women's strategic gender interest requires that they practice their skills in ways that empower them rather than reinforce their dependence. Need is for "an expansion in women's ability to make strategic life choices to provide them with resources and skills which will allow them to control their lives and livelihood suitably to accrue maximum benefits from information and communication technology. India has signed the Convention on Elimination and Discrimination Against Women 1995 and Nairobi forward looking strategy in which empowerment through communication media is given top priority. For any strategy to be effective, it should aim to:

1. Bring services closer to women;
2. Involve them in formulation of its policy, management and implementation;
3. Make women the point of control in order to delivery services directly to the beneficiary receiver.

The Self-Help Groups have played a significant role in invoking the dialogue between women and specially in the rural areas where they learnt the benefits of communication and interaction. Recently, there was a proposal by Department of Telecom to provide STD/ PCO in these SHGs which will act as a source of income as well as enable members to use it for promotion of their work. Most of the women who are illiterate and have not acquired vocational skills always regret it as it emerges in course of conversation with many of them. They think they have wasted their lives but would like their children to fare much better. They would like their children to get technical education and learn computer so as to make a better living and stand on their own legs.

Since most women in the embroidery sector are home-based workers they are invisible, unrecognised, voiceless and unorganised. They are deprived of their basic rights and they work under poor conditions which includes low wages, long hours, irregular work and delayed payments. If they can be linked by technology either the telephone, mobile or landline and internet, all these problems can find a solution. Through communication technology they can get in touch with each other, share their woes and worries as well as the ways and means to improve their situation. They can become part of a group or association thus have forum for visibility and voice. Since their work hours are irregular and home-based, if communication is at her doorstep, she can talk to her employers (for whom she works) get her wages on time and also know what the others are being paid. Since home-based workers have multiple sets of need as a part of the informal sector like social security, rights of workers and producers, better wages, maternity and health related attention and child care. All these can be addressed if these women are linked through ICT. TV and radio become useful source for dissemination of information. Telephone and internet can provide access to other needs.

Adithi in Bihar was started by Viji Srinivasan in 1988 and has 80,000 women members involved in various household jobs like leaf plate making, bidi works, as well as embroiderers. By networking and organising, *Adithi* assisted these women to commercialise their activity and reach a market. Their traditional work was recognised, products got diversified as per market demands, women got better returns for their skills.

There is a classic example of SEWA as presented by Renana Jhabvala in the Kathmandu seminar which explains how SEWA's contacts with organizations of home-based workers in India and other countries led to creation of Homenet which helped to raise the visibility and voice of home-based workers at the international level.[26]

In his paper, MM Verma discusses the approaches and strategies for women's empowerment. Women have faced subordination to men in all societies and countries around the world. Empowerment means the process of gaining and accessing control over the self and various resources in one's environment and over the ideology that determines power relationship.

Empowerment approach in social work practice includes following components:

1. Building of collaborative partnership with clients,
2. Emphasis on their environment,
3. Focus on individual as well as their social environment,
4. Recognition of women's rights responsibilities and needs,
5. Direction of professional initiatives towards helping them.

Therefore, it suggests a network of civil society organisations which need to be created for empowerment of women. This is where information and communication technology plays a role as a vital factor. Social workers have to counsel women in right perspective, suggest viable alternatives and link them to relevant civil, social organisation service agencies and systems. ICT can prove to be the binding factor but how it is to be designed and used is still an open ended question.

Empowerment of women is one area where considerable research has been carried out. Coverage is confined to visible segments of women. The detailing of status of marginalised sections as SC, ST and OBC is one such area on which research is conspicuous by its absence.[27]

The Action Plan of the U.N. Information and Communication Technologies task force 2003 at the 47th session aimed to:

1. Provide a platform to analyse how programmes for promoting education combating disease, empowerment and gender equality can be leveraged and enhanced with ICT.
2. Participation and access of women to the media and ICT and their impact on and use as an instrument for the advancement and empowerment of women needs to be recognised.

Television and Women Issues in India

There are certain positive correlations between levels of media penetration and rates of national development. Drawing lessons from western principles of the enlightenment such as rationality and progress, many thinkers concluded that the mass media were crucial tools for development and modernity in various societies.[28] The ethnography prepared by Divya C. Mcillin, at the studios and offices of Doordarshan, the national, regional language Udaya TV and in the office of the Star TV, Channel (V) and Zee TV in Banglore, India in 1997 and in 2000 showed that these networks saw their roles as entertainers first and as crucial vehicle for advertisers to reach consumers.[29] Specifically, although officials high in Doordarshan's hierarchy reported the network produced programmes targeted to women and rural residents on issues of health, sanitation, agriculture and family planning programmes, the news executives candidly stated that Doordarshan's content was increasingly entertainment-oriented with hefty daily menus of film-based programming. Ideological analyses of Doordarshan content have indicated that over the decades, development programming that presented a critical awareness of the diversity of women's groups and needs was almost or wholly absent.[30] It is obvious that the role of TV for national development, particularly about women's development and empowerment, has been far from the natural goals. Mankekar's study showed that middle class urban women in Delhi expressed their anger at the limiting portrayals of women on television, their unease about the changing roles of women and their despair that the status of women in India would ever change.[31] Efforts need to be made to shift the potential of TV for development in India. Ultimately, strategies to integrate development content that is interesting, relevant and inexpensive into mainstream programming across state sponsored and private television channels have to be accompanied by structural support in terms of legislations on issues such as minimum wage and gender discrimination in work place.[32]

India's Television penetration rate is 87 per cent and cable and satellite penetration as high as 43 per cent of television households.[33] Doordarshan network, ever since its inception in 1959, ensured that the network's programmes focussed on technological innovations in agriculture through progammes such as Krishi Darshan and on women's issues through programmes as *Mahilaon Ke Liye*. The women-oriented drama as such as "Udaan" "Hum Log" and "Rajani", sought to bring fresh air of modernisation. Women's development became synonymous with national movement.[34] From the mid seventies, television began to be used to promote development oriented messages among the Indian population. But there was no exclusive focus on women's problems and their development. Though television in India began with the avowed goals of education, modernisation and development, today's satellite channels have done more damage to the cause of women's development by regressing to highly negative values that impede women's empowerment.[35]

Role of ICT in Empowering Women – A Case Study of Micro-enterpreneurs Using Internet

In three poor neighbourhoods around Bangalore, groups of women micro-entrepreneurs have recently logged on to the power of global social networking through the internet despite being impoverished and illiterate.[36] Helping them in this attempt to escape poverty and get empowerment is a start-up called "Ubuntu At Work" which is inspired by Nobel Prize winning economist Amartya Sen's argument that a persons capability is not what he or she theoretically has, but hinges upon the person's social arrangements Vibha Pingle, a former Professor of Sociology at Rutger University has started "Ubuntu at Work" with a view to provide underprivileged women the same network that the well off have. Leveraging networks such as Face book and Twitter, Ubuntu recruits volunteers to coach the poor women and help them in identifying new business areas and developing products. In Bommanahalli suburbs of Bangalore, women recycle plastic drinking water bottle to produce green jewellery. Through social networking a Swedish jewellery designer came in to teach the poor women to make the edgy green products. Volunteers like Smita Chakravorty, a programmer at Infosys Technologies in

Bangalore became a 'friend' to women micro-entrepreneurs to understand their needs and aspirations. Chakravorty comes to Bommanahalli site, every weekend where a group is currently teaching English and Computer skills to the children of women Micro-entrepreneurs. These women are exposed to a set of people and ideas they would never have access to but for Ubuntu. Pingle realised that 99 per cent of the women she surveyed in the micro-finance networks did not even see themselves as micro-entrepreneurs. Only those poor women who built bridges outside their network were likely to escape the crush of poverty. Poor women had to open up and get self-confidence to build bridges with outside world. This was a hypothesis by setting up "Ubuntu" to provide such bridges. Two things stood out. Firstly, forming a women's self-help group was not necessarily conducive to fresh business ideas. Second, the cell phone was not adequate enough tool to develop a business and ability to use internet is necessary. The Bommanahalli suburbs of Bangalore are now producing the edge green products and marketed around the world by using social networks through internet. Volunteers run chapters have come up in several cities like Delhi, Dubai and Dublin. The Ubuntu website, Face book and Twitter help recruit the volunteers, who reach the poor women in their homes for advice and coaching. The volunteers get together on Face book to discuss current initiatives, plan training programmes and post all happenings on twitter. The products the designers and resources to train the women are aggregated on the internet. It is a test case for a collaborative business model for the poor. This also opens a new vista of role of ICT in empowering the poor women by giving them technical and professional support. Pingle wants "Ubuntu at Work" to become the Face book with cause a one-stop portal for development that connects micro-entrepreneurs across the world to their markets, by passing the multiple traditional steps. "We want to bring global resources and the global marketplace to the doorstep of these micro-entrepreneurs" say Pingle.[37] Ubuntu is an ethical concept of African Origin of the same name that emphasises community, generosity and sharing. The products, the designers and there sources to train the women are aggregated on the internet. It is a test case for a collaborated business model for the poor and marginalised women.

Case Study of Women Empowerment Through ICT in *Nabanna*, India

Poor women of rural region in Indian state of West Bengal have built a local information network called *Nabanna* by integrating ICTs into their communicative ecology with the help of facilitating agency — change Initiative – a Kolkata-based NGO. *Nabanna* is a Bengali word literally meaning first rice – a staple food in Bengal. *Nabanna* is also the name of a festival that occurs when rice is harvested. *Nabanna*'s vision is to energise the community in West Bengal and use the harvest information. Nabanna came into operation in early 2003 with the support of UNESCO. It is being undertaken in phases comprising ICT Training, information use and information sharing with the aim to have a web-based information system among poor women, private sector, research institutes and panchayats. Nabanna is about women building a community network that facilitates local information and communication with the ultimate goal of reducing poverty.[38] The network covers six regions in Baduria block and Baduria Municipality; Jagannathpur, Taraguia, Arbelia, Baduria and Rudrapur, located about 65 kilometers from Kolkata. Work around *Nabanna* is centered around two ICT centres – one located in Jagannathpur and the other at Arbelia. The Jagannathpur ICT centre has three desktops, three dot-matrix printers and telephone. The Arbelia centre has three desktops and three dot-matrix printers. Laptops and Pocket PCs are extensively used as these allows Nabanna to reach out to the poor women who cannot afford to visit ICT centres. "Change Initiatives" – a Kolkata-based NGO has successfully powered a laptop with solar energy to get going its Telecentre on Wheel Project – which is a manually run rickshaw van fitted with a laptop and solar panels to power the laptop with the support of UNESCO, New Delhi and West Bengal Renewable Energy Development Agency (WBREDA), the Telecentre on Wheel (TOW) initiative was launched at Ghora Gacha in West Bengal's Nadia district.[39] The solar panel embedded on the top allows energy generation from the sun. TOW serves the purpose very well as the two 75 watt solar panels allow generation of enough energy to power a laptop and an inkjet printer for more than four hours. The device covers four villages: Ghora Gacha, Madandanga, Kantabetia and Teligacha where youth are given training on basic computing so that they can access information in the local language Bengali from the Computer in the areas of health, education, agriculture, human right and law. This training has helped in creation of a group of *e*-literate volunteers in each village. There are the following benefits of ICT to Rural men and women:

1. Saving cost, time and trouble,
2. Better productivity – prosperity,
3. Increased Transparency,
4. Access to vital information, integration with global mainstream;
5. Enhanced awareness and utilisation of welfare schemes/poverty alleviation programmes,
6. Opportunity to exploit their own potentials,
7. Multiple uses for an Infrastructure created;
8. Value for Government investments;
9. *E*-learning,
10. Use of ICT software for monitoring activites of self-help groups.

In the first phase about 45 poor women learned knowledge management basics and learnt applications like MS-Paint and MS-Office. The poor women were taught for free: in return they undertook a voluntary service within the community. They organised groups of uneducated, poor women, which formed the basis of change initiatives' Participatory Information Networking (PIN) model. The groups are called Information groups and the model allowed these uneducated women access to ICT content. The model was tested through an information module on health, livelihood and women's rights. *Nabanna* has launched an information module on livelihood. On getting the information, 15 women from Arbelia created a sample of their needle work and handed it over to the *Nabanna* information coordinator. *Nabanna* showed the samples to potential entrepreneurs and got the first order for embroidery in Indian sarees. The order was small in size and the work was distributed on first come first serve basis. Very interestingly the information spread all over the village and the women who were not interested in this also came to observe how the programme would be conducted. Now more and more work of embroidery is being taken up by the women and they are making good earning and developing self-confidence in themselves. Now, they fix up prices for their work and maintain a proper data-base of how the work is done. Gradually, the quantity of embroidery work orders will grow and women will get opportunities to earn more. Two young *Nabanna* group members played a leadership role in successful implementation of the initiative. As soon as their wok is shown to outsiders, they started getting more orders and now embroidery is becoming a source of earning and empowerment of the poor women covered under *Nabanna* ICT project. The UNESCO Project "*Nabanna* : Networking Rural Women and Knowledge", has been declared the winner in 2003 gender and ICR with a cash prize of US $8,000. It can serve as a model for all other states of India to make similar initiatives.

Concluding Remarks

Internet usage is one of the standard indicators of the use of ICT. By 2003, there were approximately two million internet users in India. SEWA (The Self-Employed Women's Association) is one of the first organisations globally to realise the potential of using ICT for the productive growth of the informal sector. SEWA is establishing Technological Information Centres to provide computer awareness training and basic computer skills. Due to poverty, lack of education and financial resources of women, ICT by itself can not answer all the problems facing women empowerment, but it brings new information resources and can open new communication channels for the marginalised communities, namely Dalit and Muslim women. According to World Bank (2004), the main key services fail poor people – in access, quantity and quality. Jawaharlal Nehru, first Prime Minister of India in 1957 said that the greatest revolution is one that affects the status and living conditions of its women.[40]

References

1. Srinath Srinivasa, *The Power Law of Information – Life in a connected world*, Repouse Books, New Delhi, 2006, p. 30.
2. Department of Telecommunications, Ministry of Communications and Information Technology, Government of India, New Delhi, *Annual Report, 2005-2006*. Executive Summary, p. 1.
3. Barber, B.R., *Strong Democracy-Participatory Politics for a New Age*, Berkley, University of California Press, 1984, p. 274.

4. Sachdeva, R.K., 'Role of IT in Management or Organisations – Special Number on IT and Indian Administration', *Indian Journal of Public Administration*, July-Sept. 2000, Vol. XLVI, No. 7, p. 327.
5. *Britannica Ready Reference Encyclopaedia*, p. 138.
6. Turban, E. Wetherbe and Mclean M., *Information Technology for Management: Making connections for strategic Advantage*, 1999.
7. Laquey, Tracey, *Internet Companion: A Beginner's guide to global networking, London*, Addison Wesley Publishing Company, 1994, p. 20.
8. Comer Donglas E., *The Internet Book*, New York, Prentice-Hall International, 1995.
9. Joseph E. Kivlin, Ftegel, Roy and Lalik K. Sen, *Innovation in rural India*, Ohio, USA, 1971.
10. Ahluwalia Montek S. , The IT Revolution (Convocation address at S.V. University, Tirupati) *University News*, Vol. 38, No. 21, May 22, 2000.
11. *Annual Report 2006-2007*, Department of Telecommunications, Ministry of Communication and Information Technology, Government of India, New Delhi, Executive Summary, p. iii.
12. Gupta, L.N., 'Internet and Public Sector Organisations', *Indian Journal of Public Administration*, July-September, 2000, Vol. XLVI No. 3, p. 34.
13. Mahadevan K. *et al,* 'Status of Women and Population Dynamics: A conceptual Model' Mahadevan K. (Ed) *Women and Population Dynamics – Perspectives from Asian Countries*, Sage Publications, New Delhi, 1989, pp. 321-345.
14. World Bank – *Knowledge for Development, World Development Report*, Oxford, Oxford University Press, 1999.
15. *Annual Report 2005-06*, D.O.T., MC and IT, Government of India, New Delhi, Executive Summary.
16. Indian Institute of Information Technology, Bangalore – Diffusion of Information and Communication Technologies in India: Labour Market Implications for Developing Countries, Final Report, July 2003.
17. Abdul Kalam, A.P.J., Knowledge Society, (Convocation address at the Andhra University, Vishakhapatnam), *University News*, Vol. 38, No. 22, May 29, 2000.
18. *Annual Report – 2006-2007* D.O.T., MC and IT, Government of India, New Delhi, p. 67.
19. Robertson, Ronald, *Globalisation Social Theory and Global Culture*, Sage, London, 1992, p. 8.
20. Annual Report of the Ministry of Women and Child Development, Government of India, 2005-06.
21. Roy, Prodipto, *Globalisation and Socio-cultural change in India in sociology of globalisation,* (Eds.) Somayaji and Somayaji, 2006 p. 32.

22. Srinivasa, Srinath, *The Power Law of Information – Life in a connected world*, Response Book, New Delhi, 2006.
23. *Ibid*, p. 21.
24. Oommen T.K., *Contested Boundary and Emerging Pluralism*, pp. 36-37.
25. Chandoke Neera, *Beyond Secularism*, p. 21.
26. 'Women Workers in the Informal Sector in South Asia: Creating an enabling environment', Kathmandu Regional Policy Seminar organised by UNIFEM and Govt. of Nepal in conjunction with IDRC and WIEGO 18-20 October 2000.
27. Verma M.M., *Approaches and Strategies for Women Empowerment – Role of Social Work in Empowerment of the Weaker Section in India*, (ed.) Verma R.B.S. and others Serials Publications, New Delhi, 2006, p. 23.
28. Samarajuva, R., The Murky beginnings of the Communication and development field : Voice of America and the passing of Traditional Society, in N. Jayawcera and S. Amunugaine (Eds.) *Rethinking Development Communication*, Singapore, AIMC, 1987, pp. 3-19.
29. Mc.Millin D.C., 'Ideologies of Gender on Television in India', *Indian Journal of Gender Studies*, 9(1), 2002, p. 126.
30. Mc Millin D.C., Television and the Women's Question in *India, in Communication and empowerment of women*, Eds. by Kiran Prasad, the Women Press, Delhi, 2004, p. 86.
31. Mankekar P., *Screening Culture, Viewing Politics*, Durham, Duke University Press, 1999, pp. 10-15.
32. Torres R., *Towards a Socially Sustainable World Economy: An Analysis of the Social Pillars of Globalization*, International Labour Office, Geneva, 2001, pp. 110-115.
33. Mc.Millan D.C., 'Ideologies of Gender on Television in India', *Indian Journal of Gender Studies*, 9(1), 2001, pp. 1-26.
34. Singh K., *Globalisation and Employment Status of Women in India Retrieval*, April 9, 2003 from http:ww2, vinbo.it/avi/aziende/vetp/witec/doc/
35. Prasad Kiran, Rethinking Communication Policies and Empowerment of Women in India – in *Communication and Empowerment of Women – Strategies and Policy Insights from India*, Volume 1, Edited by Kiran Prasad, The Women Press, Delhi, 2004, p. 45.
36. Researcher acknowledge Indian Express for the article by Saraitha Rai – The Fifth Metro – Letter from Bangalore - *Indian Express*, New Delhi, 12 Nov., 2009, p. 12, which has formed the source material for this case study.
37. Pingle Visha, 'Logging in for a cause – Using Face book to help women micro-entrepreneurs', *Indian Express*, New Delhi, 12 Nov, 2009, p. 12.

38. Ray, Suryatirtha, *Nabanna : Gender, grassroots and ICTs*, Suryatirtha @vsnl.com. p. 1.
39. Ray, Jhumpa Ghosh, *Telecentre Goes Mobile and Green*, Vol. 18, No. 2, June 2008, www.iimahd.ernt.in/jhumpa-ray-htm.
40. Nehru, Jawahar Lal, Foreword in *Women in India*, New Delhi Publication Division, 1957, p. 2.

3

Women Empowerment

Empowerment of Women

Swami Vivekananda has said, *"Woman is the companion of man, gifted with equal mental capacities. She has the right to participate in every minute detail in the activities of man and she has an equal right of freedom and liberty with him."*

Women constitute half of the world population, perform nearly two-third of the work hours, receive one-tenth of the world's income and own less than one-hundredth per cent of the world's property. (United Nation's Report 1980). At its core, empowerment means having more control over the forces that shape one's life and increasing the choices available to and capacities of the poor (in) transforming the power structure of the society. Empowerment is an active, dynamic multidimensional process which can enable women to realise their full identity and powers in all spheres of life. Power for women has to be acquired and once acquired, it needs to be exercised, sustained and preserved to lead a life of dignity, honour and self-confidence. The empowerment process and mechanism can be easily enumerated but the real issue is the operationalisation of the same in actual life at various socio-economic levels. In the modern world, the role of women goes much beyond the home and the bringing up of children, to the political, economic and social areas of life. Liberalisation of womanhood to gain her personhood is a fundamental of human rights[1]. The progress of a nation is integrally linked with the empowerment of women. Empowerment is a multi-faceted concept and includes elements like freedom of choice and decision-making, freedom to shape one's own destiny and economic freedom. In the Tenth Five Year Plan, Government of India proposed the following monitorable targets:

(i) Reduce gender gaps in literacy and wage rates by at least 50 per cent by 2007;

(ii) Reduce maternal mortality rate to two per 1000 live births by 2007 and one by 2012;

(iii) Reduce infant mortality rate to 45 per 1000 live births by 2007 and 28 by 2012;

(iv) Reduce decadal rate of population growth between 2001 and 2011 to 16.2 per cent;

(v) Increase literacy-rates to 75 per cent by 2007;

(vi) Reduce poverty ratio by five per cent by 2007 and 15 per cent by 2012;

(vii) Provide sustained access to potable water to all villages by 2007;

(viii) Provide gainful and high quality employment to the addition to labour force.

The year 2001 was declared as the year of the Empowerment of women by the government of India and was marked by the compilation of the National Policy of the Empowerment of Women (NPEW). According to 2001 census of India, women as an independent target group, account for 495.74 million and represent 48.3 per cent of the country's total population.

Brinda Karat, noted feminist says, "The substances of women empowerment can be measured by how far women have advanced in the sphere of economic independence and equality, in political assertion, in being able to live a violence-free life and is being able to break social and cultural barriers which keep women in subordinate positions. According to Mehbooba Mufti, former Lok Sabha M.P., women empowerment should start from the family giving her equal rights in love, care, confidence, education, property and decision-making. Mahasweta Devi, writer and activist says, "Women's empowerment can only happen when each woman finds a space to express her opinion independently. President of India, Pranab Mukerjee has said, "Empowerment to me means internalisation and implementation of normative values of democracy, freedom, equality, education and equitable socio-economic development, as enshrined in our Constitution, by the vast institutional network that subsumes the organs of both state and society. R.K. Samanta has opined, "Empowerment has to be in terms of information, knowledge, skills, awareness and it has to be against powerful forces of domination and exploitation[2]. This is an inclusive term which means not only economic independence but also increase in self-confidence and decision-making ability. Empowerment is a process whereby women gain the ability to make independent choices over their activities and control over resources, become self-reliant and overcome subordination[3].

Empowerment should not be equated with rehabilitation. Rehabilitation means just equipping people with crutches, prostheses, wheel chairs etc. Rehabilitation regrettably enslaves the recipients, stunts their talent and abets corruption. The education model with accent on vocational training is the best way for empowerment. The women, SC/ST and others below poverty line will be only empowered when the support apparatus will facilitate them to stand on their own feet under their own steam. Empowerment of women will be achieved only when they are educated, develop self-confidence, develop a will to live a life of dignity and make all possible efforts with the patronage of the government and co-operative attitude of the family members. Muslim women who live below the poverty line, need to be educated, given self-confidence and support of the society to break the traditional shackles of the community. The Harvard frame-based on Sara Longive Formulation (1991) lists five levels of gender equality through empowerment.[4]

Figure showing Empowerment framework:

Levels	*Equality*	*Empowerment*
Controls (Over Life and levers of power)	↑	↑
Participations (Decision-making)	↑	↑
Conscientisation (awareness)	↑	↑
Access (Respirces/benefits).	↑	↑
Welfare (Material).	↑	↑

Empowerment will be real only when the suppressed and the exploited begin to assert their rights and when the human dignity is not a privilege of the few; when we have the political maturity to listen to the dissent of the deprived. 'Empowerment would be an empty promise unless the victims of exploitation, harassment and gender discrimination get adequate justice without delay and dignity is restored to all oppressed, poor and underprivileged members of the society. According to S.N. Dhar, "Empowerment does not only include increase in levels of income but control over income and assets and participation in Community and household decision. A woman is truly empowered if she can enhance her self-confidence and status within her family as an independent producer of wealth and provider of finance to her household."

The Oxford English Dictionary (1994) defines empowerment as: (1) to invest, legally or formally with power, to licence, (2) to bestow power upon, make powerful. Fook says that empowerment refers to techniques that aim at sharing with or giving client power.[5] According to Swift, the roots of empowerment lie in the political and philosophical foundation of our culture as the concept of democracy and its embodiment in our political institutions are based on the principles of empowering citizens to participate in decisions affecting their welfare.[6] According to Braye and Preston-Shoot, Empowerment has been defined in terms of:

1. Extending one's ability to take effective decisions.
2. Individual, groups and/or communities taking control of their circumstances and achieving their own goals, thereby being able to work towards maximising the quality of their lives.
3. Enabling people who are disempowered to have more control over their lives, to have a greater voice in institutions, services and situations which affect them and to exercise power over someone else rather than simply being the recipient of exercised power.[7] Helping people to regain their own power. Empowerment can be viewed as encompassing:
   (i) Psychological power – having the personal confidence, self-esteem and motivation to initiate change.
   (ii) Social power – having the resources of information, skills and general know-how to initiate change.
   (iii) Political power – having capacity to effectively engage in decision-making process and participations in collective decision-making.

(iv) Empowerment is autonomy, both collective and individual – encompassing several mutually reinforcing components but begins with and is supported by economic independence.[8]

Women empowerment has the following main variables:

(i) Political participation;

(ii) Economic independence;

(iii) Level of education, knowledge and skills;

(iv) Decision-making ability;

(v) Access to basic facilities like health and hygiene facilities like pure drinking water, sanitation, access to nutritious food, well-ventilated house.

(vi) Gender justice,

(vii) Ability in having the courage to disagree with husband/male members when their personal interests are hurt.

(viii) Freedom to move and interact with other members of the community.

(ix) Self-confidence and self-esteem.

(x) Ability to express views and fight against women's oppression – and social oppression.

Education is the first step in building confidence, to tap potential, to be independent and to speak one's own mind and thus get empowered. Women empowerment can only be achieved when each woman finds a space to express their opinion independently and each woman is economically self-sufficient and independent. Poverty is the biggest hurdle to empowerment. Singha Roy visualises empowerment not simply as a mechanical process of sharing, distribution or reistribution of power, (but as one which) involves far wide changes in the social and economic institutional arrangements, political ideologies traditional practices in the mind-sets of the marginalised groups through concretisation.[9] Andre Beteille regards power, authority and legitimacy as cognate concepts and points out that empowerment means different things to different people with very little guidance from social theory. Empowerment, in his view, involves a radical social transformation encompassing means and ends, human rights, basic needs, economic security, capacity-building, skill formation, conditions of dignified social existence, redistribution of power and change from hierarchical to egalitarian system.[10] Sunita Kishore and Kamla Gupta have identified three indicators i.e., evidence (of women's participation in household decision-making etc.) sources (knowledge and control of resources) and setting (present and past environment and conditioning factors) to evaluate women's empowerment.[11] In women empowerment the growth of intrinsic capability namely greater self-confidence and inner transformation of one's consciousness in order to overcome external barriers.

Dr. Amartya Sen, 1998 Nobel Prize winner in Economics, has drawn attention to the following faces of gender inequality in his book "*The Argumentative Indian – Writings on Indian Culture, History and Identity*" –

"(1) Survival inequality,

(2) Natality inequality,

(3) Unequal facilities,

(4) Ownership inequality,

(5) Unequal sharing of household benefits and chores, and

(6) Domestic violence and physical victimisation."[12]

As a result of gender bias in health care, nutrition and social attention, mortality rates of females are usually high compared with what may be expected from the local male mortality rates with India's female-male ratio of 0.93, there is a relative deficit" of woman of nine per cent of Indian male population due to a significant anti-female bias in health care, nutrition and other social influences relevant for survival. The Natality inequality reflects the fact that many parents prefer sex-specific abortions aimed at eliminating female foetuses. The availability of modern techniques to determine the gender of the foetus has made such sex-selective abortion easy and possible. In spite of all efforts of the government, girls have far less opportunity for schooling than boys. There are inequalities in social participation, especially where women are confined to their homes and incarcerated within traditional family lives. There is professional inequality in terms of employment as well as promotion in work and occupation. Ownership inequality between women and men is not a newly emerging inequality, it has existed in most parts of the world for a very long time. "Gender-based discrimination is yet another major social issue we have to address. The women who constitute almost 50 per cent of our population are yet to have an effective share in the political decision-making processes, especially in our representative institutions"[13]. Kumar and Verghese have given three main reasons for women's powerlessness – the patriarchal system which gives a subordinate status to women, women's physiological make-up which confines them to reproduction and household activities and various social-cultural factors which condition women to accept subordinate position and remain ignorant, less literate and less aware. One of the most important issues of discrimination against women is the wages that women receive notwithstanding Equal Remuneration Act. There are often unequal sharing of household benefits and chores within a family and there is unequal sharing of burden of household chores resulting in too much accumulation of labour on women and unequal division of work with bias in favour of male members. The dowry system, economic dependence of women, and social customs and traditions are some of the main causes of the neglect of the girl child and discrimination against her[14]. The National Perspective Plan for women 1988-2000 AD (1988) has made a frank, objective, free and masterly analysis of the indicators of the continued inequality, and vulnerability of women in all sectors – economic, social, political, educational, health-care, nutrition and legal which have been summarised thus:

1. Women Illiterates – over 75 per cent;
2. Rural Illiterate women – 83 per cent;
3. Women, working in unorganised sector – over 90 per cent;
4. Of these, unskilled labour in Agriculture and Construction – 83 per cent;
5. Women having full time employment in organized sector –14 per cent;
6. Maternity benefits and child care available in organised sector – 3.5 per cent;
7. Registered unemployed school graduates 51 lakhs;
8. Pregnant women who are anaemic – 65 per cent;
9. Infant mortality rate (in the first year of birth – 10 per cent;
10. Of which in slums – 124 per cent;
11. Children dying because of nutrition before the age of five years –40 per cent;

12. Sex ratio – 933 females to every 1000 males;
13. Expectation of life at birth – 51.6 as against 52.6 for males;
14. Property owned by women – less than 1 per cent;
15. On the average, a rural woman works for 18 hours a day.

Women in India are suffering due to a vicious circle of unhealthy environment, under nutrition lack of adequate spacing in children and bias against women in general. The general problem is poverty, which is inextricably linked with malnutrition, maternal and child mortality as shown in Figure 1 given below[15].

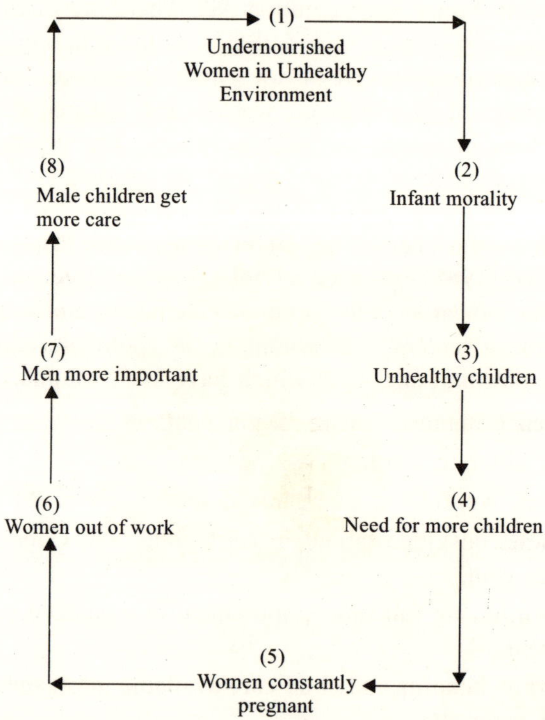

Fig. 1. ShowIng Vicious Circle of Women Poverty and Unhealthy Environment.

Poverty in India is mainly concentrated in rural India and poor people are mostly wage labourers, self-employed petty labourers and artisans. Most women belong to the non-institutionalised unorganised sector. Poverty and gender restrictions make women accept any work on any terms either at home or outside with the lowest returns. Young girls going to schools and college women at workplace often become victims of sexual harassment including such unwelcome sexually determined behaviour (whether directly or by implication) as:

(a) Physical contact and advances;

(b) A demand or request for sexual favours;

(c) Sexually coloured remarks;

(d) Showing pornography;

(e) Any other unwelcome physical, verbal or non-verbal conduct of sexual nature.

(f) Stalking – It refers to repeated harassing or threatening behaviour by an individual or group of persons. It includes following a girl or woman, appearing at a person's home or place of work, making harassing phone calls, leaving written messages or objects or vandalising a person's property. Obsessive pursuit becomes stalking when it becomes scary and it is not mutual pursuit[16]. It was only after National Commission for Women (NCW) spearheaded a movement to get IPC (Indian Penal Code) amended did laws against stalking get more teeth. Amidst the bustle of daily life, many urban women silently endure their stalkers.

There are many woes of the contract women labourers regarding sexual harassment at workplace and their exploitation knows no bounds. In spite of so many positive efforts by the government, trafficking in women and girls has assumed dangerous proportions in India. The factors conducive to prostitution as destitution, desertion, neglect, ill-treatment, strained relations, deception, illegitimate pregnancy, illicit sexual relations, ignorance, sex curiosity, sexual urge, prohibiting of widow remarriage and double standards for men and women are all well-known. The commonest form of prostitution is brothel prostitution followed by *Devadasis/Basair* System. Role of Media on gender issues, particularly of Television channels, is most disheartening.

Erosion of spiritual and moral values, breakdown of strong family ties along with psychopathological, psychological, psycho-social and socio-environmental factors contribute to a large measure for occurrence of domestic crimes in a plural society. The analysis of the problem of domestic crime and its important ramification –

domestic violence, wife battering, dowry deaths, child abuse and mal-treatment of the elderly and the handicapped, centers around the fact that while the problem is as old as is the institution of family, the perception of its criminality related aspects, is relatively recent[17]. According to International Center for Research on Women (ICRW) based in Washington, between 22 and 60 per cent of Indian women have reported being subjected to physical violence in various states[18]. The move from a belief system which saw violence within the family reasonable chastisement of women and children undeserving to be addressed as an offence, to recognizing it as a punishable crime, has been a significant advancement in the law[19]. The brutalised and subordinated existence of a large proportion of women within their social environment gives formidable challenge to the various laws safeguarding the equal rights of women. The recognition of domestic violence as a crime in India was brought about in the early 1980s after a sustained campaign by feminist groups and women activists all over the country[20]. There was a huge demand for the criminalisation of dowry deaths and domestic violence which ultimately resulted in the enactment of Section 498 A of the Indian Penal Code in 1983, Section 304 B in 1986 and the corresponding amendment in provisions of Indian Evidence Act. The criminalisation of domestic violence in the form of Section 498 A and 304 B (dowry death) are significant steps and sought for the first time to bring the issue of domestic or family violence out of the protected private realm of the family and into the public domain in India[21]. The passing of the specialised legislation in October 2006, called the Domestic Violence Act which is a significant development as it provides much-needed court law remedies to provide protection to women victims of domestic violence[22]. Naila Kabeer's definition of empowerment is significant in finding solutions to women's victimisation in domestic violence and their access to justice. She defines empowerment as "The expansion in people's ability to make strategic life choices in a context where this ability was previously denied to them[23]. Research shows that women's access to resources and enabling factors does not necessarily lead to their greater control over resources and that changes in legal statutes often have little influence on practice[24]. All too familiar are cases of rape, molestation, stripping, eve-teasing, kidnapping and abduction, and soon: domestic violence including wife battering, *sati*, female infanticide, female foeticide, dowry deaths and dowry harassment[25]. Recently, rapid growth of population and empowerment of women have led to high number of divorce cases. Many social factors are responsible for the spurt in their numbers. The most important reason is that women have started asserting their equal status in the family, refusing to be subjugated by their husbands. The domestic violence Act of 2006, covers important concerns regarding domestic violence in India. There have been significant amendments in Criminal Laws in the 1980s and 1990s regarding women's equality and violence against women in India. Many studies report that women generally do not cooperate in the investigation in criminal charges cases against their husbands as they try to preserve the sanctity of family life due to a variety of causes related to economic dependence, social stigma and emotional reasons.[26]

Two out of every five women in abusing relationships stay silent about their suffering because of shame and family honour. Lack of awareness about their rights and lack of knowledge about how to seek help in the case of private sphere renders these women more vulnerable to continued and escalating abuse at home.[27] The capacity to aspire" is defined as the forward looking capacity of individuals and groups to envision alternatives and to aspire to different and better future.[28] Martha Nussbaum uses the term "adaptive preference" to illustrate the phenomenon which explains that women often internalise low possibilities for themselves because of their life experience[29]. Women need to be empowered in terms of developing the capacity to transform their choices into desired actions and outcomes. Poorer and subordinate groups experience inequalities not only with respect to economic resources (including "human capital") but also with respect to social, cultural and political factors[30]. The primary responsibility for the empowerment of women is really a societal responsibility[31]. Corruption is a big road block for empowering people, particularly poor women. The dynamics of empowerment are complex and multi-faceted. Power and the potential for empowerment are linked to all levels of society, including its macro, meso and micro–dimensions[32]. In order to promote empowerment, it is necessary to understand the power dynamics in a given society. A complicated institutional and human dynamics of the family and household can be just a step towards the ultimate enhancement of empowerment for women – Joy Deshmukh – Ranadive has suggested Empowerment Linkages as depicted in

Figure 1. "Macro level changes, in the from of political and economic intervention by both state and non-state actors, have a direct impact on micro (domestic) level by changing opportunities for domestic units and individuals. Macro level factors, together with social structure at the community level also act upon the meso environment which consists of villages and neighbourhoods. Changes in the macro environment in turn alter the domestic environment as shown in Figure 2.[33]

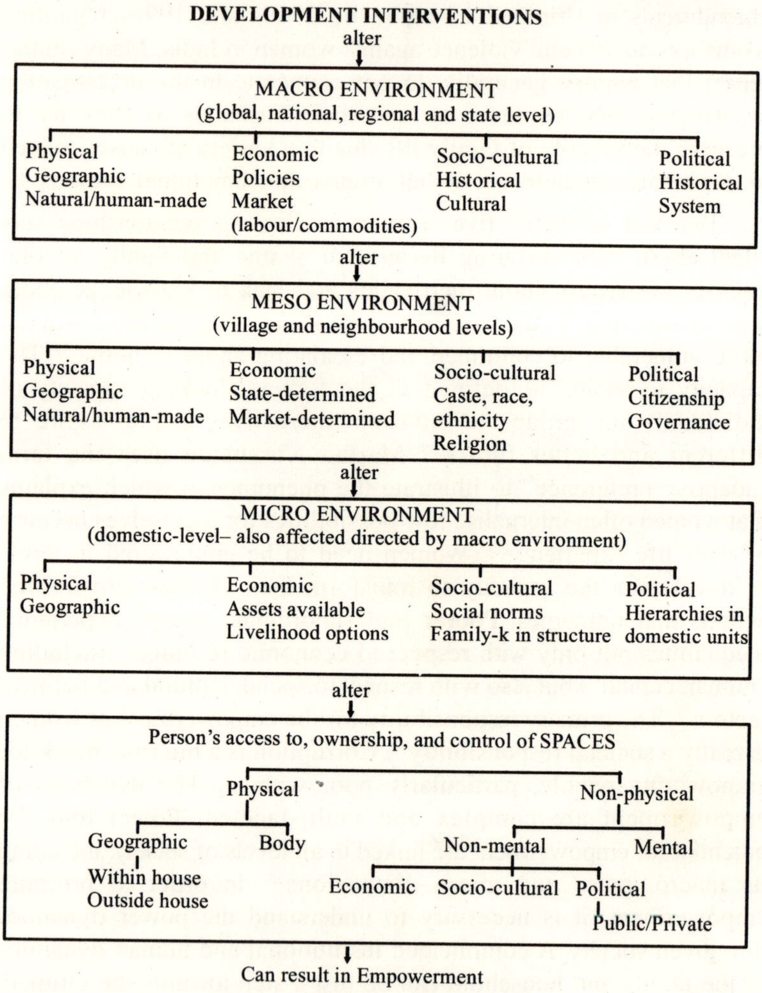

Fig. 2: Empowerment Linkages

In the Indian context unfortunately the road ahead is a bumpy one and expecting legal equality for women is somewhat a pipe–dream mainly due to:

1. Socio-cultural impediments and tradition-bound customs which shackle women;
2. Ignorance, illiteracy, superstition and self-sacrificing attitude of women.
3. Social, economic and financial hurdles faced by women when seeking justice.
4. Biased/discriminatory attitudes and delays by our law enforcement machinery (Police and Administrators)"[34].

Two persistent problems that affect a significant portion of Indian women are poverty and violation of their human rights. Where poor women have an inherent potential for empowerment and transformation, an external stimulus is considered necessary to unleash the process and micro-credit programmes can improve women's access to economic resources and generic basic needs thus enabling them to have access to independent sources of saving and credit[35]. Increasing consciousness and awareness building is an important component of the process of empowerment. Women empowerment can be viewed as a "continuum of several inter-related and mutually reinforcing component:

1. Awareness building about women's situation discrimination and rights and opportunities as a set of gender equality.
2. To inculcate a sense of group identity and power of working as a group.
3. Capacity building and skill development.
4. Participation and greater control.
5. Action to bring greater equality between men and women.

Hoshain, Schuler and Riley in their longitudinal study on dimension of empowerment have brought out that participation in credit programmes has a positive effect on:

1. Mobility,
2. Ability to make small purchases;
3. Ability to participate in major decisions

4. Ownership of productive assets
5. Legal and political awareness
6. Participation in public campaigns and protests
7. Reduced vulnerability to domestic violence.

It is to be understood that empowerment can not be delivered, it must be self-generated and self-acquired. Empowerment has been stated as one of four essential components of human development paradigm – others being productivity, equity and sustainability as per Human Development Report (1995).

"Arise, awake and do not stop till the goal is achieved" says – Swami Vivekanand. According to the Word Bank's empowerment source book, empowerment is the expansion of assets and capabilities of poor people to participate in, negotiate with, influence, control and hold accountable institutions that affect their lives[36]. Empowerment of women is one of the Central Concerns of the Tenth Plan (2002-2007) which spells out a three-pronged strategy for it:

(1) Social Empowerment: Create an enabling environment for development of women and give them easy and equal access to all the basic minimum services so that they can realise their full potential.

(2) Economic Empowerment: Ensure provisions of training, employment and income generation activities to make women economically self-reliant.

(3) Gender Justice: Eliminate all forms of gender discrimination so that women are able to enjoy equal rights not only in theory but also in practice.

Empowerment to women has been made by the Constitution of India by granting universal adult franchise and in terms of legal and administrative measures as well as enabling support to improve the working and living conditions of women, many initiatives have been taken since 1947 to empower women. Empowerment of women through education is most important in India. Today there are thousands of women in higher jobs and professional careers like engineers, doctors, educationists, bureaucrats and managers. Empowerment of women through preservation of indigenous knowledge traditions. "Political empowerment is both a weapon and device in the struggle of women for emancipation from poverty, disease and illiteracy, for by active involvement in the decision-making machinery for the country at all levels to ensure and carve a place for themselves and their girls, daughters, the future citizens of this nation[37]. Domestic empowerment is another dimension wherein women will have better ability to take decisions in the context of their families and households. Economic independence, active political participation at various levels, decision-making power in family and households, access to basic amenities and ability to actively participate in social activities are the main elements of women empowerment. It is the gradual process by which powerless gain greater control over their lives, break socio-cultural barriers which keep women in subordinate positions. Empowerment has to be earned, lived and asserted. No one can empower an unwilling person who is not self-confident and not ready to assert for her rights, privilege and powers. What is needed is awareness. Multifaceted efforts are required to create gender sensitivity among women and also among enlightened man who may support the women's cause. The Constitution of India has guaranteed equality, liberty and dignity to the women of India but women need to be sensitised about these provisions and their own fundamental rights even after six decades of independence. There are laws repugnant to the Constitution of India e.g.:

"(1) Personal and family laws discriminate not only between men and women but between women and women as well.

(2) Army Act, Navy act, Air Force Act and Service Rules discriminate against women.

(3) A woman in India is not the natural guardian of her children.

(4) As there is no community of poverty, a woman is not entitled to an equal share in the property of the husband.

(5) There is no money value to the work of women in home.

(6) A Hindu woman is not entitled by birth to a share in the joint property nor can she ask for partition of the property.

(7) A Muslim woman is discriminated against in matters of marriage, divorce, maintenance and inheritance: (a) Polygamy is permitted (not polyandry); (b) By pronouncing *"Talak"* three times a wife can be divorced; (c) a male child is entitled to a share of two females.

(8) A Parsi woman, if marries out of the community, she ceases to be a Parsi and a Parsi daughter is discriminated against in matters of inheritance"[38].

In a country of one billion, women empowerment has no meaning unless it touches the economically or socially weak segments of population. A series of legislations and changes in government policies, affirmative action including reservation in education and jobs has led to a frame for better provision of education, health and employment for weaker segments of the society and deprived sections. Empowerment of women cannot be truly meaningful without a minimum level of good quality education, basic heath services and child nutrition, a reduction of the unacceptable high level of infant mortality and the extremely high levels of maternal mortality – 500 to 600 per one hundred thousand births[39]. There are many lacunae and loopholes which need to be pointed out and even legally fought at various forums. The *Sati* Prevention Act was passed in 1987 but glorification of *sati* continues in many states like Rajasthan and others. There is need for the change of value system and social change must come from sensitisation of young women, girls and men. There is continued inequality and vulnerability of women in all sectors—economic, social, political, education and health-care, nutrition and legal. Sensitisation process must highlight these glaring inequalities of the society. In spite of all efforts, the menace of dowry, violence against women, sexual harassment, damaging portrayal of women in India, infanticide, foeticide, trafficking of women, domestic violence are all growing and the sensitisation process must bring out these challenges before women who are going to be empowered – A psychic and socio-psychological revolution in the minds of both men and women is needed. Empowerment is an active multi-level process and has to be acquired by women themselves. Once acquired it needs to be exercised, sustained and pressurised by a vigilant group of empowered women. The empowerment mechanism needs to be built, preserved and constantly reinforced by constant sensitisation process. Empowerment of women can be operationalised by the following sensitisation processes:

"(1) Removing sex bias in our curriculum and by designing courses incorporating women's dimensions.

(2) Emphasising the multiple roles of women.

(3) Developing the ability to think creatively about situations, the hurdles to face, possibility of change the coping mechanism etc.
(4) Overcoming social, cultural and traditional beliefs.
(5) Encouraging late marriages.
(6) Sensitising them to laws related to property, marriage, divorce, minimum wages, maternity leave benefit etc.
(7) Encouraging them to take careers seriously.
(8) Encouraging to believe in their own ability and a sense of self-worth.
(9) Making them aware of the possibilities of self-employment.
(10) Educating parents on the importance of making women economically self-sufficient[40]."

After the latest amendment to the Hindu Succession Act, women have now become equal shareholders in family property." We need to have clear policies for empowerment of women. Organising women to be economically productive citizens is both a challenge and a fulfillment. According to Anubhuti Vishnoi, (*Indian Express*, 19 Nov. 2009, New Delhi) Govt. of India has approved a revision of Mid-day Meal scheme and Rs. 5,000 Crore plan to ensure Information and Communication Technology at schools. The salary of cook and the helper at each school will be Rs. 1,000 each. The revised scheme will cost the Government about 14,000 crore over the plan period. The ICT @ schools scheme formulated by the HRD Ministry plans will convert government schools to "smart" schools with internet access, digital cameras, scanners projectors and audio-recorders. As many as one secondary, higher secondary and govt. aided schools will be covered under the scheme. Each school will be equipped with at least one computer laboratory with 10 networked computers to begin with.[41] Process of Sensitisation about empowerment of women needs to be initiated for police, judiciary, administration and even the common man. Custodial care for women, human rights of women, education and training for women and gender issue are topics where the male bias is apparent and therefore sensitisation programmes must be started for police, judiciary, administrators and law-makers Bonded labour, family planning, education for women, nutrition and health-care for women are topics on which common citizens and law-makers need to be sensitised and educated. Empirical evidence supports the view that sensitisation process needs to be initiated in the following critical areas:

"(1) Inadequacy of institutional mechanism for the advancement of women;
(2) Persistent and institutionalised discrimination against the girl child;
(3) Feminization of poverty;
(4) Gender blindness in macro-economic policies;
(5) Invisibility of women's contribution to the economy and environmental sustenance;
(6) Poor participation by women in decision-making structured by women in accessing legal entitlements.
(7) Gender gaps in literacy, education and health;
(8) Barriers encountered by women in accessing legal entitlements.
(9) Gender biased societal norms[42]."

As a measure of empowerment Govt. of India has launched a number of schemes for the empowerment of women and girls. Allocation of some major schemes on women's employment and self-helps groups is shown in Table 1 below:

Table 1. Govt. of India Allocation of Resources[43]

S.No.	*Schemes for Empowerment*	*Year 2003-04 Rs. crore R.E.*	*Year 2004-05 Rs. crore R.E.*
1.	STEP	8	16
2.	*Swayam Siddha*	8	16
3.	Rajive Gandhi National Creche Scheme for Working Women	—	—
4.	Hostels for Working Women/Girls	4	6
5.	*Rastiya Mahila* ------	—	—
6.	NREGS	—	—
7.	*Sampoorna Grameen Rozgar Yogana*	9,640	4,590
8.	*Swarna Jayanti Gram Swarorzar Yojana*	720	900
9.	*Swarna Jayanti Shabri Rozgar Yogana*	94	122
10.	Priya Darshini Scheme	—	—

Source: Economic and Political Weekly – Yamini Mishra, Bhumika Jhamb – An assessment of UPAI through a gender budget ——— Notes – August 29, 2009, Vol. XLIV, No. 35 p. 65.

All women need to be sensitised about the above given critical areas that call for immediate action for empowerment of women in India. The litmus test for empowerment is whether poor and subordinate groups have effectively advanced their particular interests through their own choice and action. The specific empowerment intervention encompass a diverse set of actions to promote participation, increase transparency, build capacity among poor groups and strengthen accountability mechanism in development processes[44]. Empowerment is to be spelt out within a value framework. The empowerment lies in their capabilities and readiness to make the best use of resources – human, natural and financial, to meet the needs of all[45].

Women were empowered with equal rights w.e.f. 26 January, 1950. In *Bodhisattva Gautam* vs *Subhra Chakraborty*, ISSC 1996: 490), the Supreme Court followed the Delhi Domestic Working Women Forum and awarded an interim compensation of Rs. 1,000 per month to the victims of the rape till the trial court decided her charges. This is one of the most praise worthy pronouncement of the Supreme Court on the area of the compensatory jurisprudence in the Indian legal history. A three-judge bench of the Supreme Court in [*Vishaka vs State of Rajasthan* (6 SCC 1997): 241] made a significant contribution in evolving the code against sexual harassment at workplaces.

The National Commission for Women Act 1990 (No. 20 of 1990) has been enacted with a very large number of functions to safeguard the interest of women and to empower them. The Supreme Court of India in the Criminal Original Jurisdiction in the case *Visaka and others versus State of Rajasthan* (Writ Petition (Criminal) Nos. 666-700 of 1992) has given a landmark judgement pertaining to gender equality and protection from sexual harassment. India is the first country in the world to adopt family planning officially but unfortunately still population of India is increasing because many sections of the society have not adopted family planning methods. One of the main problem of women is the birth of children, their spacing and the health of the mother.

India is still basically agrarian with approximately 70 per cent of the population involved in agriculture and altered activities for earning their livelihood. One-third of the agricultural labour force and nearly half of the self employed farmers are women. Agriculture sector employs nearly 84 per cent of all economically active women in the country. Rural women are the integral part of agriculture system. Farm women are usually employed in arduous filed operations i.e., pods crushing, stubbles collection, sowing behind plough, transplanting, weeding, interculturing, harvesting, thrashing and agro-processing.[46] Investment in improving the health and nutritional food to women will pay direct dividends to the nation by increase the capacities of the women as producers, as well as those of their children in the long run.

Education for girls in women is one of the most essential areas for empowerment. During the last 60 years there has been quantitative growth of education of women. Undoubtedly, there has been quantitative growth of education since India became a republic in 1950 as given in Table 2 below:

Table 2: Qualitative Growth in Education

Sl. No.	*Items*	*Figure in 1950-51*	*Figure in 2005-06*
1.	Literacy Rate	18.3%	64.8%
2.	Female Literacy Rate	8.9%	53.7%
3.	Schools	0.23 millions	1.28 millions
4.	General Colleges	370	11698
5.	Gross Enrollment Ratio in Elementary Education	32.1%	94.85%
6.	Gender Parity Index at Elementary level	0.38	0.92
7.	Public Expenditure on Education as per cent of GDP	1.5%	3.46%

Source: Yojana – September 2009 p. 27.

Number of girls per hundred boys enrolled in schools shows steady increase over the years as given in Table 2 ahead.

Table 3: Number of Girls per Hundred Boys in School

Year	Primary Class (I – IV)	Upper Primary (VI – VIII)	Secondary and Higher Secondary Class (IX – XII)
1990-91	71	58	50
2000-01	78	69	63
2004-05 (Provisional)	88	80	71

Source: Yojana – September 2009, p. 33.

The success achieved in education of girls in our country in the post-independence period is the result of a number of schemes put in place by the government for bringing girls to school and holding them there. Table 3 shows, the increase in enrollment of girls from 1990 to 2005. While the stress on the education of girls has been the cornerstone of most plans and policies related to education, some of the notable schemes that have come up in recent years are as follows:

Sarva Shiksha Abhiyan: This is an effort to universalise elementary education by community-ownership of the school system. One of the objectives of the scheme is to bridge all gender and social category gaps at Primary stage by 2007 and Upper Primary by 2010. The scheme has special features focussing on education of girls, which include provision of free textbooks to all girls upto class VIII, separate toilets for girls, back to school camps for out-of-school girls, bridge courses for older girls, recruitment of 50 per cent women teachers, early childhood care and education centres, in/near schools in convergence with ICDS programme, teachers' sensitisation programmes to promote equitable learning opportunities, gender-sensitive teaching-learning materials including textbooks, intensive community mobilisation efforts, 'innovation fund' per district for need-based interventions for ensuring girls' attendance and retention.

National Programme for Education of Girls at Elementary Level (NPEGEL): The National Programme for Education of Girls at Elementary Level (NPEGEL) has been formulated for providing additional support for education of underprivileged/disadvantaged girls at elementary level. NPEGEL is a part of SSA and is implemented under its umbrella but as a distinct and separate gender component plan of SSA.

Kasturba Gandhi Balika Vidyalaya: This is a new scheme for setting up upto 750 residential schools with boarding facilities at elementary level for girls belonging predominantly to the SC, ST, OBC and Minorities in identified educationally backward blocks where the rural female literacy is below the national average and gender gap in literacy is more than the national average. The scheme will be coordinated with the existing schemes of Department of Elementary Education and Literacy viz., Sarva Shisha Abhiyan (SSA) National Programme for Education of Girls at Elementary Level (NPEGEL) and Mahila Samakhya Scheme (MSS). The objective of KGBV is to ensure access and quality education to the girls of disadvantaged groups of society by setting up residential schools with boarding facilities at elementary level.

Mahila Samakhya Scheme: The *Mahila Samakhya* Scheme was started in 1989 to translate the goals enshrined in the NPE into concrete programme for the education and empowerment of women in rural areas particularly those from socially and economically marginalised groups through informal learning. The MS scheme recognises the centrality of education in empowering women to achieve equality. The *Mahila Sanghas* or Women's collectives at the village level provide the women a space to meet, reflect, ask questions and articulate their thoughts and needs and make informed choices. The programme has focussed on awareness of the need to educate the children, especially girls, which has resulted in a direct impact on enrollment and retention of girls in schools.

Government has started a number of schemes for women empowerment. Some important ones are: *Balika Samriddhi Yojana, Kishori Shakti Yojana, Mahila Samakhya, Mahila Shiksha Kendra, Nari Adalat, Swayam Sidha* and IWEP (Integrated Women Empowerment Programme). The formation of SHG (Self-Help Groups) where women get together to start some small enterprise with micro-credit from banks like NABARD (National Bank of Agriculture and Rural Development). The basic principle on which a SHG is formed is micro-saving[47]. At present, more than 200 such SHGs are operating in the country and 90 per cent of these are run by women. The Social Security Bill 2005, covers the entire country and all workers in the unorganised sector with monthly income of Rs. 5,000/- and below and covers self-employed workers, home-based workers, small farmers and wage workers. The benefits include, minimum social security cover comprising (1) old age pension for workers above 60 years, (2) health insurance for self, spouse and small children, (3) maternity benefits for women and (4) insurance to cover death and disability arising out of incident. Women involved in handicrafts and other home-based work do not get sufficient attention and face problems like low wages, lack of institutional funds flow, difficulty in getting raw material and in marketing etc[48]. Empowerment of minorities, SC/ST and other OBCs is a national Commitment. "As a practical course, all secular forces, including Muslims, should work for implementation of the Sachar Committee Report. For instance, all benefits guaranteed to the Hindu Scheduled Castes, including political reservations, should be extended to SC Muslims also, just as they are extended to Buddhists and Sikhs. OBC Muslims should also be treated like OBC Hindus. The 15-point programme for the economic benefits of the minorities should also be welcome." Development of the integrated basket of media proves to be a highly powerful tool in sensitising the people about female foeticide and infanticide and the dangers of negative ratio for the future of the society. Documentaries based on this social menace are screened in all public places like cinema theatres and are relayed on television.[49] As the census 2001 figure indicate in the recent past there has been a spurt in the killing of the female in the womb itself. The invention of modern ultrasonographs has added fuel to the fire and greedy practitioners and their network of contactmen are involved in this barbaric act of female foeticide.

According to Ministry of Women and Child Development, Govt. of India, the following have been eleven special initiatives taken for empowerment of women[50] and their Social and economic rehabilitation: (1) Upgrading nutrition intake, through supplementary nutrition, micro and macro nutrient deficiencies, health check up of pregnant and lactating mothers under ICDS programme benefitting 91 lakh mothers. (2) to enable greater mobility and safe and inexpensive accommodations to working women, 917 working women hostels in position benefitting 57,264 women; (3) special hostel under process; (4) *Swayam Siddha* – empowering SHGs for income generation through micro-credit and other facilities – 650 block, 67971 groups and 9,89,485 beneficiaries; (5) *Swa Shakti* training and skill development in 36 trades for securing employment, 167 proposals benefitting 9560 beneficiaries were processed upto December 2005; (6) STEP – The Scheme of "Support of Training and Employment Programme" for women mobilised women into groups and providing them with comprehensive package of services of access to credit, training, skill upgradations, market linkages etc. – 19,200 beneficiaries benefited in 2005-06 (Upto 15.01.2006); (7) *Swa-Shakti*—a rural women development and empowering programme through SHGs and micro-credit: 17647 SHGs and 1213 clusters formed; (8) *Rashtriya Mahila Kosh* – provision of micro-finance to start income generation activities – 16,246 beneficiaries assisted in 2005; (9) spearheading gender budget initiatives in Central and State Government; (10) 585 condensed courses of education benefitting 14,625 women; (11) 5070 awareness generation camps involving 125 lakh women. Although there are so many schemes and projects for women the stark realities are as follows according to NSSO survey:

(1) The top bracket of spending class are almost double among upper castes compared to OBCs.

(2) 12 per cent households among upper castes figure among those who spend Rs. 1,155 and above per month among OBCs while the figure for the highest bracket in urban Areas – Rs. 2540 or more – is 13 per cent for upper castes and three per cent for OBCs.

(3) SCs are at the bottom with just 10 per cent in the top group in urban areas and three per cent in rural areas[51]."

The Tenth Plan (2002-2007) outlay for various schemes and programmes of the Ministry of Women and Child Development and Empowerment was Rs. 13,780 crore. The details of year wise Annual Plan allocation and actual expenditure from 2003-04 to 2005-06 are given in Table 4 below.[52]

Table 4: Plan Outlay and Expenditure

Year	*Allocation*	*Expenditure*	*Per cent E/A*
2003-2004	2600.00	2051.99	78.92 per cent
2004-2005	2400.00	2399.78	99.99 per cent
2005-2006	3872.29	3790.72	97.82 per cent
Rupees in crores, as on 10.03.2006			

The fight against poverty is not a campaign – it is a mission of empowerment.

Tenth Five Year Plan (2002-2007), adopted three-fold strategy for empowering women. These are: Social Empowerment, Economic Empowerment and Gender justice in all spheres viz., political, economic, social, civil, cultural etc.[53] The National Common Minimum Programme (NCMP) of the United Progressive Alliance Government (UPA) is to "empower women politically, educationally, economically and legally" Govt. of India National Perspective Plan (1988-2000), categorically urged for effective participation of women in local democratic bodies with the following recommendations for ensuring participation of women in local bodies:

1. Reservation of 30 per cent seats at Village Panchayat to Zilla Parishad level and local municipal bodies.
2. Reservation of 30 per cent of executive heads of all bodies from the Village Panchayat to district and certain percentage of the chief executives of Panchayati Raj bodies at lower, middle and higher levels for women.
3. Declaring a certain percentage of constituencies in the lower tier of Panchayat Raj as exclusively women's constituencies.

A study conducted by Dilip Kumar Ghosh regarding women representation in West Bengal Panchayats, has established the reality that introduction of quota can not yield the desired results. Quota is an enabling tool, but it is not an end in itself. Any substantial improvement requires the change in attitude and shift from traditional approaches on the part of those who are at the helm of affairs.[54]

In India, the most vulnerable section of the population, appropriately called the weaker sex is women and among women widows are the most backward due to the sudden change in their socio-economic status with the death of their husbands. The life style of widows is very bad in India irrespective of the stratum to which they belong. Widows are neglected even in the category of women and worst of all, she is looked upon as inauspicious. Widowhood is a very stressful situation bringing about several socio-economic cultural-emotional deprivations.[55] Widowhood is a period of crisis in the life of women. Widows are forced to lead a life of deprivation and misery.

Constitutional directives regarding non-discrimination on grounds of sex in education and employment, processes of modernisation industrialisation and urbanisation, migration of single families to urban areas, western education, awareness of better standards of life etc enabled women, especially middle class, to enter professional careers of physicians, and surgeons, teachers, engineers, lawyers, administrators, scientists, managers, health technicians and office ministerial and gazetted staff.

The basic issues that came to one's mind are as under: "How empowered are the women professionals and working women? Does the socio-economic educational and family background influence their career choices? How far do the family responsibilities clash with career commitments? What problems do the women professionals face at home and at work place? How far are their careers helpful to them in the process of empowement. Jaya Kothai Pillai in her book "*Women and Empowerment*" has given some research findings of some of these issues. Few studies indicate that priority given to family demands were barriers to career development[56]. They had to accommodate to husband's careers and had to opt for positions compatible with their family roles[57]. Many professionals women are interested in combining employment with marital and family commitments as two pay cheque family becomes more empowered economically and even in social orders. Women professional and executives do feel empowered, develop self-confidence and self-esteem, and are more sensitive to the feelings of others. However, according to Erik Erikson; "there is always a historical lag between any emancipation and the inner adjustment of the emancipated; it takes much longer time to emancipate what goes on deep down inside us – whatever prejudices and inequalities have managed to become part of our impulse life and our identification formation – than – the time it takes to define professed values and to change legalities." Many professional women feel that they are assets to their family and double family income has enabled them to improve the quality of their life[58]. The 73rd Amendment to the Constitutions of India has given good opportunities to women as 33 per cent seats are reserved for women candidates in Panchayat elections and it is generally considered a very positive step towards political empowerment of women. Smt Sushma Swaraj has said,

"Even though the government is working consistently to empower women, the empowerment process will not be complete till we empower women completely." After independence, the age-old customs and prejudices discouraging the employment of women have been fast disappearing with constitutional provisions guaranteeing equal rights to women and special reservations to SC/ ST and OBC. Large number of women are taking up regular jobs and empowering themselves economically. The majority of young women opt for jobs with the predominant motive of leading a purposeful life. Many women adopted career jobs to become economically independent and getting a feeling of fulfillment. A research study revealed that 68.5 per cent of the respondents to her survey, succeeded in making a viable adjustment between the work role and family life[59]. Another significant fact that has emerged from a number of studies is that a vast majority (97.5 per cent) of the respondents had come to believe that their jobs had given them respect and prestige in society. During the last fifty years, a large number of women have been economically empowered and emancipated but still India has to go a long way to empower all the eligible women population. However, the nations adopt all possible measures and policies to empower women economically and socially. The women professional in India are certainly on the move towards empowerment with confidence. For empowering women, the experience of Self-Help Groups in the 1980s, yielded encouraging results. *Swayam Siddha* is an integral scheme for women's empowerment through formation of Self-Help Groups. The main achievements of Swayam *Siddha schemes* are as under:

(i) 67,971 women self-help groups have been formed against the target of 65,000.

(ii) 9,89,485 beneficiaries were covered against the target of 11,37,500.

(iii) 6,234 clusters have been formed.

(iv) Basic training on the important aspects have been imparted to SHGs.[60]

There are three brief case-studies highlighting benefits of joining SHGs *(Swayam Siddha)*. *Roshni Seva-shakti Mahila Samooh* of Jharkhand comprises 13 members of which 11 members are from ST category (Dalit). All the 13 members are saving Rs. 20/- per month and their savings is Rs. 9,710. The group received a cash credit of Rs. 25,00 and were given training in piggery and goat rearing. After receiving training they took a joint loan of Rs. 15,000 and started piggery and goat rearing activity. The members take care of the activity by rotation and earn Rs. 500 per member per month. In another case Sannarangamma (of Karnataka) and her family were in abject poverty, struggling for survival. After joining Shri Rajeshwari *Swa-Shakti* SHG, she was trained for "petty business" set up under Enterprise Development programme. She started her own shop with micro-credit fund of Rs. 5,000 and today gets a daily profit of Rs. 40 to 50. In another case Smt. Jagadhar, member of the Mahalakshmi group received training under animal husbandry programme after which she started her own dairy activities. She collects/procures milk from other SHG members and sells it in Gulbarga city. She now earns on an average Rs. 200 per day.

In India from ancient times, young girls and women have been engaging themselves in embroidery and crafts as a part-time hobby. The Varanasi Sarees, Lucknow Jarri and Chikan work and Kutchi embroidery of Gujarat have been famous all over the world for their artistic designs. Deep in the arid reach of Kutch, thousands of women embroiders are ushering the vibrant colours of their folk craft into beautiful designs and artistic creations. As a high artistic handicraft it requires tremendous hard work dedication and patience. A voluntary organisation Shrajan has successful provided economic freedom and empowerment to women spread across 114 villages over 500 sq. kms.[61] It has revived the fading art and helped rural women create sustainable income and has empowered women to some extent.

Achievements of Swa-Shakti Projects

The *Swa-Shakti* Projects jointly funded by IFAD, World Bank and Govt. of India, was launched in October 1999. The project culminated on 30 June 2005 and was implemented in 335 blocks of 57 districts of 9 states viz. Haryana, Bihar, Chhattisgarh, Gujarat, Jharkhand, Madhya Pradesh, Karnataka, Uttar Pradesh and Uttaranchal. The overall objectives of the *Swa-Shakti* Programme has been to bring out socio-economic empowerment of women self-help group, micro-credit and income generating activities (IGAs).

The project has established 17,647 SHGs against the original target of 7,400 covering about 2,44,000 women. All the groups have received the basic training in SHGs concept, book keeping, accounts, leadership, group dynamics and credit management. The project has aimed at the formation of clusters of SHGs which is an important strategy for survival. 1,164 clusters have undergone basic training on cluster concept whereas 536 cluster have undergone exposure visit during the project period. Linkages with the credit institutions have been impressive which is evident from the fact that a total of 12,256 groups were linked with banks with total bank credit of Rs. 34.59 crores, 333 business counselling centres which are providing appropriate support services in terms of counselling and guidance on enterprise development have been formed and 420 business counselling consultants in total have been trained. By and large the programme has benefitted the most disadvantaged groups viz., Scheduled Castes (Dalits) (27%); Scheduled Tribes (18%); women headed households (11%) marginal farmers (43%) and the landless households (1%). It provides self-confidence, mobility, voicing demands, accessing credit from banks and developed the habit of systematic savings.

The women's empowerment in domestic sphere makes two assumptions. The first is that empowerment is basically a property of social or cultural systems rather than of individual experiences and traits. The second is that empowerment is multi-dimensional with imperfect associations among its different dimensions. Levels of women's empowerment in the private and public spheres are often dissimilar : there are many cultures that give women domestic power of certain types but deny their power in public sphere[62]. For example, Thai wives typically engage in income-earning activities and they are independent in the arena of birth control but they are sexually submissive to their husbands and largely excluded from politics[63]. An important source of inter-community variation in women's participation is community values and norms about gender roles[64]. Empowerment is a multi-dimensional group-based process. Individual traits and experiences such as education, health, or paid employment may influence women's empowerment but they do not automatically determine it. Measuring the impact of attempts to empower poor women is obviously very difficult, complex and infracted. Domestic family relations and household domestic power dynamics between husband and wife are notoriously difficult to measure. The difficulties of measuring the dynamics of family powers are compounded when researchers want to employ quantitative techniques. Research studies show a variable relationship between women's paid employment and different aspects of their empowerment. Mason has stated that although paid work is positively associated with having a greater say in the household's economic decisions in five countries namely India, Pakistan, Malaysia, Thailand and Phillipines, the strength of this relationship varies, being relatively weak in Pakistan and the strongest in Thailand. In India, Malaysia and Phillipines, women's paid employment is unrelated to having a say in decisions about family size, to enjoying freedom of movement or to being unafraid to disagree with the husband. However, many research studies show that paid work does indeed empower women. Education, employment and higher age group of women do empower them but it is difficulty to quantify as it differs from individual to individuals and cultural norms of the society. Masons has admitted that although his study provides some valuable insights into the problems of measuring women's empowerment, the study does not pretend to provide the final word on either the determinants of women domestic empowerment or the best way to measure and analyse it[65]. An individual's control of economic resources – human capital, earned income or liquid assets, generally help women in economic empowerment. Studies of receipts of micro-credit in Bangladesh find that borrowing tends to enhance women's incomes and their empowerment as measured through survey questions about decision-making autonomy and freedom of movement[66]. Empowerment measures used by researchers are mainly five indicators namely; (1) Economic decision-making; (2) Family size decision making; (3) Freedom of movement; (4) Afraid to disagree with husband; (5) Husband beats or hits wife. Measurement of empowerment is practically not possible as it is a very complex phenomenon, partly psychological, cultural and personal.

Support to Training and Employment Programme for Women (STEP)

Launched in 1987, STEP seeks to provide updated skills and new knowledge to poor and asset-less women in the traditional sectors, such as, agriculture, animal husbandry, dairying, fisheries, handloom, handicraft, *khadi* and village industries, sericulture, social forestry and wasteland development for enhancing their productivity and income generation to empower them for self-employment. A comprehensive package of services, such as health care, elementary education, crèche facility, market linkages etc., are provided besides access to credit. During 9th plan period about 2,55,635 women were covered under 66 projects launched in 19 states. Dairy sector, handlooms, handicrafts, sericulture, piggery and poultry received maximum support. In the year 2004-05, projects were sanctioned to benefit and empower 15,900 women. In Delhi upto 10.01.2006 Rs.10.87 lakh were sanctioned with beneficiaries under STEP scheme. In Delhi, *Bisnouli Sarvodaya Gramodyog Sewa Sansthan* project was sanctioned with handicraft trade having 500 beneficiaries.

Swawlambam Programme

Swawlambam women's economic development programme was previously known as NORAD (Nowegran Agency for Development Cooperation) and was started with the objective to provide training and skill to women to facilitate them to obtain employment or self-employment on sustained basis. The target group under the scheme are the poor and needy women from weaker sections of society such as Scheduled Castes and Scheduled Tribes etc. It provides training in computer programming, medical transcription, radio and TV repairs, watch assembling, garment-making, embroidery, handloom weaving etc. Financial assistance is also arranged.

National Policy for the Empowerment of Women (2001)

1. Main Highlights

Within the framework of a democratic polity, our laws, development policies, plans and programmes have aimed at women's advancement in different spheres. In recent years, the empowerment of women has been recognised as the central issue in determining the status of women. The National Commission for Women was set-up by an Act of Parliament in 1990 to safeguard the rights and legal entitlements of women. The 73rd and 74th Amendments (1993) to the Constitution of India have provided for reservation of seats in the local bodies of Panchayats and Municipalities for women, laying a strong foundation for their participation in decision-making at the local levels. The Mexico Plan of Action (1975), the Nairobi

Forward Looking Strategies (1985), the Beijing Declaration as well as the Platform for Action (1995) and the Outcome Document adopted by the UNGA Session on Gender Equality and Development and Peace for the 21st century, titled "Further actions and initiatives to implement the Beijing Declaration and the Platform for Action" have been unreservedly endorsed by India for appropriate follow up.

However, there still exists a wide-gap between the goals enunciated in the Constitution, legislation, policies, plans, programmes, and related mechanisms, on the one hand and the situational reality of the status of women in India, on the other. Gender disparity manifests itself in various forms. Social stereotyping and violence at the domestic and societal levels are some of the other manifestations. Discrimination against girl children, adolescent girls and women persists in various parts of the country. Consequently, the access of women particularly those belonging to weaker sections including Scheduled Castes/Scheduled Tribes/Other Backward Classes and Minorities, majority of whom are in the rural areas and in the informal, unorganised sector – to education, health and productive resources, among others, is inadequate. Therefore, they remain largely marginalized, poor and socially excluded.

2. Goal and Objectives

The goal of this policy is to bring about empowerment of women. Specifically, the objectives of this policy include:

(i) Creating an environment through positive economic and social policies for full development of women to enable them to realise their full potential.

(ii) The *de-jure* and *de-facto* enjoyment of all human rights and fundamental freedom by women on equal basis with men in all spheres – political, economic, social, cultural and civil.

(iii) Equal access to participation and decision-making of women in social, political and economic life of the nation.

(iv) Equal access to women to health-care, quality education at all levels, career and vocational guidance, employment, equal remuneration, occupational health and safety, social security and public office etc.

(v) Strengthening legal systems aimed at elimination of all forms of discrimination against women.

(vi) Changing societal attitudes and community practices by active participation and involvement of both men and women.

(vii) Mainstreaming a gender perspective in the development process.

(viii) Elimination of discrimination and all forms of violence against women and the girl child; and

(ix) Building and strengthening partnerships with civil society, particularly women's organisations.

3. Policy Prescriptions

(i) Judicial Legal Systems: Judicial Legal system will be made more responsive and gender sensitive to women's needs, especially in cases of domestic violence and personal assault. New laws will be enacted and existing laws reviewed to ensure that justice is quick and the punishment meted out to the culprits is commensurate with the severity of the offence. The Policy would aim to encourage changes in laws relating to ownership of property and inheritance by evolving consensus in order to make them gender just and empower women.

(ii) Decision-making: Women's equality in power sharing and active participation in decision-making, including decision-making in political process at all levels will be ensured for the achievement of the goals of empowerment. Affirmative action such as reservations/quotas, including in higher legislative bodies, will be considered whenever necessary on a time bound basis. Women friendly personnel policies will also be drawn up to encourage women to participate effectively in the developmental process.

(iii) Mainstreaming a Gender Perspective in the Development Process: Policies, programmes and systems will be established to ensure mainstreaming of women's perspectives in all developmental processes, as catalysts, participants and recipients. Wherever there are gaps in policies and programmes, women specific interventions would be undertaken to bridge these. Coordinating and monitoring mechanisms will also be devised to assess from time to time the progress of such mainstreaming mechanisms.

4. Economic Empowerment of Women

(A) Poverty Eradication: Since women comprise the majority of the population below the poverty line and are very often in situations of extreme poverty, given the harsh realities of intra-household and social discrimination, macro economic policies and poverty eradication programmes will specifically address the needs and problems of such women. Steps will be taken for mobilisation of poor women and convergence of services, by offering them a range of economic and social options, along with necessary support measures to enhance their capabilities.

(B) Micro Credit: In order to enhance women's access to credit for consumption and production, the establishment of new, and strengthening of existing micro-credit mechanisms and micro-finance institutions will be undertaken so that the outreach of credit is enhanced. Other supportive measures would be taken to ensure adequate flow of credit through financial institutions and banks, so that all women below poverty line have easy access to credit.

(C) Women and Economy: Women's perspectives will be included in designing and implementing macro-economic and social policies by institutionalising their participation in such processes. Such measures could include:

(i) Reinterpretation and redefinition of conventional concepts of work wherever necessary e.g., in the Census records, to reflect women's contribution as producers and workers.

(ii) Preparation of satellite and national accounts.

(iii) Development of appropriate methodologies for undertaking (i) and (ii) above.

(D) Globalisation: From the micro-level studies that were commissioned by the Department of Women and Child Development, it is evident that there is a need for reframing policies for access to employment and quality of employment. Strategies will be designed to enhance the capacity of women and empower them to meet the negative social and economic impacts, which may flow from the globalisation process.

(E) Women and Agriculture: The programmes for training women in soil conservation, social forestry, dairy development and

other occupations allied to agriculture like horticulture, livestock including small animal husbandry, poultry, fisheries etc., will be expanded to benefit women workers in the agriculture sector.

(F) Women and Industry: The important role played by women in electronics, information technology and food processing and agro-industry and textiles has been crucial to the development of these sectors. Suitable measures will be taken to enable women to work on the night shift in factories. This will be accompanied with support services for security, transportation etc.

(G) Support Services: The provision of support services for women, like child care facilities, including crèches at work places and educational institutions, homes for the aged and the disabled will be expanded and improved to create an enabling environment and to ensure their full cooperation in social, political and economic life.

5. Social Empowerment of Women

(A) Education: Special measures will be taken to eliminate discrimination, universalise education, eradicate illiteracy, create a gender-sensitive educational system, increase enrolment and retention rates of girls and improve the quality of education to facilitate life-long learning as well as development of occupation/vocation/technical skills of women. Reducing the gender gap in secondary and higher education would be a focus area. Sectoral time targets in existing policies will be achieved, with a special focus on girls and women, particularly those belonging to weaker sections including the Scheduled Castes/Scheduled Tribes/Other Backward Classes/ Minorities.

(B) Health: A holistic approach to women's health which includes both nutrition and health services will be adopted and special attention will be given to the needs of women and the girl at all stages of the life cycle. The reduction of infant mortality and maternal mortality, which are sensitive indicators of human development, is a priority concern. Measures will be adopted that take into account the reproductive rights of women to enable them to exercise informed choices, their vulnerability to sexual and health problems together with endemic, infectious and communicable diseases such as malaria, TB, and water-borne diseases as well as

hypertension and cardio-pulmonary diseases. Strict implementation of registration of births and deaths would be ensured and registration of marriages would be made compulsory. Women's traditional knowledge about health care and nutrition will be recognised through proper documentation and its use will be encouraged. The use of Indian and alternative systems of medicine will be enhanced within the framework of overall health infrastructure available for women.

(C) Nutrition: In view of the high risk of malnutrition and disease that women face at all the three critical stages viz., infancy and childhood, adolescent and reproductive phase, focussed attention would be paid to meeting the nutritional needs of women at all stages of the life-cycle. Wide spread use of nutrition education would be made to address the issues of intra-household imbalances in nutrition and the special needs of pregnant and lactating women.

(D) Drinking Water and Sanitation: Special attention will be given to the needs of women in the provision of safe-drinking water, sewage disposal, toilet facilities and sanitation within accessible reach of households, especially in rural areas and urban slums.

(E) Housing and Shelter: Women's perspectives will be included in housing policies, planning of housing colonies and provision of shelter both in rural and urban areas.

(F) Environment: Women will be involved and their perspectives reflected in the policies and programmes for environment, conservation and restoration. Women will be involved in spreading the use of solar energy, biogas, smokeless *chulahs* and other rural application so as to have a visible impact of these measures in influencing eco-system and in changing the life styles of rural women.

(G) Science and Technology: Programmes will be strengthened to bring about a greater involvement of women in science and technology. These will include measures to motivate girls to take up science and technology for higher education and also ensure that development projects with scientific and technical inputs involve women fully. Special measures would be taken for their training in areas where they have special skills like communication and information technology.

(H) Women in Difficult Circumstances: In recognition of the diversity of women's situations and in acknowledgement of the needs of specially disadvantaged groups, measures and programmes will be undertaken to provide them with special assistance. These groups include women in extreme poverty, destitute women, women in conflict situations, women affected by natural calamities, women in less developed regions, the disabled widows, elderly women, single women in difficult circumstances, women heading households, those displaced from employment, migrants, women who are victims of marital violence, deserted women and prostitutes etc.

(I) Violence Against Women: Institutions and mechanisms/ schemes for assistance will be created and strengthened for prevention of such violence, including sexual harassment at work place and customs like dowry; for the rehabilitation of the victims of violence and for taking effective action against the perpetrators of such violence. A special emphasis will also be laid on programmes and measures to deal with trafficking in women and girls.

(J) Rights of the Girl Child: All forms of discrimination against the girl child and violation of her rights shall be eliminated by undertaking strong measures both preventive and punitive within and outside the family. These would relate specifically to strict enforcement of laws against pre-natal sex selection and the practices of female foeticide, female infanticide, child marriage, child abuse and child prostitution etc. There will be special emphasis on the needs of the girl child and earmarking of substantial investments in the areas relating to food and nutrition, health and education.

(K) Mass Media: Media will be used to portray images consistent with human dignity of girls and women. The media would be encouraged to develop codes of conduct, professional guidelines and other self-regulatory mechanisms to remove gender stereotypes and promote balanced portrayals of women and men.

6. Operational Strategies

(A) Action Plans: All Central and State Ministries will draw up time-bound Action Plans for translating the Policy into a set of concrete actions, through a participatory process of consultation with Centre/State Departments of Women and Child Development

and National/State Commissions for Women. The Plans will specifically including the following:

(i) Measurable goals to be achieved by 2010.

(ii) Identification and commitment of resources.

(iii) Responsibilities for implementation of action points.

(iv) Structures and mechanisms to ensure efficient monitoring, review and gender impact assessment of action points and policies.

(v) Introduction of a gender perspective in the budgeting process.

Collection of gender disaggregated data by all primary data collecting agencies of the Central and State Governments as well as Research and Academic Institutions in the Public and Private Sectors will be undertaken.

(B) Institutional Mechanisms: Institutional mechanisms, will be through interventions as may be appropriate and will relate to, among others, provision of adequate resources, training and advocacy skills to effectively influence macro-policies, legislation, programmes etc., to achieve the empowerment of women. National and State Councils will be formed to oversee the operationalisation of the Policy on a regular basis. The National Council will be headed by the Prime Minister and the State Councils by the Chief Ministers and be broad in composition having representatives from the concerned Departments/Ministries, National and State Commissions for Women, Social Welfare Boards, representatives of Non-Government Organisations, Women's Organisations, Corporate Sector, Trade Unions, financing institutions, academics, experts and social activists etc. These bodies will review the progress made in implementing the Policy twice a year. National and State Resource Centres on women will be established with mandates for collection and dissemination of information, undertaking research work, conducting surveys, implementing training and awareness generation programmes, etc. While institutions at the district level will be strengthened, at the grassroots, women will be helped by Government through its programmes to organise and strengthen into Self-Help Groups (SHGs) at the *Anganwadi*/Village/Town level. The women's groups will be helped to institutionalise themselves into registered societies and to federate at the Panchayat/Municipal level.

7. Resource Management

Availability of adequate financial, human and market resources to implement the Policy will be managed by concerned departments, financial credit institutions and banks, private sector, civil society and other connected institutions. This process will include:

(a) Assessment of benefits flowing to women and resource allocation to the programmes relating to them through an exercise of gender budgeting.

(b) Adequate resource allocation to develop and promote the policy outlined earlier based on (a) above by concerned departments.

(c) Developing synergy between personnel of Health, Rural Development, Education and Women and Child Development Department at field level and other village level functionaries'.

(d) Meeting credit needs by banks and financial credit institutions through suitable policy initiatives and development of new institutions in coordination with the Department of Women and Child Development.

The Department of Women and Child Development being the nodal Ministry will monitor and review the progress of the implementation of the Component Plan from time to time, in terms of both quality and quantity in collaboration with the Planning Commission. Efforts will be made to channelise private sector investments too, to support programmes and projects for advancement of women.

8. Legislation

The existing legislative structure will be reviewed and additional legislative measures taken by identified departments to implement the Policy. The specific measures required would be evolved through a consultation process involving civil society, National Commission for Women and Department of Women and Child Development. In appropriate cases, the consultation process would be widened to include other stakeholders too. Following specific measures will be taken to implement the legislation effectively:

(a) Strict enforcement of all relevant legal provisions and speedy redressal of grievances will be ensured, with a special focus on violence and gender related atrocities.

(b) Measures to prevent and punish sexual harassment at the place of work, protection for women workers in the organised/ unorganised sector and strict enforcement of relevant laws such as Equal Remuneration Act and Minimum Wages Act will be undertaken.

(c) Crimes against women, their incidence, prevention, investigation, detection and prosecution will be regularly reviewed at all Crime Review forum and Conferences at the Central, State and District levels.

(d) Women's Cells in Police Stations, Encourage Women Police Stations, Family Courts, *Mahila* Courts, Counseling Centers, Legal Aid Centers and Nyaya Panchayats will be strengthened and expanded to eliminate violence and atrocities against women.

(e) Widespread dissemination of information on all aspects of legal rights, human rights and other entitlements of women, through specially designed legal literacy programmes and rights information programmes will be done.

9. Gender Sensitisation

Training of personnel of executive, legislative and judicial wings of the State, with a special focus on policy and programme framers, implementation and development agencies, law enforcement machinery and the judiciary, as well as non-governmental organisations will be undertaken. Other measures will include:

(a) Promoting societal awareness to gender issues and women's human rights.

(b) Review of curriculum and educational materials to include gender education and human rights issues.

(c) Removal of all references derogatory to the dignity of women from all public documents and legal instruments.

(d) Use of different forms of mass media to communicate social messages relating to women's equality and empowerment.

10. Panchayati Raj Institutions

The 73rd and 74th Amendments (1993) to the Indian Constitution have served as a breakthrough towards ensuring equal access and increased participation in political power structure for women.

11. Partnership with the Voluntary Sector Organisations

The involvement of voluntary organisations, associations, federations, trade unions, non-governmental organisations, women's organisations, as well as institutions dealing with education, training and research will be ensured in the formulation, implementation, monitoring and review of all policies and programmes affecting women.

12. International Cooperation

The Policy will aim at implementation of international obligations/ commitments in all sectors on empowerment of women such as the Convention on All Forms of Discrimination Against Women (CEDAW), Convention on the Rights of the Child (CRC), International Conference on Population and Development (ICPD+5) and other such instruments.

Rashtriya Mahila Kosh

Rashtriya Mahila Kosh (National Credit Fund for Women) was established in the year 1993 with the initial corpus of Rs. 31 crore. This corpus since has been recycled four times to reach cumulative loaning operations of Rs. 178 crore. RMK has the main objective of facilitating credit support or micro-credit support to the poor women for income generating, productions, skill development and housing activities in order to make them economically independent and thus give them economic empowerment. It mainly channelises its support through Women Development Corporations, Cooperative Societies Self-Help Groups formed under *Swayamsiddha* or *Swa-shakti* etc., it provides smaller loan assistance, maximum upto Rs. 5.00 lakhs to smaller and newer organisations having at least six month experience in formation of self-help groups, thrift, credit and recovery management. Under main loan scheme credit is provided to poor women for income generating activities through experienced NGOs having three year minimum experience. Under revolving fund scheme, organisations having five years experience in the field of micro-credit with satisfactory track record can be granted upto Rs. five crores as loans. RMK charges interest @ Rs. eight per cent P.A. RMK has organised many awareness cum business development workshops. It also provides training programmes for NGOs/voluntary organisations. So far 16,246 women have been benefitted by RMK with the help of 1,083 SHGs. 24 states are covered by RMK. In Delhi state Rs. 324.72 lakhs were sanctioned, Rs. 283.12 lakhs have been disbursed and 139.08 have been recovered, giving benefits to 3,785 beneficiaries since inception to 31.01.2006. Ind Care Trust, New Delhi (F. 66 Green Avenue, Colonel Bhatia Road, Vikas Nagar, Hastasal, New Delhi – 110 059 is the nodal agency under RMK scheme. RMK has a strategic vision to expand its programme uniformly all over the country to empower more and more economically poor women of the country as an apex micro-credit institution.

Family Counselling Centres for Empowering Rescuing and Rehabilitating Women

The objective of the Family Counselling Centres is to provide preventive and rehabilitating services to women and even families that are victims of atrocities and family maladjustments. FCCS are located in Police headquarters, jails and red-light areas. Pre-marital counselling centres are working at various girls colleges in Delhi. These centres lay emphasis on pre-marital counselling and other areas of psycho-social crisis for young women. Rape crises intervention centres are functioning in Delhi.

Help Line for Women

This scheme is operational from 2002-03 with a 24-hour phone emergency outreach programme for accessing women/girls needing immediate protection and shelter. The objectives of the programme are as under.[67]

1. To provide services to women and girls in need of special care and protection and to ensure that proper care is provided till they are rehabilitated.
2. To provide crisis intervention services.
3. To provide referral services like short-stay home, free legal aid, police assistance, counselling, hospitalisation etc.
4. To arrange suitable rehabilitation services for the target group.
5. To provide counselling.
6. Awareness, opinion-building and documentation.
7. Assistance to women affected by natural calamities.

8. Documentation of the type of cases being registered to understand the trends and magnitude of the problem in society.

Dr. Girija Vyas, Chairperson, National Commission for Women, has said, "A woman in a live-in relationship should be entitled to maintenance if she is deserted by the man". The Commission has sought a change in the definition of "wife" as described in section 125 of Cr.PC which deals with maintenance and suggested that it include women involved in live-in relationships. The move aims to harmonise other sections of the law with Domestic Violence Act that treats a live-in-couples relationship on par with a legally married husband and wife. NCW also sought another significant amendment to Section 125, saying that adultery should no longer be grounds for denying maintenance to women[68]. Girija Vyas, Chairperson NCW has said, "We have found in 70 per cent of divorce cases, adultery is used to discredit the woman. Not only is she thrown out of the house, but is also denied her rights. Not any more, said Vyas, even if the marriage is not registered, if the woman can provide enough proof of a long-term relationship, her claim will stand"[69]. The minister said that the first ceiling for OBC reservation was fixed at Rs. one lakh annually in 1993 which was increased to Rs. 2.5 lakh in 2004. The report would soon be taken to the Cabinet so that the Government can take a decision in this matter as soon as possible[70]. Recently, the government has taken a decision to fix the ceiling for creamy layer at Rs. 4.8 lakh annually.

In Delhi Central Social Welfare Board runs 38 help lines and was granted Rs. 72.45 lakh as per on 21.12.2005. It also runs orientations training programmes.

Micro-credit Interventions

Micro-credit intervention programme has been recognised the world over as an effective tool for poverty alleviation and empowering poor by improving their socio-economic conditions. In India micro-credit is making a strong headway in its efforts to reduce poverty and empower the rural poor.[71] *Rashtriya Mahila Kosh* has computerised its activities with Nodal Agencies and high value NGOs partners by restoring to development of software for automating activities of RMK which, *inter alia*, includes web enabled loan disbursement and recovery monitoring system, on time submission of loan application forms and status of release of loan. Thus, ICT has been very useful with respect to micro-credit intervention programmes.

Swadhar Programme for the Rescue and Relief of Women in Distress

This scheme was launched by the Government during the year 2001-2002 for the benefit of women in difficult circumstances with the following objectives:[72]

1. To provide primary need of shelter, food, clothing and care to the marginalised women, girls living in difficult circumstances, who are without any social and economic support.
2. To provide emotional support and counselling to such women.
3. To rehabilitate them socially and economically through education, awareness, skill up-gradation and personality development through behavioural training etc.
4. To arrange for specific clinical, legal and other support for women/girl in need with other organisations in both Government and non-Government sectors on case to case basis.
5. To provide helpline (24 hour telephone facility).
6. To provide such other services as will be required for support and rehabilitation to such women in distress.

Widows deserted by their relatives, women prisoners released from jail and without family support, women survival of natural disasters, trafficked women and girls rescued or run away from brothels, women victims of terrorism/violence, mentally challenged women, women with HIV/AIDS and similarly placed women/girls in difficult circumstances can get support and assistance from *Swadhar* programme.

Sam Pitroda has said: "the key to empowering (people – men and women) is to provide knowledge, tools, technology and techniques, to change their mind-set from negative cynicism to positive optimism with hope for the limitless opportunities in this ever-changing world. True knowledge can empower people at all levels and make them aware of the rights and responsibilities. The main road blocks to women's empowerment are the gender bias that operates at all levels, the neglect of the girl child, the feminisation of poverty in modern times, the ill-effects of the process of globalisation on workers in the unorganised sector (where 85 per cent women work), the adverse effects of SAP on the very livelihood of the poor, the anti-poor policies of the government on management of natural resources and the country's unfavourable macro-economic balance which is threatening the process of empowerment that has been achieved by the poor[73]. In Delhi there are two NGOs, who have been granted loans by the *Rashtriya Mahila Kosh*".

1. *Chetanalaya* – 9-10 Vir Singh Marg, New Delhi – Rs. 15 lakh sanctioned.
2. Ind Care Trust – F. 66, Green Avenue, Colonel Bhatia Road, Vikas Nagar, New Delhi – Rs. 18 lakh sanctioned.

In a revolutionary decision, the Supreme Court, in a judgment dated 19.10.1994, directed the Government to evolve a scheme to mitigate the sufferings of victims of rape and to constitute Criminal Injuries Compensation Boards to pay them compensation. The protection of women from Domestic Violence Act 2005 (No. 43 of 2005) provides for more effective protection of the constitutional rights of women, who are victims of violence of any kind occurring within the family. It defines domestic violence to include actual abuse or threat of abuse that is physical, sexual, verbal, emotional or economic. It also covers harassment by way, unlawful dowry demands to the woman. It provides for appointment of protection officer.

Women's study centers all over the country are doing important job of preparing a database about the conditions and requirements of women; conducting research and creating awareness about the problems of women. The Centre for Women's Development studies in New Delhi is a premier institution which provides extensive reading material on women's issues.

Television Campaign

A large number of small films are being telecast on Doordarshan DD/network and private T.V. channels. Some of the noted publicity campaign through electronic media are as under:

1. *Lalli* – on Trafficking,

2. Human Chain – Women's Empowerment,
3. Census – Falling female sex ratio,
4. Empowered Girl – Empowerment of girl child,
5. *Mujhe Mat Maro* – Female Foeticide,
6. *Mujhe Betc Hai Na* – Gender discrimination,
7. *Mujhe Beti Hi Chahiye* – Encouraging Birth of girl child,
8. Child Sex Abuse – Child Sex Abuse,
9. Speak up – Sexual harrasement,
10. *Naye Sadi ka Naya Tarana* – Girl child abuse/girl child education,
11. Scroll social messages on dowry, child labour, educational empowerment of women, child marriage, domestic violence, breast-feeding, complementary feeding, female foeticide and personal hygiene and sanitation have been telecast on DD News channel for every five minutes for 24 hours from December 2005 and will continue from time to time. During India-Sri Lanka cricket ODI series 2005, five spots on child marriage, falling female sex ratio (census), child marriage, dowry and domestic violence were telecast during various matches held at Mohali, Jaipur, Pune, Ahmedabad, Rajkot and Vadodara.

Researcher has formulated one of the hypothesis as under – "The National Policy for the Empowerment of Women (2001) in India has not been effectively implemented and has remained an empty slogan". Although great strides have been made in many fields but the goal of advancement, development and empowerment of women has not been substantially achieved. In the context of globalisation, there is a need for reframing policies so that it may not lead to wider economic disparities, the feminisation of poverty, increased gender inequalities through deteriorating working conditions and unsafe working environment, particularly in the special context of women embroidery workers. Special empowerment of women with regard to education, health, nutrition, drinking water and sanitation, housing and shelter, environment, right of girl child, violence against women has not given the desired results although some progress in various fields has definitely been made. Poverty eradication and economic empowerment of women is a very stupendous task and can not be achieved in a few years in a vast country like India. National Policy for the Empowerment of Women (2001) is a vast area for implementation and there are many problems, difficulties and handicaps in its fullest implementation. In the context of National Policy for Empowerment of Women (NPEW), it can be said that we have marched on the road only a few miles and we have yet to go a few thousand miles. An impressive campaign of social engineering has been undertaken in India for the empowerment of women, by Indian Legislatures, both at the Federal and State levels. We all know too well that it is not a matter of scheme or resources. Implementation, enforcement and involvement of individuals and communities, are even more important. The formidable foe is the societal role perception of women. Economic empowerment, professional competence and integrity of women are looked down upon even today that is the reason why the numerous legislations passed to help women to occupy equal place in society often seem to be granting concessions that are rendered in-fructuous for they are unimplementable. Enforcement of Child Marriage Restraint Act, the Dowry Prohibition Act, *Sati* Prevention Act, Immoral Traffic Prevention Act are glaring examples. India's vision about women empowerment has been identified as under:[75]

"Indian women of today are culturally rooted, globally oriented, healthy, educated, self-reliant, secure in her home and safe outside with access to all the rights of a citizen with opportunity to continue in all walks of life."

References

1. Justice V.R. Krishna Iyer – Foreword in the book *Emancipation and Empowerment of Women* – By Dr. (Mrs.) V. Mohini Giri – Gyan Publishing House, New Delhi, 2005 – p. 11.
2. Samanta R.K. *Empowering Rural Women 2005*, The Women Press Delhi.
3. Dhar S.N., *Micro-Finance and Women*, Northern Book Centre, 2005.
4. Quoted in Shakti, *Multi-disciplinary Perspectives on Women Empowerment in India*, Eds. by Ranjana Harish and V. Bharathi, Hari Shanker, Rawat Publications, Jaipur, 2003. p. 102.
5. Fook, J., *Radical Case Work: A Theory of Practice*, Sydney – Allen and Unwin, 1993, p. 102.
6. Swift, C., Empowerment: An anti-dote for folly, *Prevention in Human Services* 3, 1984 (viii), xi-xv.

7. Brays, S. and Preston – Shoot, M., *Empowering Practice in Social Case Work*, Buckingham: Open University Press, 1995, p. 48.
8. Verma, R.B.S., Empowerment: Concept, Objectives and Strategies in *Empowerment of Weaker Sections in India*, Serials Publications, New Delhi, 2006, pp. 54-55.
9. Roy, Singha, (ed.) *Social Development and Empowerment of Marginalised Groups*, Saga, New Delhi, 2001, p. 14.
10. Beteille, Andre, 'Empowerment', *Economic and Political Weekly*, 34, 1999 (589-597), pp. 10-11.
11. Kishore, Sunita and Gupta, Kamla, 'Women's Empowerment in India and its State', *Economic and Political Weekly*: 39(7), Feb 14, 2004-694.
12. Sen, Amartya, *The Argumentative Indian – Writings on Indian Culture, History and Identity*, Penguin Books 2005. New Delhi. p. 224.
13. Som Nath Chatterjee, M.P. and Speaker, Lok Sabha – Posted on line to *Indian Express*, Tuesday August 16, 2005 at 0053 hours IST – India Empowered to the Govt. of India 2006. p. 7.
14. Jaya Kothai Pillai, *Women and Empowerment*, Gyan Publishing House, New Delhi 1995, p. 37.
15. Tariher I. *Development and Disintegration of Family, Assignment Children*, 1976, 6:29-37-168.
16. Marcus A Clay, 'Taking Stalk of the Town', *Times of India*, *Chennai Times*, 19th June 2008.
17. Dr. Krishna Mohan Mathur, *Crime, Human Rights and National Security*, Gyan Publishing House, New Delhi, 1996, P.21.
18. Anuradha Rajan, 'Women are battered all over the world', ICRW Report, *The Sunday, Times of India*, New Delhi, 22nd August, 1999.
19. Dobash R.E. and Dobash R.P. (eds). *Rethinking Violence Against Women*, London Sage 1998; Mac Kinnon. Cathrine, *Are women Human and other International Dialogues*, Belknap – Harvard University Press 2006; Merry Sally Engle, *Human Rights and Gender Violence: Translating International Law into Local Justice*, the University of Chicago Press, 2006.
20. Singh Kirti, Obstacles to Women's Rights in India, in Rebecea Cook (ed). *Human Rights of Women; National and International Perspective*, University of Pengylvanie Press 1994.
21. Kothari, Jayana, Criminal Law on Domestic Violence: Special Article, *The Economic and Political Weekly,* 12 Nov. 2005.
22. Vineet Kapoor, Women's access to Justice Domestic violence, Governance and Human Rights, *The Indian Police Journal,* Vol. LIV. No. 2, April-June 2007.
23. Kabeer, Naila, Reflections on the measurement of women's Empowerment, in *Discussing women's Empowerment: Theory and Practice*, *Sida Studies*

3 Stockholm: Swedish International Development Cooperation Agency, 2001.

24. Malhotra, Anju and Sidney Ruth Schuler 'Women's empowerment as a variable in International development' in Deepa Narayan (ed) *Measuring Empowerment : Cross Disciplinary Perspectives*, World Bank 2005.
25. Dr. (Mrs.) V. Mohini Giri, *Emancipation and Empowerment of Women*, Gyan Publishing House, New Delhi, 2005.
26. Merry, Sally Engle, *Human Rights and Gender Violence*, The University of Chicago Press 2006; Kotharei Jayana, 'Criminal Law on Domestic Violence', Special Article, *The Economic and Political Weekly* 12 Nov. 2005.
27. Visaria Lila, *Violence Against Women in India – Evidence from Rural Gujarat*, International Centre for Research on Women, USA, 1999.
28. Narayan Deepa, *Measuring Empowerment; Cross Disciplinary Perspective*, The World Bank 2005.
29. Nussbaum – Martha, *Women and Human Development: The Capacity Approach*, Cambridge University Press, 2000.
30. Pathi Peterch, Catalina Smulovitz and Michael Walton, *Evaluating Empowement*, 2006.
31. Dr. (Mrs) V. Mohini Giri, Preface to her book, *Emancipation and Empowerment of Women*, Gyan Publishing House, New Delhi, 2005.
32. Joy Deshmukh – Ranadiva, Gender Power, and Empowerment : An analyses of household and family dynamics in *Measuring Empowerment – Cross Disciplinary Perspective* ed. By Narayan Deepa. Oxford University Press, 2006.
33. Joy Deshmukh – Ranadive, '*Gender Power and Empowerment – An Analysis of Household and Family Dynamics*' in Narayan Deepa– *Ibid* – chapter 5.
34. Dr (Mrs.) V. Mohini Giri, *Emancipation and Empowerment of Women*, Gyan Publishing Home, New Delhi, 2005. p. 35.
35. Neera Burra, Joy Deshmukh Ranadive and Ranjani K Murthy (eds.), *Micro Credit, Poverty and Empowerment – Linking the Triad*, Sage Publications, 2005.
36. Narayan, Deepa (ed) *Empowerment and Poverty Reduction: A Sourcebook*, Washington D.C. – World Bank. 2002, p. 14.
37. Dr (Mrs) V. Mohini Giri, *Emancipation and Empowerment of Women*, Gyan Publishing House, New Delhi. 2005, p. 184.
38. Jaya Kothari Pillai, *Women and Empowerment*, Gyan Publishing House, New Delhi. 1995. p. 10.
39. B.K. Chaturvedi, 2006, *op. cit,* p. 35.
40. Jaya Kothai Pillai, 1995. *op. cit.,* pp. 62-63.

41. Vishnoi, Anubhuti, Mid-day Meal Scheme – Smart School Plan on Cabinet table, *Indian Express,* New Delhi, 19 Nov. 2009.
42. Dr (Mrs.) V. Mohini Giri, *Emancipation and Empowerment of Women*, Gyan Publishing House, New Delhi. 2005. pp. 112-113.
43. (Source *Economic and Political Weekly* – Yamini Mishra, Bhumika Jhamb – *An assessment of UPARI through a gender Budget* ——— Notes – August 29, 2009, Vol. XLIV No. 35 p. 65.
44. Narayan, Deepa (ed.) *Empowerment and Poverty reduction: A Source Book* Washington D.C. World Bank, 2000.
45. Medha Patkar, Environmental Activist – Indian Empowered to me, *Ibid*, p. 130.
46. Tiwari, Poonam, *Agricultural Sustainability through Women Empowerment in Women in India – Issues, Perspectives and Solutions*, Ed. By Rameshwari Pandya, New Century Publications, New Delhi, 2007, p. 225.
47. Dhar S.N., *Micro-Finance and Women*, 2005, pp. 100-125.
48. Sainab Rahman, *Empowerment of Rural Indian Women*, 2007, p. 84.
49. A Salim Sultan and K. Shan, Sensitizing the right to survival of the female child – Lessons from TN-FORCES Model-in *Empowerment of the Weaker Section in India* by R.B.S. Verma and Raj Kumar Singh – Serials Publications, New Delhi 2006, p. 2009.
50. Annual Report – *2005 -2006*. Ministry of Women and Child Development, Govt. of India, p. 6.
51. Subodh Ghildiyal, 'Empowerment only on Paper? NSSO Survey Brings out chasm between OBCs and SCs in literacy, property', *Times of India*, New Delhi Nov 2, 2006.
52. Annual Report – *2005-06*, Govt. of India, Ministry of Women and Child Development, p. 16.
53. Ghosh, Dilip Kumar, *Women representation in West Bengal Panchayats, in women in India – Issues, Perspectives and Solutions*, New Century Publications, New Delhi, 2007, eds. By Dr. Rameshwari Pandya, pp. 36-37.
54. *Ibid.*, p. 59.
55. Shankuntala C. Shettar and Shanta Bangare, 'Empowerment of Rural Widows – A case study in Karnataka' – in *women in India – Issues, Perspectives and Solutions*, Eds. By Dr. Rameshwari Pandya, New Century Publications, New Delhi, 2007, p. 101.
56. Sinha Pushpa, *Role, Conflict among working women*, Anmol Publications, New Delhi, 1987.
57. Kapur – Promilla, *Marriage and Working Women in India*, Vikas Publishing House, Delhi, 1987.

58. News Item in *Times of India*, March 2006.

59. Arora. Anand, *The Women Elite in India*, Radiant Publishers – New Delhi 1990 p. 172.

60. Annual Report 2005-2006 Ministry of Women and Child Development, Govt. of India, p. 25.

61. Chanda Shroff, Crafts as Means to Eeconomic, Spiritual Freedom, *Times of India*, November 23, 2006.

62. Mason, Karen Oppenheim, 'Measuring women's Empowerment – Learning from Cross-National Research', in Narayan Deepa – (Ed.) – *Measuring Empowerment – Cross Displinary Perspective*, 2006.

63. Knodel, Chanra – Trithirong and Debavalya, *Thailand's Reproductive Revolution : Rapid Fertility Decline in a Third World Setting*; Madison: University of Wisconsin Press, 1987.

64. Mason Karen Oppenheim and Herbert L. Smith, *Women's Empowerment and Social Context : Results from Five Asian Countries, Gender and Development Groups*, World Bank, Washington D.C., 2003.

65. Mason, Karen Oppenheim, *Measuring Women's Empowerment : Learning from Cross-National Research.*

66. Kabeer, Naila, 'Money can't Buy Me Love, Re-evaluation Gender, Credit and Empowerment in Rural Bangladesh', *Discussion Paper 363* Institute of Development Studies, University of Sussex, Brighton U.K., 1998; Also Hashemi, Syed M., Sidney Ruth Schuler and Ann P. Riley, Rural credit Programmes and women's Empowerment in Bangladesh – *World Development* 24 (4), 1996, 635-53.

67. Annual Report 2005-06, Ministry of Women and Child Development, Govt. of India, p. 167.

68. Himanshi Dhawan, Maintenance for live-in-partners sought by law, *Times of India*, Chennai, 30 June, 2008.

69. Dr. Girija Vyas, Key Demands, *Times of India*, Chennai. 30 June, 2008.

70. Raise Creamy layer Income Ceiling:- Panels – *Times of India* – two July 2008.

71. Singh, S.K. and Pandy, S.P., *Empowerment of Scheduled Caste Women*, Serials Publications, New Delhi, 2007, *vii-viii.*

72. Annual Report 2005-06, Ministry of Women and Child Development, Govt. of India, pp. 33-34.

73. Arunachalam Jaya, *Women's Equality – A Struggle for Survival*, Gyan Publishing House, New Delhi, 2005.

74. *National Commission for Women* – Search for a vision statement on Women Empowerment vis-à-vis Legislation and Judicial Decisions. p. 6.

75. *Ibid.*

4

Muslim Women and Empowerment

The role of women in Muslim society has changed significantly over the years and their position has varied from shifting social, economic and political circumstances. During the last two decades women have been caught between traditionalists and modernists as they compete for dominance in Islamic society.[1] Muslim women are hoping to improve their condition on many fronts-be-they social, economic or political others. Muslim women who live as minority community in India are also affected by the sexist and authoritarian attitudes of their male members and impact behaviour in terms of marriage, divorce, abuse, exclusion of women from the mosques and decision-making bodies. In this context empowerment of Muslim women throws numerous challenges, hurdles and problems. Muslim women are facing great challenges from within and without. However, the current desire for change on part of the Muslim women is perhaps borne out of the fervent belief in Indian democratic polity and enlightened interpretation of Quran having full faith in the spirit of Quaranic verses. Shabana Azmi, Ismat Chugtai, Qurratul-En-Haider, Najma Heptullah, Mohsina Kidwai, Justice Miram Sahiba Fatima Bibi, to name only few, have attempted their best to highlight the reformatory dimensions about the status of Muslim women in India.

Muslim Women and the Emerging Awareness for Change

There is a feeling among academics that Indian Muslim community, in general and that of Muslim women in particular, for diverse socio-economic and religious reasons, are relatively less responsive to change inducing forces[2]. In this book Dr. Azim had identified the change retarding as well as change promoting factors with special reference to Muslim women. The following are the major constraints coming in the way of development, modernisation and empowerment of Muslim women. Firstly, illiteracy or low level of education of parents and the attitude of old people to change are the major constraints in the development of Muslim women[3]. Secondly, the religious leaders/*Maulvis* are obstructing Muslim women from enjoying the fruits of modern education and keeping them in isolation and stagnation. Recently, in a Taliban *fatwa*, Darul Uloom Deoband has decreed that it is *"Haram"* and illegal according to Sharia for a family to accept a woman's earning.[3] Cleric at the largest Sunni Muslim seminary after Cairo's Al. Azhar has said, "It is unlawful (under the Sharia Law) for Muslim women to work in the government or private sector where men and women work together and women have to talk with men frankly and without a veil".[4] The *fatwa* however drew flak among other clerics and Rasheed, the Naib Imam of Lucknow's main Eidgah mosque in Ashbagh has said, "Men and women in Sharia are entitled to equal rights. If men follow the Sharia, there is no reason why women can't work with them." ANHAD founder and the social activist Shabnam Hashmi said, "I don't recognise the Deoband. I think they are interfering in Muslim women's lives." Waris Mazhari, Jamia Millia Islamia research scholar and a former Deoband student has said, "The life of the Prophet and his companions provides us a standard that Muslims should follow. During the Prophet's time, women used to worship in mosques and work along with men. No such restrictions were imposed. Men used to even seek guidance from the Prophet's wife, Aisha, who has also fought in a war Jang-e-Jamal."[5] Urdu press tears into latest fatwa and Urdu columnists and opinion makers are outraged and shocked beyond belief at the Deoband fatwa. In this stinging editorial titled "*Kya Deoband sun raha hai*? (Is Deoband listening?) the Sahafat (May 13) attacked the Islamic seminary's lack of understanding about cotemporary world". Which world do these people who issue such *fatwa* inhabit? If they think they spoke of today's world, they have missed the train", commented the editorial. The *Inquilab*, Mumbai's leading Urdu daily wondered how the Muslim women who were part of workforce globally could be advised not to work. Referring to the Prophet's wife, Khadija, who was a successful business women, the papers stressed the need to propel Muslim women into mainstream and not to pull them back".[6] The legal equality of men and women in Islam is a fact which has never been in dispute among Muslims. There is no legal right belonging to the man for which a corresponding female right can not be cited."[7] The *Maulvis* in general are misguiding the illiterate Muslim masses and discouraging them from adopting progressive practices.[8] Thirdly, lack of family planning among the poorer sections, larger domestic responsibilities in unplanned families, and low economic position of the Muslim women pose problems in adopting modern methods and values. Fourthly, lack of adequate separate schools and college meant exclusively for girls is one of the constraints in the educational development of Muslim women. Fifthly, lack of able leadership among women, "most of the existing leaders seem to have a vested interest in their backwardness so that they can create vote-banks by whipping up religious dearth of enlightened leadership at all levels of the Muslim community.[9]

They (Muslim women) are depressed, they are ignorant and they have been placed under many fetters of customs and artificial traditions not sanctioned by Islam. They receive proper Islamic education, become conscious of their rights as well as their duties and they can easily break their chains. At present, being ignorant of Islamic teachings, they think that traditions and customs they have been forced to observe are part of Islamic teachings. Education – proper educations is their dire and essential need.[10] Muslim women are gradually trying to break the shackles coming out of old out-dated socio-economic system in India and adopting modern ways of life and living. Government of India has enacted Domestic Violence Act, 2005 which was approved by the then President A.P.J. Abdul Kalam on September 12, 2005. In India, National Crimes Record Bureau (NCRB) registers a case of cruelty by husbands and relative every nine minutes.[11] Unfortunately, most police officers are not even aware of the provisions of the Domestic Violence Act, 2005. Muslim women need economic empowerment by organising women into self-help groups under various poverty alleviation programme viz., *Swarnjayanti Gram Swarozgar Yojana* (SGSY) and Support of Training and Employment Programme (STEP).

As the economic conditions keep changing from time to time, Islam, in accordance with its character as a universal religion did not lay down any rigid rules regarding the movement of women outside their homes and their joint participation with men in political, social and economic activities.[12] Lack of security and a discriminating attitude towards Muslim women is felt widely. However, there is considerable variation in the gravity, intensity and magnitude of such a feeling across various states. Communal tension or any untoward incident in any part of the country is enough to make Muslims fear for their safety and security.[13] While there is considerable variation in the conditions of Muslim women across states, the community exhibits deficits and deprivation in practically all dimensions of development. The situation is particularly grave in the states of West Bengal, Bihar, Uttar Pradesh, Delhi NCR and Assam. The provisioning of education through Urdu medium is precarious in Uttar Pradesh, Jharkhand, Bihar, Delhi NCR and Andhra Pradesh. Dr. Amanullah Fahad had identified the following major problem areas:

1. Family laws pertaining to marriage and divorce that reinforce the image of relationships based on a hierarchy with the rights of the husband superceding those of the wife and that prevent women from being in control of their lives.
2. Violence against women which occurs in the home, community and as a consequence of warfare which is claimed by some to be allowed by Islam when it is not.
3. Abuse of certain Islamic practices that affect women negatively such as polygamy and temporary marriage, when applied out of context and without abiding by Islamic restrictions.
4. Excluding women from religious activities such as attendance in the mosque which has clearly been established as the Muslim women's right.
5. Failure to promote the importance of a woman's contribution to society beyond child bearing.
6. Failure to enable women to take advantage of rights of property ownership and inheritance outlined by Islam.
7. Focussing on the behaviour of women as a market for morality in society and subjecting them to harassment, intimidation and discrimination.

8. Lack of awareness of the important role of men in contributing significantly in sharing house-hold responsibilities and child-rearing as exemplified by Prophet Muhammed (PBUH).[14]

However, it is heartening to note that modernisation and positive change-promoting factors are gradually emerging in Muslim community in many parts of the country. They have begun to realise that to make their daughters independent and employable, education is important.[15] The number of Muslim women in the field of employment is slowly but perceptibly increasing after independence. The younger generation of Muslim women is getting educated and seeking employment and they get respect and recognition by the enlightened Muslim community. Muslim women in cities, colleges and universities are discarding seclusion and the number of young women, who do not wear *burkha* is on the increase. There is gradually more autonomy for the Muslim women to visit parks, cinema houses, eating places, exhibitions and educational schools. They possess little more freedom compared to their rural counterparts, to cast their franchise in elections and have freedom to spend money at their own discretion. Modern Muslim women involve themselves in taking decisions on matters relating to household, marriage, etc. Gulf employment of the men folk has perforce made the Muslim women to take various decisions independently.[16] Social activities of Muslim women have gone beyond the four walls of the house and they have started reaping the benefits of modernisation, globalisation and democratisation of the Indian society. Muslim women are now realising the need to reduce the family size by adopting various family planning methods. On the whole, the emerging trends of increasing modernisation, following small family planning norms, coming out of seclusion, education to the daughters, and modern attitude to marriages are heartening. The wind of change is blowing strong and sure. "The current desire for change on the part of the Muslim women is perhaps more borne out of the part of the fervent belief in the image of the Muslim women as communicated by god in the Quran of a liberated, vital human being who can work in cooperation with men on many levels to contribute to the betterment of society".[17] The role and status of modern Muslim women in India is gradually changing with the shifting social, economic and political circumstances and the vital role played by the information technology, particularly internet, radio and television. An educated middle class is emerging among Indian Muslims. Although still a small class, they are well aware of changing society and need for change among Muslim women. The educated Muslim women exposed to democratic politics, electronic and print media are becoming aware of their rights and no longer prepared to accept what is being imposed on them in the name of religion.[18] During the last two decades there have been many positive indicators of change.

A new Muslim middle-class is gradually emerging during the last two decades but this middle class in "the newborn psychological version of the aristocratic Muslim elite of pre-partition India."[19] Many of the members of the English-speaking Muslim elite in Delhi and north India neither have an understanding of the problems of the common Muslims nor do they have an interest in the matter. In the world of entertainment there is a great deal of empowerment but it is an elite phenomenon. Muslim women are gradually emerging as a vocal group having an adequate knowledge of India's secular image and their role. A group of Muslim women developed a standard *Nikhanama* (marriage contract) and forced the Muslim personal law board to adopt it. Many Muslim women are already on the move and some got together and constituted their own board called Muslim Women Personal Law Board. Islamic feminism is slowly and gradually emerging. Some Muslim women NGOs have come together and formed *Bhartiya Muslim Mahila Morcha* and decided to operate within Indian constitutional provision within Islamic frame work and held its First Convention in Delhi in early December 2009. There are many hopeful signs about awareness of change and commitment to change to keep pace with other communities of India. India being secular democratic country, there is much more political and social space to Muslim women in India compared to their sisters in many other Muslim countries.[20] Justice Rajinder Sachar Committee report has observed that since independence India has achieved significant growth and development. In 1999-2000 a survey was got conducted by the government of India for estimation of levels of poverty and the tabulated results are shown in Table 1 as follows:

Table 1: Population of Religious Communities Living below the Poverty Line

	Per cent Below Poverty Line (Rural)	*Per cent Below Poverty Line (Urban)*
Hindus	27.80	21.66
Muslims	27.22	36.92
Christians	19.82	11.84
Sikhs	2.95	10.86
Others	33.05	18.51

India has been successful in reducing poverty and improving crucial human development indicators such as levels of literacy, education and health. However, not all religious communities and social groups have shared equally the benefits of the growth process. Among these of 13.4 per cent of the population, are seriously lagging behind in terms of the most of the human development indicators.[21] The protection of women from Domestic Violence Act, 2005 is a revolutionary law and aims at providing protection to wife or female live-in-partners from the husband or his relatives. Domestic violence under the act included actual abuse or the threat of abuse whether physical, sexual, verbal, emotional or economic harassment by way of unlawful dowry demands to the women or her relatives is covered. It is estimated that around 50 to 70 per cent of women in India were victims of domestic violence in some form or the other. The law addresses sexual abuse of children of forcing girls to marry against their wishes as well. Now, a man cannot beat his wife and husbands cannot come home and rape the girls/daughters. A woman can not be burnt alive by her husband or in-laws. This act is for those women who genuinely need help. Under this act, offenders can be jailed for maximum of one year or fined upto Rs. 20,000 or both. This law is an empowering act for all women of India including Muslim women. While the perception of deprivation, particular among Muslim women, is widespread among Muslims there has been no systematic effort since independence to analyse the conditions of religious minorities in the country. The non-implementation of recommendations of several earlier commissions and committees have made the Muslim community wary of any new initiatives. Tired of presenting memorandums, many wanted results.[22] The Muslim situation should be looked upon not as a problem of a minority but as a national concern. They carry a double burden of being labelled as "anti-national" and as being "appeased" at the same time. Women in general are the torch-bearers of community identity. It is said that for large number of Muslim women in India today, the only "safe" space (both in terms of physical protection and in terms of protection of identity) is within the boundaries of home and community. The identity crisis combined with the apparent lack of commitment on the part of the government. Often results in a perverse response even to well-intended programmes. However, there is considerable variation in gravity, intensity and magnitude of such a feeling across various states. There is an underlying feeling of injustice in the context of compensation to communal riots victims. Attitude of the police and law enforcing agencies is not balanced. Muslims live with an inferiority complex during violent communal conflicts and border areas. Fearing for their security, Muslims are increasingly resorting to living in ghettos across the country.[23] The Muslim community constitutes an integral part of India. They constitute largest minority. They are divided into two sections, Ashrafi and non-Ashrafi. Muslims are viewed as backward when compared to other socio-religious communities. Women are generally weaker section. Their overall socio-economic condition is bad. They are illiterate and compared to others they are very backward. The concentration of girls in *Madarsas* is high so they get religious education. Their participation in the modern secular stream is very low. Due to *purdah* system and poverty, women are rendered illiterate. One factor of illiteracy is early marriage between 14-18 years. They are withdrawn from education. The economic participation of Muslim women is low. They are confined to homes to assist husbands in family occupation. As far as inheritance of parental property is seen, they got a fair deal in Islam but in reality, do not get fair share. During the last sixty-five years, the socio-economic status of common Muslim women has not shown any perceptible improvement. Women in Muslim community are not a homogeneous lot and there is a vast diversity due to class differences, religious practices and other socio-economic factors. Education and economic status are important determinants. Their socio-economic status reflects lack of social opportunity which is exacerbated by their marginal status within an overall context of social disadvantage for most Muslim women. Most Muslim women remain invisible workers in the informal economy. Lack of information contributes to the reinforcement of cultural stereo-types serving to obfuscate their life experiences and struggles. Notion that Muslim women status derives from Muslim law is prevalent.[24] Even in 2008 there is a picture of glaring inequalities – social economic and political – that consistently define and circumscribe women's life – all women and Muslim women in particular. Trends in economic and social well-being reveal that, amidst all the celebration of cultural diversity, social improvement and economic growth that has taken place in the country (more notably in some regions than others), women and specially Muslim women are lagging behind.[25] There are great group inequalities and discrimination in at least three areas: education, socio-economic status and work. Similarly, there is great gender inequality persistent in the areas of marriage, mobility and autonomy across the board. The overall general standard of living of Muslim women is very poor and rather deplorable. Islam and Hinduism are two great religions and they have to stay together with each other. Maulana Abdul Kalam Azad insisted that "it was India's historic destiny that many human races and cultures should flow to her, finding a home in her hospitable soil and that many a caravan should find rest here...... eleven hundred years of common history (of Islam and Hinduism) have enriched India with our common achievements. Our manners and customs bear the stamps of our joint endeavours. India has developed a shared composite culture and women are gradually emerging out empowered in various fields. However, within the household, there is much exploitation of Muslim women by men which goes unmentioned and unnoticed when we use poverty measures which simply treat households as units and ignore intra-house aspects of exploitation. We need measures which illuminate unequal access to resources between men and women in the household.[26]

A comparison of data collected by the National Sample Survey Organisation (NSSO) in 1999-2000 and in 2004-2005 shows that in rural areas attendance of Muslim boys (5-14 years old) increased by nearly 12 per cent compared to about nine per cent for other communities and for Muslim girls, it increased to 16 per cent compared to about 13 per cent for others. As a result, 76 per cent of Muslim boys and 71 per cent of girls were attending schools in 2004-2005 quite close to boys 84 per cent and girls 71 per cent from the Hindu community. In urban areas, the pace of increase in school attendance in 5 – 14 years age group was practically the same as Muslim boys compared to other communities while it was almost double, at 12 per cent of Muslim girls compared to Hindu girls. A large number of studies show that many male household heads do not contribute all their wages to household needs but keep varying proportions for discretionary personal expenditure. Men's spending is often on non-merit goods such as alcohol, tobacco, gambling and extra-marital affairs, which not only deprive other household members of income in the short term but can also, exact financial, social and psychological costs down the line and women are generally silent sufferers. The recent data collected by National Sample Survey Organisation (NSSO) in 1999-2000 and 2004-2005 indicates that more Muslims are still struggling to find jobs and there is employment crunch. The NSSO report no. 521 shows the following data (Table 2):

Table 2: Employment Crunch, Educated Unemployed, 15 Years and Above (Per cent) (2004-2005)

	Secondary and above	*Diploma certificate*	*Graduate*	*Post-graduate*
Rural				
Hindu	9	7	7	4
Muslim	14	11	15	6
Urban				
Hindu	7	5	5	4
Muslim	7	8	10	5

The recent trends of employment still show much lower opportunities even for educated Muslims. In rural areas while seven per cent of Hindu graduates were unemployed, among the Muslims it was 15 per cent. A similar trend is visible in older age group of 15-19 years.[27] In an article on "What Muslims really want",

Prof. Dipankar Gupta has clearly highlighted "overtime the reliance of Muslim victims on Islamic institutions has faded somewhat. These displaced Muslims need jobs and they are not easy to come by."[28] After the Sachar Committee report exposed the backwardness of Muslims in every sphere of life including education, UGC has established that largest minority has lagged behind in higher education.

Gross Enrollment Ratio in higher education was

Christians	19.85 per cent
Hindus	13.13 per cent
Sikhs	10.77 per cent
Muslims	7.70 per cent

The enrollment ratio of Christian women is 19.98 per cent, three times higher than Muslim women who are 6.16 per cent.[29] A substantial larger proportion of Muslim household in urban areas are is less than Rs. 500 p.m. spends and needs to be empowered. Generally speaking, women are keen voters with Muslim women being keener than Hindu women. The level of political awareness evident in the knowledge of candidate and party names is fairly high-even though the majority of respondents were unaware of the 73rd and 74th Amendments, three quarter supported reservations for women in legislatures; moreover they expressed an interest in contesting elections especially at the local level.[30] When it comes to exercising the right to vote, Indian women, including Muslim women, show a greater determination than voters in some more advanced democracies. Empowerment of women raises many issues. How can we understand women's collective agency in today's globalising organisations in promoting women's empowerment? What types of interventions have emerged and what do they do differently than in the past? In the specific Indian context, how have inequalities beyond gender been addressed within the women's movement with changing opportunities and constraints?[31] To answer these questions, macro level (national) analysis with a meso and micro-level analysis is needed on a regular basis from time to time. Empowerment as a term has been used intensively now-a-days and the discourses on empowerment are constructed around a cluster of recurring concepts of social power, right, respect, autonomy, interests and control.[32] The present work has concentrated on role of information and communication technology on women empowerment in India. There is a pervasive belief that Muslim women have less autonomy

Table 3: The Distribution of Workers by Occupation Groups 2004-2005 of Workers Aged 15-64 Years.

Occupational categories	*Hindus*				*Muslims*	*Other minorities*	*All*
	All Hindu	*SCS/STS*	*OBSC*	*UC*			
			Males				
Professional Technical and related workers	4.1	2.1	2.9	8.1	3.0	5.0	4.0
Administrative, Executive and Marginal workers	3.9	1.5	3.1	8.1	4.7	6.2	4.3
Clerical and related workers	3.6	2.2	3.0	6.4	1.9	4.3	3.5
Sales workers	9.1	4.9	8.5	15.0	16.2	9.9	10.0
Service workers	3.9	3.7	4.1	3.8	3.1	3.2	3.8
Farmers, Fishermen, Hunters Loggers and related workers	51.5	58.3	53.9	39.7	35.8	47.7	49.5
Production and related workers, equipment operators and labourers	23.8	27.3	24.5	18.8	35.2	23.7	25.2
Workers not classified by occupation	0.0	0.0	0.0	0.0	0.1	0.0	0.0
Total	100	100	100	100	100	100	100

contd...

Table 3 (contd...)

Occupational categories	*Hindus*				*Muslims*	*Other minorities*	*All*
	All Hindu	*SCS/STS*	*OBSC*	*UC*			
			Males				
Professional Technical and related workers	3.5	1.4	2.3	9.9	3.8	4.0	3.7
Administrative, Executive and Marginal workers	1.3	0.9	1.2	3.2	2.9	3.7	1.6
Clerical and related workers	1.1	0.4	0.8	3.1	0.5	0.7	1.2
Sales workers	3.0	2.1	3.3	3.9	4.8	5.2	3.1
Service workers	4.4	4.9	4.0	4.4	4.9	5.6	4.5
Farmers, Fishermen, Hunters Loggers and related workers	75.6	79.7	76.9	65.4	51.5	48.4	73.7
Production and related workers, equipment operators and labourers	10.9	10.6	11.5	10.1	31.5	32.3	12.2
Workers not classified by occupation	0.0	0.0	0.0	0.0	0.1	0.1	0.0
Total	100	100	100	100	100	100	100

Source: Sachar Committee Report on Social, Economic and Political Status of the Muslim Community of India, New Delhi 2006, p. 119.

and mobility than Hindu women and are more likely to be denied education and work opportunities, owing to restrictions imposed on women's freedom by Islamic codes.[33] The women's autonomy in India, including in Tamil Nadu where women enjoy greater autonomy than their northern counterparts, is far more limited than that of women in other parts of Asia, for example Malaysia, Philippines and Thailand. As far as decision-making is concerned, women participate in decision-making but final decision is taken by father/husband. Authority structure is vested in male member of family.[34] The distribution of workers in each socio-religious category by occupation groups 2004-2005 of all workers aged 15-64 is given in Table 3.

The National Council of Applied Economic Research's (NCAER's) rural survey of 1999 had limited scope to the conventional census categories of literacy, educational level, work, fertility and so on. The National Family Health Surveys (NFHSs first and second rounds) extended their enquiry to include data on exposure to media contraception, violence and autonomy. The Women's Research and Action Groups (WRAGs) study of 15,600 Muslim women, elicited information on their response to Muslim personal law. However, these studies remained sharply focused on a few issues – law, fertility, reproductive health and educations. Since there is no official recognition of caste among Muslims, they are frequently distinguished in terms *Ashraf* (high born) and *Aijlas* (low born) groups. The Muslim women's Survey (MWS) at the empirical level, attempted to generate a national profile of Muslim women, covering a wide range of issues conducted in the year 2000 with 9451 Muslim and Hindu women respondents. A number of micro studies on Muslim Women reveal that the majority are among the most disadvantaged, economically impoverished and politically marginalised sections of Indian society today. During the last twenty five years in the wake of the Shah Bano controversy in 1985-86, the Deorala *sati* in 1987, the tragedy of the Babri Masjid in 1992 and frequent bomb blast in Hindu dominated areas, the intensification of communal politics in India, gender politics of minority community has became more complex and acute. Polygamy in Islam is a right reserved to men. The Quranic verses relating to polygamy stress the need for equal and just treatment of wives as a condition of polygamy, but orthodox interpretation confines equality to measurable technical criteria such as the provision of maintenance (*nafqa*) and the apportionment (*qasim*) of the husband's time among the wives; as for the "inclination of the heart". (*Maylal Qaib*).[35] Muslim women study indicates, it is not the existing social accounting, officially classification systems and the gender-biased definitions of works and employment contributing to the statistical veil over Muslim women's work. The fault does not lie solely with the policy-makers and male investigators but also with the ordinary men and women motivated by the prevalent attitudes and status codes that restrain them from providing accurate descriptions of women's productive activities.[36] In Muslims, husbands are the authority to decide whether female members should work outside or not. There are low earnings of Muslim women in unprotected wage sector and it gets further aggravated by the overall social discrimination within families, which discourages women from acquiring the skills and education needed to enter the labour market.[37] Muslim women especially poor women are both bankable and reliable as workers, if a modicum of economic and community support is made available through special interventions. Women participation in the political process is minimal except for voting activity, due to low level of literacy, lack of mobility and freedom to take decisions on their own. Akshaya is good example of using ICT for local self-governing institutions in Kerala. It has three objects – (1) access to infrastructure by setting access points, (2) IT literacy training, (3) making available relevant content; piloted in Malappuram community radio. Kudumba Shree Mission for women problems. Receipt system – computerising records. Jagratha Samithy – women can access the Panchayat Jan Seva Kendra officials for blood bank, BPL application form and exam results.

According to MWS (Muslim Women Survey) regarding socio economic status of Muslims, the unmistakable fact is that they are generally poor and disadvantaged due to educational backwardness and the inevitable effect of under-representation of Muslims in public employment and resource generating bodies. Recent empirical studies have confirmed that the Muslim share in regular worker category and regular wage salary occupations in the organised sector is minimal as opposed to other communities.[38] Self-employed Muslims predominantly are tailors, weavers, transport casual workers, car mechanics, rickshaw pullers, carpenters, mason and menial workers or daily wages mainly because they face disadvantage in the formal job market.[39] NSAER Rural Survey of socio-economic status reveals that Scheduled Castes and Scheduled Tribes are the poorest group with the Muslims only slightly above them. The Muslim Women Survey (MWS) reports that close to 60 per cent Muslim respondents were illiterate, lower than Scheduled Caste and Tribes proportion. The proportion of Muslim women who are illiterate is substantially higher for rural North India. The Muslim women survey indicates that Muslim girls schooling is poor and the various reasons for dropping out are as under:-

1. School too far away,
2. Transport not available,
3. Education not considered necessary,
4. Failures in class,
5. Required for household work,
6. Required for work on farm/family business,
7. No proper school facilities for girls in the village/locality,
8. Financial constraints,
9. Family objections,
10. Death of father/mother,
11. Required for care of siblings,

The Muslim leadership of the post-partition India campaigned for Muslims to declare Urdu as their mother tongue and to consider it as a symbol of their cultural identity. In India the Urdu Press is by and large a Muslim Press. During the last ten years or so, there is a noticeable change about education of Muslim girls. When mothers are educated, they send them to public schools. These days all the Muslim children whose fathers earn Rs. 1,500-2,000 only go to public schools and they do accomplish something.[40] There are 15 Urdu medium government schools in the Capital and seven Muslim community managed schools. In old Delhi there are four high schools upto class XII and ten upto class X for girls. A very encouraging change that has taken place with regard to Muslim women is that they are now coming out in large numbers to be educated and have a great desire for economic autonomy.

There is shortage of teachers. A report in the *Hindu* (May 31, 2004) noted that "Urdu is one of the official languages in the capital region but negligence by the society is turning Urdu medium schools into factories of failure. The class XII results declared over the weekend shows a poor 28 per cent success for Urdu schools compared to 84.90 per cent for English and Hindi medium schools. The pass percentage for class X in Urdu medium schools is a mere 25 per cent."[41] Most of the Urdu schools in the capital function from sparely-lit rooms and dilapidated structure with moth eaten furniture and stinking lavatories. Though poor and illiterate, but Muslim girls are keen on getting education. Mothers are desperate to educate their daughters.

Lack of female teachers and absence of basic amenities combined are the key factors that hold back women's education in the north India.[42] Specifically low socio-economic status and financial constraints are important factors in Muslim women's education particularly in north India. The MWS indicates that 60 per cent Muslim and 55 per cent Hindu women get married by the age of 17 years. Muslim girls are generally getting married without observing the legal age norm to reduce burden on parents, lack of education, to reduce a chance of love affairs and availability of good match at younger age. Generally, Muslim girls are culturally groomed for marriage through a range of prescriptive injunctions and normative practices, and are 'socialised' into accepting marriage and motherhood as their principal life long career. House-work, child bearing and child-rearing, caring for the aged and ailing and working to supplement the family income generally proceed in that order.[43] Muslim women by tradition are generally wearing *purdah* when going out. There is paucity of literature on Muslim women because *purdah* removed women from scrutiny, both literally as well as figuratively. Nasreen Fazalbhoy writes that this is so because the analysis of Muslims has been concentrated on a few areas and has been largely defined by attitudes prevalent in the larger social milieu.[44] Many studies suggest that, like other women, Muslim women too are not homogeneous and are differentiated among the fault-lines of class, caste, community and region. However, there minority location does qualitatively transform women's experience and perceptions in very distinct ways and this transformation is central to understanding the development of women's subjectivity and consciousness. Generally, a great deal of heated discussion is witness in India about gender bias of personal law and the appeasement of Muslims.[45] Stereo-types of Muslim women, entrenched by the trinity of multiple marriages, triple *talaq* and *purdah* have held them hostage for almost several decades that they have become difficult to dislodge. In last fifty years, the Muslim community has built up a slowly emerging new image. An expert committee of the Indian Council of Social Science research addressed a memorandum to the government expressing its dissatisfaction at recent trends in women's employment and the erosion of women's productive roles (which) emphasises women's position primarily as consumers and bearers of children. The committee has recommended that at least 25 per cent of investment and promotional activities in the small scale and cottage industries sectors and public works and services in the trading and commercial sector be earmarked to increase economic opportunities for women.[46] In 1977, there were 218 small scale units throughout the country giving training to women in handicrafts, handlooms, agro-units, small scale industries and ancillary units to larger industries. The state of Uttar Pradesh has set up training-cum-shelter workshop for destitute women and grants-in-aid are generously given to poor women to purchase sewing, knitting and weaving machines. *Nari Niketans* are being established in various tribal blocks where women and girls are trained in gainful trades. Empowerment of Muslim women can be measured by various economic and social indicators. The level of income per month has been considered as the indicators of the economic empowerment.

Three indicators used to identify the social empowerment are: (1) Business knowledge and established market links by women beneficiaries; (2) Mobility outside the home; 3) Participations in the intra family decision-making process.[47] The empowerment of Muslim women should aim at striving towards acquisitions of following: (i) Higher literacy level and education, (ii) Better health care for here and her children; (iii) Equal ownership of productive resources; (iv) Increased participation in economic and commercial sectors; (v) Awareness of their rights; (vi) Improved standard of living; (vii) Achieve self-reliance and self-confidence.

The Muslim Women Survey (MWS) is the first comprehensive baseline survey of Muslim women in India, indeed of women anywhere covering a wide range of issues and conducted in the year 2000 with 9541 Muslim and Hindu women respondents.[48] The MWS has focused on women. Fifty-two per cent of India's total Muslim population is concentrated in the three states of Uttar Pradesh, Bihar and West Bengal. Muslims form a majority in Jammu and Kashmir (64 per cent). In five states, their populations are above the national average: Assam (28.43 per cent), Kerala (23 per cent), West Bengal (23.16 per cent), Uttar Pradesh (17 per cent) and Bihar (14 per cent). Another state with a sizeable Muslim population is Karnataka (11 per cent). According to Rehana Sikri, certain conclusions appear to indicate the directions in which special efforts are needed to improve the lives of women. Legislation is not lacking in most countries for the protection of women in the fields of personal rights and in the labour market.[49] Women number about 498.7 million according to the 2001 census of India. Women constitute about 31.56 per cent of the work force. In India the objective of empowering women is to provide them with self-respect, self-reliance and socio-economic empowerment. The ninth Five Year Plan (1997-2002) adopted the strategy of women's component plan under which not less than 30 per cent of the funds/benefits were earmarked for all women-related sectors and women-specific programmes. The tenth five year plan (2002-07), undertook steps to further strengthen the policy of women's component plan. The working group on empowerment of women for the eleventh Five Year Plan (2007-11) constituted by the Planning Commission in 2006, has emphasised the strengthening of Self-Help Groups (SHGs) and community-based organisations for the empowerment of women. The task force on women and children under the chairmanship of K.C. Pant, submitted its report in April 2002 and *inter alia*, recommended the setting up of an inter-ministerial standing committee in the department of women and child development. The task force reviewed the whole gamut of legislations concerning women and recommended amendments of 22 laws to make them more effective under the women economic programme now named *Swavalamban*, the employment linked training is provided to women in various traditional and non-traditional trades. The selected viable economic activities for women are pottery, weaving, handicrafts, painting, printing, workshop, electric repairs, typing, tailoring and jewellery work. Self-Help Groups are generally engaged in the following business activities namely handloom weaving, palm-products making, livestock rearing, brick-making, toy making, phenoil manufacturing, sanitary napkin manufacturing, furniture repairs and making, agarbatti manufacturing, rope manufacturing, sweet stall and bakery, nurseries, rock-collieries, waste management agriculture. Muslim women participation in work is 60 per cent in self-employment category. Muslims appear to have distinct employment profile, marked by the pre-ponderance of self-employment of both men and women.[50] The Muslim Women Study reports particularly low level of Muslim women's work participation 14 per cent). Family responsibilities, child-bearing and rearing, lack of education, lack of skills, lack of permission from husband, lack of employment opportunities, getting married in conservative families, lack of mobility, *purdah* system and disinclination to work are some reasons for not working. According to Schumpeterian concept of innovative entrepreneurs, women who innovate, imitate or adopt a business activity are called "women entrepreneurs". There are the following main constrains of women entrepreneurship:

1. Lack of motivation, managerial and behavioural competences.
2. Absence of mentoring and women role models.
3. Lack of collateral security.
4. Lack of proper training and knowledge.
5. Overdependence on intermediaries.
6. Unable to get competitive prices.
7. Family life style and role-conflict.[51]

In India the women's participation in the 9th Plan has been estimated to be upto 20 per cent with the number of women entrepreneurs estimated to about 5,00,000. Women entrepreneurs are motivated by integral factors as the family background, educational background and passion to do something independently. Muslim entrepreneurs are very few though no formal statistical data is available. Self-Help Groups with the help of banks can promote small entrepreneurs. The following institutions can be potentially involved in self help; linked micro-credit programmes:

1. Cooperative Societies or branches of Cooperative Banks.
2. Around 60,000 branches of 27 Public Sector Commercial Banks.
3. Rural Banks, and
4. Smaller Private Banks.

India's share in the global micro-credit market in 2003 was 13 per cent of all clients and 16 per cent of the poorest clients. As per 2001 census, micro-enterprises sub-sector accounts for 25 per cent of employment of all main workers. India has started the following policies for economic empowerment of women:

Policies for Economic Empowerment of Women

1. Support to Training and Employment Programme (STEP).
2. Training-cum productive centre.
3. *Rashtriya Mahila Kosh* (RMK).
4. *Indira Mahila Yojna* (IMY).
5. National Commission for Women (NCW).
6. National Policy for Empowerment of Women.
7. Parliamentary Committee for Empowerment of Women.
8. Rural Women's Development and Empowerment Project (RWDEP).
9. *Swarnjayanthi Gram Swarojgar Yojana* (SGSY).
10. Integrated Rural Employment Guarantee Scheme.
11. Self-Help Group-cum Micro Credit Scheme.

Challenges Faced by Women Entrepreneurs

1. Financial constraints,
2. Over-dependence on intermediaries,
3. Scarcity of raw materials,
4. Intense competition,
5. High cost of production,
6. Low mobility,
7. Family commitment and support,
8. Social attitudes,
9. Adverse effects of risk-bearing,

10. Lack of education,
11. Low need for achievement.[52]

Kiran Mazumdar Shaw, Chairman and Managing Director, BIOCON India started her entrepreneurial career in 1987 at the age of twenty-five, promising herself that she would one-day becomes a poster-girl of India women entrepreneurs. The entrepreneur has been generally referred to "as any person in effective control of commercial undertaking". In words of Robert Hisrich (1985), entrepreneur is the process of creating something, different with value by devoting the necessary time and effort, assuming the accompanying financial psychological and social risks and receiving the results rewards of monetary and personal satisfaction. According to government of India, a women entrepreneur is defined as an enterprise owned and controlled by women and having a minimum finance of 51 per cent of the capital and giving at least 51 per cent of the employment generated in the enterprise to women. In India women entrepreneurs need to be promoted, developed and nurtured. The following strategies can help in promoting and nurturing women entrepreneurs and particularly Muslim women:

1. Literacy level of women has to be enhanced and management education should be encouraged.
2. Entrepreneurship education and training at all levels has to be introduced (up to P.G. Levels).
3. Women entrepreneurship research and applications from time to time have to be documented.
4. Entrepreneurship education should be imparted in secondary schools and colleges with special emphasis on women.
5. Women should be made aware of various credit facilities, financial incentives and subsidies.
6. Family members should encourage, motivate, support and inspire young girls to become entrepreneurs.

The government of India has taken initiatives for empowerment of women from time to time. Development of Women and Children in Rural Areas (DWCRA) is a scheme of the Central Government which was launched in 1982 to support women's income generating activities through a group of 15 to 20 women in each group by motivating them through providing financial assistance. *Indira Mahila*

Yojana (IMY) was launched in August 1995 to give education, awareness, income generation capacity and empowerment to women. NAYE (National Alliance of Young Entrepreneurs) assists women entrepreneurs by providing access to capital, infrastructure and markets; identifying investment opportunities, sponsoring delegating participation in trade fairs, exhibitions, arranging buyer – seller meets and specialised conferences. *Mahila Mandal* Programme under central social welfare boards provides financial assistance to eligible women entrepreneurs. *Rashtriya Mahila Kosh* (RMK) was established in 1992 with a fund of Rs. 31 crore to meet the needs of poor women by giving them loan. The IDBI has set up the *Mahila Udyam Nidhi* (MUN) and *Mahila Vikas Nidhi* (MVN) schemes to help women entrepreneurs. *Swarna Jayanti Gram Swarozgar Yojana* (SGSY) was launched by the ministry of rural development in April 1999, and has focussed on mobilisation of rural poor into Self-Help Groups (SHGs) in their building skill upgradation, training, assistance in taking up different economic activities, credit linkage, infrastructure technology and marketing support as important elements of development strategy for poor families. SGSY has the following features:

1. The SHG members must be below poverty line,
2. 12 to 20 members in a group,
3. Should live in a particular village,
4. Weekly meetings,
5. Internal lending,
6. Prompt repayment,
7. Involvement of SHG activities,
8. Opening of bank account,
9. Regular transaction.

The upgradation of the women's productive activities by the provisions of income-generating employment outside the home may intervene in the cycle of rural poverty and high fertility, characteristics of predominantly rural economies. Eight pre-requisites are proposed for such employments; (i) Women should have control over the income generated; (ii) Jobs should be in villages and small towns; (iii) They should be outside agriculture; (iv) They should focus on small scale, labour intensive light industries; (v) Work should be centrally located away from home; (vi) Jobs should attract only or primarily women in early reproductive years; (vii) Production should be organised on principles of economic and social cooperation and (viii) Additional social services and incentives should be provided.[53] Arvind was started by the National Bank for Agriculture and Rural Development (NABARD) to provide loans upto Rs.10 lakh to women who work collectively in agriculture for their economic development. The NABARD data released in the financial year 2003 reveals that more than 8,67,041 of SHGs have been framed and functioning successfully in India. The year 2005 witnessed an all-round growth in SHG bank lineage programme in various states. The goal of NABARD was to credit link another 10,00,000 SHGs with banks covering Rs. 10 crore rural bodies by 31st March 2008. Women entrepreneurs manufacturing solar cookers in Gujarat, small foundries in Maharashtra and T.V. capacitors in Orissa have proved beyond doubt that given the opportunities, they can excel their male counterparts. Smt. Shahanaz Hussain, beautician is one name of the most successful Muslim women entrepreneur in our country. Muslim women have full opportunities to avail all facilities and training from various schemes of the government for their economic empowerment. Muslim women need family support, motivation from male members and adequate education to take over the task of entrepreneurship.

The 2001 census enumerated Muslim population at over 1348 million and by 2006, it would be over 150 million in India. Population of all major religions have experienced large growth in the recent past, but the growth among Muslims has been higher than the average. Between 1961 to 2001 Muslim populations increased rapidly from 47 million to 138 million. This amounts to an increase of 194 per cent just short of trebling and much higher than the average increase of 134 per cent.[54] This has been a hindrance to their economic growth and empowerment.

Married, Employed .... Not Empowered in some States but Delhi, Goa and Northern States are Better:[55]

The National Family Health Survey found that better educated women had greater access to money and rights to decision-making within the family. The advantage was pronounced for women who were earning cash and had 12 years of formal education. An NFHs survey on around 40,000 married women across the country found the following:

1. Less than half the respondents were employed women.
2. Of them only 64 per cent were paid cash, compared to 92 per cent men.
3. 11 per cent of the women were paid in kind, 25 per cent were not paid at all.
4. The number of women earning cash is highest in Delhi (95 per cent) and the lowest in Himachal Pradesh.
5. Less than 25 per cent of them were able to decide on their own about how to spend their salary.
6. 57 per cent make this decision jointly with their husbands.
7. 16 per cent of respondents have no control over the money they earn.
8. 10 per cent could not even take decisions about visiting family and friends.
9. 25 per cent had no say on issues related to their health.
10. 44 per cent of employed women work for a family member while 15 per cent are self-employed, leaving 40 per cent working for outside individual or firms.
11. 58 per cent of employed women worked on farms, only 15 per cent were employed in sales, administration and technical professions.
12. The proportion of women able to decide how to dispose off their own earnings rises as they grow older or are more educated although the increase is marginal.
13. Rajasthan, J&K, Orissa, Tripura, West Bengal are some of the states where women have no say in money matters.
14. Delhi, Goa, Nagaland, Mizoram, Assam, Manipur and Tripura are some states where women participate in decision-making.[56]

Access to Information Technology and Communication

Information Technology has a very important role to play in empowerment of women at all levels. In low-literacy societies non-print mass media i.e., Radio and television are very important source of information and entertainment. Last three decades have witnessed a dramatic expansion of television to different parts of the country. Television viewing increased by 68 per cent between 1978 to 1983 and the number of women viewers rose by 33 per cent.[57] The arrival of television has clearly reduced the importance of radio/ Print media/newspapers/magazine etc. provide lot of local and state/ international news about politics, economy and culture. Since the level of education in Muslim women is very low, access to print media is low compared to Hindu women. A very small percentage of Muslim women read print-media regularly. About 45 per cent Hindu and 42 per cent women watch television regularly. As Muslim women become more educated and liberated, the frequency of their reading newspapers/magazines and books increase. Young Muslim women are more exposed to different types of mass media. Television viewership figures suggest that exposure to mass media goes beyond the constraint of ability to buy.[58] In certain areas of north India, compared to television, radio is relatively cheaper and within the reach of Muslim women with less formal education and lower socio-economic status. Television is a positive influence on society and particularly Muslim women. Transnational Islamic movements provide discursive fields within which Muslim women in *Kachchh* are above to contest prescriptive notions of male, body honour and piety. It reflects on the articulation of collective identity and its gendered dimension, as manifested in conjunctive of global discourse – Islamic reform as well as NGO led political economic emancipation.[59] It is argued that global transnational idioms are reconciled with secular liberal market discourse. India where many communities have lived together for centuries with its secular, democratic and progressive society must build up a culture of mutual faith, understanding, tolerance and acceptance. However, Indian prejudices, famously, may have originated in one faith, but seeped into the culture of other faiths as well. But surely such attitudes are a matter of past that we seek to store in the attic of oblivion as we look for a modern future.[60] Mikhail Gorbachev, the noble prize winner has said "it is better to discuss things, to argue and engage in polemics than make perfidious plans of mutual destruction." Extremist clerics have misled Muslims by promoting bias against Muslim women with a consistency that is the prerogative of a closed mind. They have done their best to separate Muslims from modernity, now they want to divorce Muslims from the modern economy.[61]

Empowerment of Muslim Women in India – Myth or Reality

The status of Muslim women varied enormously from one state of India to another, and even within cities, urban and rural areas of different parts of country. Muslim women's status can be analysed in terms of their participation in decision-making, access to the opportunities in education, training, employment and income, health and demographic details like life-expectancy, mobility, family-planning and many other such areas, such as gender justice, protection against violence so as to allow them to realise their full potential. As far as empowerment of Muslim women are concerned, the most critical areas for concern can be as under:

1. Poverty and very low economic status,
2. Education – illiteracy,
3. Health and maternity problems,
4. Violence against women,
5. Armed conflict in some areas like Jammu and Kashmir and north eastern region of India,
6. Economic activities of women and women's employability levels,
7. Participation of women in decision-making,
8. National, state level and district level machinery to safeguard interests of women and girls,
9. Human rights of women,
10. Access to the media for women and balanced reporting on women issues,
11. Environmental sustainability at home and the area of residence,
12. The girl child and her empowerment,
13. Gender justice and gender equality,
14. Institutional arrangement for the empowerment of women,

15. Laws empowering Muslim women and their effective implementation,
16. Adequate policies and laws for protecting working mothers women in stress and older women living alone,
17. Inability to utilise the full potentials of information and communication technology due to various handicaps and limitations.

In a recent judgment the Supreme Court, while upholding an appeal filed by Cannanore district Muslim educational association challenging a Kerala High Court decision that association had no right to run a higher secondary course in the Sir Syed college run by it has upheld that as a religious minority, it has a fundamental right under Article 30 to establish and administer educational institutions of its choice.[62] This is one of the many ways to empower the Muslim community to set up academic institutions to cater for the needs of the minority community and spread educations in the country.

The Tenth Five Year Plan has laid down the approach for empowering women, shown in Chart I.

The Eleventh Plan, 2007-12 laid out the following five points agenda for women empowerment:

(i) Ensuring economic empowerment,

(ii) Engineering social empowerment,

(iii) Enabling political empowerment,

(iv) Effective implementation of women-related legislations.

(v) Creating institutional mechanism for gender mainstreaming and strengthening delivery mechanisms.[63]

TENTH FIVE YEAR PLAN–WOMEN EMPOWERMENT APPROACH

CHART – I

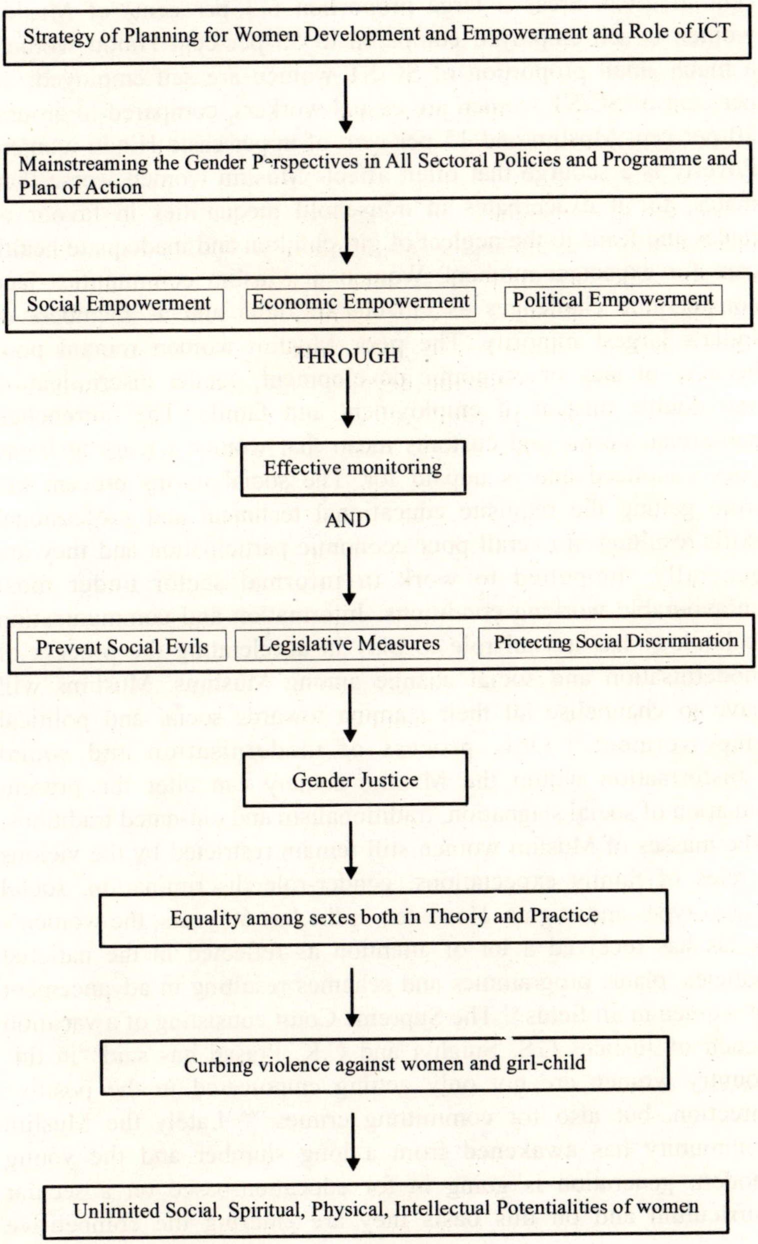

The Sachar Committee Report, shows that work participation rate among Muslim women is 25 per cent and as low as 18 per cent in urban areas a large proportion (73 per cent) of Muslim women is self-employed compared to 55 per cent Hindu women, a much small proportion of SC/ST women are self-employed; 45 per cent of SC/ST women are casual workers, compared to around 20 per cent Muslim and 15 per cent of upper caste Hindu women. Poverty is a scourge that often affects Muslim women worse than males, for it exacerbates in household inequalities in favour of males and leads to the neglect of girl children and inadequate health care for expectant mothers. Women in Muslim communities face considerable challenges as citizens of India and as members of India's largest minority. The poor Muslim women remain poor because of lack of economic development, gender discrimination and double burden of employment and family. The entrenched patriarchal norms and customs mean that women's work at home goes unnoticed and is unpaid for. The social norms prevent her from getting the requisite educational technical and professional skills resulting in overall poor economic participation and they are generally compelled to work in informal sector under most unfavourable working conditions. Information and communication technology has a vital role to play in accelerating the process of modernisation and social change among Muslims. Muslims will have to channelise all their stamina towards social and political empowerment.[64] Only process of modernisation and social transformation within the Muslim society can alter the present situation of social stagnation, traditionalism and out-dated traditions. The masses of Muslim women still remain restricted by the vicious circles of family expectations, gender-role discrimination, social stereo-types and stigma. However, in the last 60 years, the women's status has received a lot of attention as reflected in the national policies, plans, programmes and schemes resulting in advancement of women in all fields.[65] The Supreme Court consisting of a vacation bench of Justices G.S. Singhvi and C.K. Prasad has said "in this country women are not only getting empowered in the positive direction, but also for committing crimes."[66] Lately the Muslim community has awakened from a long slumber and the young modern generation is going in for education-based on a secular curriculum and on this basis they are entering the competitive global market. The basic issue is – whether the Muslim women are worse or better off compared to (a) others including Hindu women/ SC/ST women and OBC women/and their own position from 15 or 20 years ago? India is a plural society with lot of diversities, having a multi-cultural and multi-centered polity with federal system of governance. In rebuilding India's democratic secularism the minorities (Muslims) in particular have a major role to play – in close liason with the democratic secular elements within the Hindu social fold in a progressive developing economy.

India is a plural and democratic society in which oppositions and contradictions thrive and nowhere is this more so than with regards to women. If we have women, who are among the most progressive and the world, we also have women who are among the most backward, poor and voiceless. During communal riots, Muslim women have suffered immensely as many of them have lost their husbands, parents and children and many have lost the only earning member of the family. For women empowerment self-employed women need to be provided marketing linkages and credit facilities, in view of the economic boycott call of the Muslims by some organisations. The English language in India today segregates people more firmly than class, caste and community in haves and have-nots.[67] It is, therefore, necessary that young generation of Muslim girls should get English education for getting empowered and finding their place under the sun. Where Muslim women are concerned, the large influx of sensitive reporters in English media has helped. Due to various media compulsions, the serious, positive and broad-based issues regarding Muslim women, their economic and political needs, their assimilation in the workforce and their reactions to national events mostly go unreported, while select information that confirms the stereo-type of Muslim women as illiterate and sacred pawns in the hands of religious leaders is widely put out.[68] Indian media has generally been unable to provide equally important space to the work, health, education, their positions in society and experience within families of Muslims. Citing an example of Shah Bano's case, the editor of Manushi, Madhu Kishwar wrote "by singling out Muslim men and Islam in this way, Justice Chandrachud converts what is essentially a women's right issue into an occasion of gratuitous attack upon a community.[69]

Government of India and state governments have undertaken the following initiatives in the area of women empowerment:

- Welfare and support services,
- Employment and training,
- Socio-economic programme,
- *Swayamsiddha*,
- Swa-shakti project,
- *Balika Samriddhi Yojana*,
- Plan of action to combat sexual exploitation of women and children,
- Declaring 2001 as Women's Empowerment Year,
- Instituting National Commission for Women,
- Rashtriya Mahila Kosh,
- National Institute of Public Cooperation and Child Development,
- Central Social Welfare Board,
- Food and Nutrition Board,
- Information and Mass Education,

Muslim community has an important part to play in bringing about a change in the attitude of their young children so that they may become educated, balanced and open-minded citizens of Indian plural, secular and forward-looking society. Muslim women in particular have a greater role in this task of upbringing their children as modern, educated well-informed future citizens of the country. The instrument of education is one of the major tools for empowering Muslim women. The focus on educational planning for Muslim women should be shifted from their traditional role as housewives and mothers to non-traditional rules as producers, partners and partakers in national development. Ninth Five Year Plan (1997-2002) had a commitment for empowering women as agents of social change and development and has recommended the following main strategies:

- To create an enabling environment for women to exercise their rights both within and outside home, as equal partners along with men through early finalisation and adoption of "national policy for empowerment of women".

- To expedite action to legislate reservations of not less than one-third seats for women in the Parliament and in the state Legislative Assemblies and thus ensure adequate representation of women in decision-making.
- To adopt an integrated approach towards empowering women through effective convergence of existing services, resources, infrastructure and manpower in both women–specific and women-related sector.
- To adopt a special strategy of "women's component plan" to ensure that not less than 30 per cent of funds/benefits flow to women from other developmental sectors.
- To organise women into Self-Help Groups and thus mark the beginning of major process of empowering women.
- To accord high priority to reproductive child health care.
- To universalise the on-going supplementary feeding programme – Special Nutrition Programme (SNP) and Mid-Day Meals (MDM).
- To ensure easy and equal access to education for women and girls through the commitments of the special action plan of 1998.
- To initiate steps to eliminate gender bias in all educational programme.
- To institute plans for free education for girls upto college level, including professional courses.
- To equip women with necessary skills in the modern upcoming trades which could keep them gainfully engaged besides making them economically independent and self-reliant.
- To increase access to credit through setting up of a development bank for women entrepreneurs in small and tiny sectors.[70]

India is committed to the cause of empowerment of women including women of minority community. However, the journey towards progress is long and arduous. In a world of challenge and competition, both the state and the community (society) have to constantly attend to the changing needs in order to empower themselves. Empowerment of Muslim women is a reality though there are number of constraining factors and handicap in fully implementing the mission as can be depicted by the following chart:

Chart Showing the Vision of Empowerment of Muslim Women

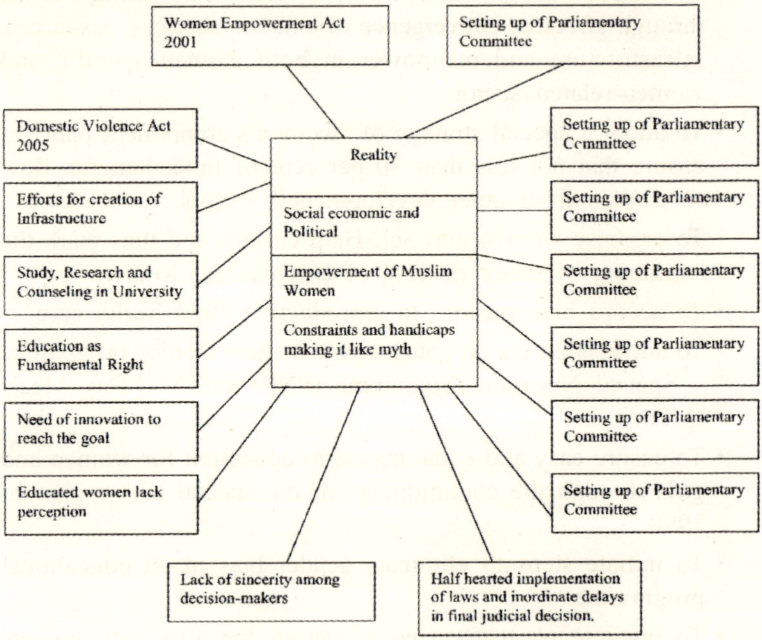

According to *Indian Express*, New Delhi, Saturday, May 22, 2010, Atiya Zabeen, daughter of a tailor Jamil Ahmed living in the walled city and an Urdu-medium student, secured 88 per cent with distinction in all five subjects, in her class XII examination. At her school 97 per cent students cleared the examination.[71] For the last six year, the school's Uurdu medium wing of Govt. Sarvodaya Bal Vidyalaya, Pataudi House, Delhi, held top most position with 100 per cent XII class result pass percentage-wise. This, despite the facts, the students struggle with lack of text books, trained-teachers and without infrastructure. Coming from National School for Open Schooling, Nundrisha, whose both parents are from Kashmir, secured 89 per cent marks in XII class. This shows girls willingness to get empowered. Zainab Rahman writes – empowerment is not a commodity that can be handed over to the Muslim women.

Power is an analytical category that denotes strength or control. It is something that has to develop from within. One cannot empower women if they are unwilling or if they are not equipped for it. Empowerment comes to women when they strive hard for it. (Rahman–2005)[72] Apathy, fear, ignorance and vulnerability as Muslim women within patriarchal patterns of behaviour are the main problems and these can be overcome by higher education, exposure to the I.C. Techniques and inner-motivation to achieve something in life with self-confidence and self-dignity. However, the journey towards empowerment has begun and so far only a few miles journey has been done while the arduous journey is long, full of challenges and fears. According to Asghar Ali Engineer "there is a big difference in what is theologically projected and ground reality. It may not be wrong if I venture to say, Muslim women have been defying theological code for over a century now".[73] Indian media, which is interested in sensationalising issues, refuses to highlight Muslim women's achievements and continues to portray them as submissive to traditional authorities and meekly accepting their situations. This image of Muslim women has to change and reality, which is much more complex, has to be understood.[74] The determined struggle on the part of Muslim women will force many more theologians to revise their position and take Quran and not medieval theology seriously on women issues. As educated middle class is emerging among Indian Muslims.[75] Time has certainly come for Muslim women in India to be proactive for improving their lot. The number of Muslim women activities is on the increase. Women empowerment has developed over the years through four main approaches namely WID (Women in Development), WAD (Women and Development), GAD (Gender and Development) and laws framed by the governments from time to time. Formulation of gender aware data system on literacy, education level, employment and earnings, health and well-being can help in proper planning and policy-making for the empowerment of the Muslim women in India. Gender Employment Measure (GEM) has been formulated to take into account aspects relating to economic participation and decision-making by women. The process of empowerment of Muslim women is definitely perceptible. From being a liability, Muslim women has become an asset.[76] Recently, declared CBSE results of XII class have very reassuring trend depicting empowerment of minority community in Delhi. As per available data Government Sarvodaya Bal Vidyalaya, Pataudi House, Delhi, held top most positions with 100 per cent result. For the last six years, the school's Urdu medium wing has been registering 100 per cent pass percentage.[77] Education is one of the significant social indicators having bearing on the achievement in the growth of an individual as well as community. Literacy rate of female Muslims, according to Census 2001 is 50.1 per cent as against Hindu women which have 53.7 per cent. This is one indicator of Muslim women empowerment. Education is to be highly suitable for providing employment and thereby improving the quality of life, the level of human well-being and access to basic social services within each of the religious groups. There is no homogeneity as regards women's status. Women belonging to the same religion might yet have very different conditions of life which are influenced by their earning capacity, employment, rural-urban setup, educational level and so on. Within every minority group, some women subsist Below the Poverty Line (BPL) while others enjoy a higher standard of living.[78]

References

1. Fahad, Dr. Amanullah, *Islamic Women – The Modernists Approach*, Jnanda Prakashan, New Delhi, 2009, Preface p. 1.
2. Azim, Saukath, *Muslim Women-Emerging Identity*, Rawat Publications, Jaipur, 1997, Foreward, p. 1
3. *Ibid.*, p. 218.
4. Siddiqui, Pervez Iqbal, Deoband Fatwa: It is Illegal for Women to Work, Support Family, *Times of India*, New Delhi, Wednesday, May 12, 2010, p. 1.
5. *Times of India*, New Delhi, Wednesday, May 12, 2010, Fatwa Against Working Women Contradicts Islam. p. 17.
6. Wajihuddin, Mohammad, Urdu Press Rears into Latest Fatwa, *The Times of India*, News Delhi, Friday, May 14, 2010, p. 12.
7. Siddiqui, Mohammad Mazheruddin, *Women in Islam – Institute of Islamic Culture*, Lahore, Pakistan, 1999, 12th edition p. 61.
8. Azim, Saukath, *op cit*, p. 219.
9. *Ibid.*, pp. 219-220.
10. Siddiqui, Mohammad Mazheruddin, *op cit*, pp. 180-181.
11. Goel, Aruna, *Women Empowerment – Myth or Realty*, Deep and Deep Publications, New Delhi, 2009.

12. Siddiqui, Mohammad Mazheruddin, *op cit*, pp. 172-173.
13. Sachar Committee Report on Social, Economic and Educational Status of the Muslim Community in India, Govt. of India, News Delhi, Nov. 2005, p. 13.
14. Fahad, Dr. Amanullah, *Islamic Women – The Modernists Approach,* Jnanda Prakashan, New Delhi, 2009, pp. 33-34.
15. Azim Saukath, *op cit*, p. 216.
16. Azim Saukath, *ibid*, p. 217.
17. Fahad, Dr. Amanullah, *op cit*, p. 35.
18. Engineer, Asghar Ali, *Muslim Women in Indian Society*, http://www.IndianMuslims.info/book/htm/2009 p. 2
19. Mitra Chandan, *The Print Media and Minority Images in Muslim and Media Images*, News versus views, Edited by Ather Farouqui, Oxford University Press, New Delhi, 2009, p. 45.
20. Engineer, Asghar Ali, *Muslim Women in Indian Society*, *op cit*, p. 4.
21. Government of India, Prime Minister's High level committee, Cabinet Secretary Report on Social Economic and Educational status of the Muslim Community of India, November 2006, p. 2.
22. Justice Sachar Committee Report on Social, Economic and Educational Status of Muslim Community in India, Government of India, Cabinet Secretariat, Nov. 2006, p. 2.
23. Report on Social, Economic and Educational Status of Muslim Community in India, Government of India, Nov. 2006.
24. Kazi, Seema, *Muslim Women in India*, Minority Rights Group International, 1999, p. 9.
25. Hasan, Zoya and Menon, Ritu, *Unequal Citizens – A Study of Muslim Women in India*, Oxford Press, 2006, p. 231.
26. Jane, S. Jaqueth and Gale Summerfield (eds.), *Women and Gender Equity in Development Theory and Practice – Institutions, Resources and Mobilization*, Duke University Press, London, 2006, p. 97.
27. Sharma, Subodh, Jobless Rate Among Muslim Graduates Double the Figure for Hindus, *Times of India*, New Delhi, 27th October 2008.
28. Gupta, Dipanker, *Times of India*, 17th March, 2009.
29. Falahi, Mumtaz Alam, *UGC* Study on Muslim Backwardness, *Muslim India*, Jan, Feb 2009, p. 28 Two Circles.net
30. Hasan, Zoya and Menon, Ritu, *Unequal citizens – A Study of Muslim Women in India*, *op cit*, p. 218.
31. Subramanian, Mangla, *The Power of Women's Organising – Gender, Caste and Class in India,* Rawat Publications, Jaipur, 2007, p. 1.
32. Bantiwala, S., *The Meaning of Women's Empowerment*, New concepts from action, pp. 127-138.

33. Jegeebhoy, Shireen and Sathar Zeba, Women's Autonomy in India and Pakistan. The Influence of Religion and Region, *Population and Development Review*, December 2001, p. 687.
34. Khanam, Azra, Social Profile of Muslim OBC Women: A Study of Pihan in *Islam and the Modern Age*, Vol. XXXIX No. 3, Aug. 2008, p. 184.
35. Sikri, Rehana, *Women in Islamic Culture and Society – A Study of Family, Feminism and Franchise*, Kanishka Publishers Distributors, New Delhi, 1999, p. 43.
36. Deshpande, Ashwini, *Casting of Sevitude : Caste and Gender Inequality in India*, in Kathleen Blee and France Winddance (eds) *Feminism and Anti-Racism International Struggle*, New Yrok, NY University Press, 2001, pp. 328-48.
37. Hasan, Zoya and Menon, Ritu, *Unequal Citizens – A Study of Muslim Women in India, op cit*, p. 126.
38. Das, Maitreyi Bordia, Employment and Social Inequality in India – How Much do Caste and Religion Matter, Ph.D. Dissertation, 2002, p. 4.
39. Shariff, Abusaleh, Socio-economic and Demographic Differentials between Hindus and Muslims in India – *Economic and Political Weekly*, Nov. 1995, p. 2948.
40. Hasan, Zoya and Menon Ritu, *Educating Muslim Girls – A Comparison of Five Indian Cities*, Women unlimited, New Delhi, 2005, p. 77.
41. *Quoted* by Hasan, Zoya and Menon Ritu, Women Unlimited, New Delhi, 2005, p. 80.
42. Gupta, Piyali Sen and Gulia, Juba, Enrollment, Drop-out and Grade Completion of Girl Children, *Economic and Political Weekly*, April 2002, pp. 1621-37.
43. Hasan, Zoya and Menon, Ritu, *Unequal Citizens – A Study of Muslim Women in India,* p. 98.
44. Fazalkbhoy, Nasreen, Sociology of Muslims in India – A Review, *Economic and Political Weekly*, 27 June, 1997, pp. 1547-51.
45. Zoya Hasan (ed.) *Forging Identities: Gender, Communities and the States*, Koli for Women, New Delhi, 1994.
46. Sikri, Rehana, *Women in Islamic Culture and Society – A Study of Family, Feminism and Franchise*, *op cit*, p. 14.
47. Selvaraj, Sikri and Kannusamy, K., *Empowerment of Women in the Present Scenario: Issues and Challenges in India: Economic Empowerment of Women*, New Century Publications, New Delhi, edited by Ganesamurthy, V.S., May 2007, p. 26.
48. Hasan, Zoya and Menon, Ritu, *Unequal Citizens – A Study of Muslim Women in India*, *op cit*, p. 9.

49. Sikri, Rehana, *Women in Islamic Culture ands Society – A Study of Family, Feminism and Franchise*, *op cit*, p. 8.
50. Hasan, Zoya and Menon, Ritu, *Unequal Citizens – A Study of Muslim Women in India*, *op cit*, pp. 101-102.
51. Raheem, A. Abdul and Prabhu, C., *Women Entrepreneurs – Problems and Perspectives in India. Economic Empowerment of Women*, Edited by Ganesamurthy V.S., New Century Publications, New Delhi, 2007, pp. 3-4.
52. Rajini, R., *Challenges Faced by Women Entrepreneurs in India: Economic Empowerment of Women*, Edited by Ganesamurthy, S., New Century Publications, New Delhi, May 2007, pp. 167-169.
53. Sikri, Rehana, *Women in Islamic Culture and Society – A Study of Family, Feminism and Franchise,* Kanishka, New Delhi, 1999, p. 12.
54. Sachar Committee Report on *Social Economic and Educational Status of the Muslim Community in India*, Government of India, New Delhi, Nov. 2006, p. 29.
55. Nagarajan, Rama, Times Insight Group – Married, employed ….. but not empowered, *Times of India*, New Delhi, November 2, 2008, p. 15.
56. The National Family Health Survey 2008 – Unfair Deal, *Times of India*, New Delhi, 2 November, 2008.
57. Mankekar, Purnima, *Screening Culture, Viewing Politics: Television Womanhood and Nation in Modern India*, Oxford University Press, New Delhi, 2001, p. 6.
58. Gupta, Nilanjan, *Switching Channels Ideologies of Television in India*, Sage Publications, New Delhi, 1998.
59. Ibrahim, Farhana, Islamic 'reform' the Nation State and Liberal subject: The Cultural Politics of Identity in *Kachchh Gujarat, Contributions of India Sociology*, May – Aug. 2008, Vol. 42, No. 2.
60. Of animal and the inhuman form – Editorial, *The Sunday Guardian*, New Delhi, 16 May 2010.
61. Akbar, M.J., Byline – "Comforts, Dangers of Sin and Stupidity", *The Sunday Guardian*, New Delhi, 16 May 2010.
62. Express News Service, New Delhi, Ministries can set up Academic Institutes – Supreme Court, *Indian Express*, New Delhi, 22 May 2010, p. 12.
63. Goel, Dr. Arun, *Women Empowerment Myth or Reality*, Deep and Deep Publications Pvt. Ltd., New Delhi, 2009, pp. 60-61.
64. Mehta, Vinod, Muslim and Medial Images – Where Things went wrong in Muslims and Media Images, *News versus Views*, edited by Ather Farouqui, Oxford University Press, New Delhi, 2009, p. 32.
65. Report of the National Commission for Religious and Linguistic Groups, Ministry of Minority Affairs, 2007, p. 41.

66. Women getting empowered to commit crimes, *Indian Express*, New Delhi, 25 May, 2010, p. 7.
67. Pandey, Mrinal, Indian Press, The Vernacular and the Mainstream Babel – In Muslim and Media Images, *News Versus Views*, edited by Ather Farouqui, Oxford University Press, New Delhi, 2009, p. 28.
68. *Ibid.*, p. 55.
69. Kishwar, Madhu, *Manushi*, No. 32, 1986.
70. Govt. of India, Planning Commission Ninth Five Year Plan 1997-2002, Vol. II, p. 322.
71. Sinha, Chinki, Tailor's Daughter Comes out with Flying Colours – CBSE Declares Results, *Indian Express*, New Delhi, May 22, 2010, p. 4.
72. Rahman, Dr. Zainab, *Empowerment of Rural Indian Women – Study of Uttarakhand*, Kalpy Publications, Delhi, 2007, p. 28.
73. Engineer, Asghar Ali, Muslim Women and Change – *Bhavan Journal*, April, 15, 2010, Bhartiya Vidya Bhawan Journal, Mumbai, p. 47.
74. *Ibid*, p. 49.
75. Engineer, Asghar Ali, Muslim Women in Indian Society – http://www.IndianMuslims.ionfo/book/export/htm.23009
76. Interview Falimida Saifullh, December 1999, Quoted by Zoya Hasan and Ritu Menon in *Educating Muslim Girls - A Comparison of Five Indian Cities* – Women Unlimited, New Delhi, 2005, p. 147.
77. Sinha, Chinki, Urdu Medium Schools, *Indian Express*, New Delhi, May 22, 2010, p. 4.
78. National Comission Report for Religious and Linguistic Groups, Ministry of Minority Affairs, Government of India, 2005, p. 42.

5

Dalit Women and their Empowerment

"India is a place of multiple identities and therefore the study of discrimination and exclusion should be understood at multiple spheres ... there is denial of opportunities to all the historically marginalised sections, but it varies in degree".[1] Dalit women are particularly the greatest victims of social discrimination, exclusion, economic poverty, unemployment and exploitation. Therefore, there is a need to invent policies that can create more and more space for them with the ultimate aim of providing them social, political and economic empowerment along with gender justice. Justice V.R. Krishna Iyer says in *State of Kerala* vs. *N.M. Thomas*, "A bare reading (of Article 341 and 342 of the Constitution) brings out the quintessential concept that they (Scheduled Castes and Scheduled Tribes) are no castes in the Hindu fold but an amalgam of castes, races, groups, tribes, communities thereof found on investigation to be the lowliest and in need of massive state aid and notified as such by the President. On July 17th, 1997 K.R. Narayanan, a member of Dalit Community, was elected President of India. This is the first time in the fifty-year history of India that a Dalit has been elevated to such a high position supported by the traditional political parties. Nevertheless on June 30, 1997, a gang of high caste men attacked nine Dalits, who were travelling on a bus in the district of Madurai, Tamil Nadu. These two events exemplify the condition of Dalits in India in general. The Dalit's assertions and the higher castes resistance are the two sides of life in India today.[2] In *Indra Sawhney* vs. *UOI* 1992, (Supp. C3) SCC 217, Para 94 A and 462) nine judges constitutional bench of the Supreme Court has held that Scheduled Castes and Scheduled Tribes are included in the wider term, "Backward class of citizens". 1981 Census shows that there are 22 dominant castes in the country which have accounted for 55.36 per cent of the total Scheduled Caste. There are however more than 1000 other smaller castes which account for remaining 44.46 per cent.[3] Dalit political parties are now gradually asserting their power that cannot be easily ignored in the political formation in India.[4] Bahujan Samaj Party (BSP) led by Ms. Mayawati in Indian politics is mobilising people to form an identity in order to gain space and power in politics in the country and ultimately to be recognised and respected as a community. The economic approach of the state in the empowerment of the Dalits has in the past led to a dilution of the Dalit mass movements. The economic approach tends to focus on the "politics of demand" that only addresses the material aspects of life but the cultural approach focuses on the politics of command that transforms the worldview of the people.[5] The Government of India through the Constitution has notified the Scheduled Castes and Scheduled Tribes in pursuance of Article 341 and 342 for each state and Union Territory. After independence caste has become an important dimension of political mobilisation. The politics of reservation for Dalits has fuelled intra-caste conflagration among the reserved communities with a dual paradoxical dilemma of having to forge Dalit unity against the oppressive upper castes and also to engage with the divisive forces emanating from within the Dalits.[6] Brinda Karat, the well-known feminist and Communist Party leader has been the General Secretary of the All India Dalit Women Association (AIDWA) for more than a decade. In her book "*Survival and Emancipation – Notes from Indian Women's Struggle* (2005), he has admitted that the Dalit women's movement has been grappling with certain problematic issues which have time and again created confusion over the movement's agenda and status. She believes that women's issues are not the forte of women alone. Instead women have to struggle with men to fight various forms of injustices. Dalit women's subjugation has been characterised by their experience of two distinct patriarchal structures/situations: a Brahmanical form of their caste status, as well as the more intimate forms of control by Dalit men over the sexual and economic labour of their women.[7] Dalit women generally face many problems, injustices and discriminations.

Between Dalits there are broadly some major categories historically. *Jatav, Chamar, Mala, Madiga, Mang, Mahar* have the caste legends explaining their origin and status. Second is their structural exclusion and inferior status indicated by Brahmanical texts as for instance *Atchur, Asprishy, Antyaja, Chandala, Asuras, Dasas* or *Dasyas, Rakshasas, Pariah, Haryan* and *Panchamas* etc. The Third category of nomenclatures was a result of the administrative and political and economic discourse, e.g., depressed class, exterior class or Scheduled Castes and so on. Finally, comes a category of generic identities that the ex-untouchables themselves adopted such as "Adi-Andhra", "Adi-Dravida" Bhumi Putra and Dalit which came in vogue in 1972 in Maharashtra with the formation of Dalit Panthers Movement.[8] In Bihar, Nitish Kumar, Chief Minister has taken the social justice process for political empowerment of the Extremely Backward Classes (EBCs) naming 21 Dalit groups rechristening them as "Maha Dalit" or greater Dalit. Dalit women are generally victims of gender-based violence which threatens the well-being, rights and dignity of women. Violence against Dalit women includes not only physical violence but also sexual, psychological and emotional abuse. Violence against Dalit women includes sexual harassment, trafficking in women, forced prostitution, sexual abuse of female children and battering. Isolation is a form of violence when women are not allowed to talk to anyone and control over what they do, and where they want to go. Violence against Dalit women should be viewed as one of the most crucial social mechanisms by which they are forced into a subordinate and disempowered position. Violence against Dalit women remains the greatest challenge facing Indian society in the 21st Century. Such violence are impediments to the achievement of the objectives of equality, development and empowerment of Dalit women. Then phenomenon against Dalit women arises mostly from patriarchal notions of ownership over women's bodies, sexuality, labour, reproductive rights, mobility and level of autonomy. Dalit women had been the victims of social exclusion. "Social exclusion means" the inability of an individual to participate in the basic political, economic and social functioning of society and it involves the denial of equal access to opportunity imposed by certain groups in society upon others.[9] Exclusion involves both the act of restricting access and the consequences that[10] follow principal forms of deprivations. Amartya Sen differentiates between active exclusion which means blocking opportunities through deliberate policy interventions on the part of government or private agents and passive exclusion, which does not rely on these interventions, but may lead to similarly negative outcomes.[11] In order to have an inclusive society we need essentially three values of human development such as peace, freedom and equality. Planning Commission (2006) has even recognised this by saying India's economic growth is unequal and not equally shared by all exclusion has historically served to deny that Dalits access to economic growth is unequal and not equally shared by all. The exclusion has historically served to deny Dalits access to economic resources and social dignity. The Constitution of India provides 15 per cent reservation as proportionate to their population in education and jobs for empowerment of Dalits throughout India.

Dr. B.R. Ambedkar, who chaired the Committee that drafted India's democratic Constitution, concluded his presentation with a powerful pointer: "On the 26th January (the founding of the Indian Republic with its new Constitution), we are going to enter into a life of contradictions. In politics we will have equality and in social and economic life, we will have inequality."[12] Ambedkar himself played an important part in the policy of affirmative action in favour of the disadvantaged social groups ("the Scheduled Castes and Scheduled Tribes)" included in the Constitution of the Indian Republic. Article 17 of the Constitution of India states that the practice of untouchability is abolished and its practice in any form forbidden. How far society has accepted this is a question which needs to be probed, investigated and highlighted. The social and religious reformers the place of pride must be given to Buddha, Mahavira, saints like Gyaneshwar, Tukaram and Kabir, who made valiant effort to modify the strictness of the old spirit of caste exclusiveness. They sought to raise the untouchable classes to a position of spiritual power and social importance almost equal to that of Brahmins.[13] Dalit have waged along arduous and bitter struggle for more than 100 years against oppressive caste discrimination, economic exploitation, marginalised political participation and an unjust social order and have forced upper castes to accept the fact that constitute an important force in politics. For more than a century, Dalit women were looked down in all aspects of life and discriminated in the disguise of tradition and culture.[14] About 90 per cent of Dalit women are rural, most are landless or marginal farmers who live in abject poverty and grinding labour. The major beneficiaries of education and employment reservations for Scheduled Caste (SCs) and Scheduled Tribe (STs) are men from relatively forward castes among the Dalits. Dalit women have not been able to get equal access as men to benefits reserved for SC/ST. Due to triple oppression of caste, class and gender, Dalit women have the least access to education and other opportunities for economic and social mobility. The low status of women from insignificant economic status ascribed to them may be due to continued economic dependence on men along with illiteracy, low levels of skills, lack of access to training, credit etc.[15] Dalit women's disempowerment in the social context can be traced back to illiteracy, tradition-ridden values, social isolation, class violence, caste system, dependence on the elite sections, dependence on intermediaries and dependence on money lenders.

Dalit women generally live in slums which are areas where buildings are unfit for human habitation by reasons of dilapidation, over-crowding, faulty arrangements and design, narrow street, lack of ventilation and light, absence of bathing room, lavatory and drainage, lack of proper water supply and electricity and unsanitary living conditions. Poverty as well as discriminating attitude towards Dalit women are responsible for inadequate access to health services, nutrition and other basic facilities. Women eat last at home and do without food if there is any shortage as men and children are fed first.[16] Lack of opportunities, lack of articulation, seclusion of women, non-participation in decision-making, divorce or desertion, atrocities by liquor addicted husband, female infanticide, gender violence, oppression to male member due to patriarchal system are some of the main sources of Dalit women disempowerment. In the economic context, poverty, low wages, no asset base, no access to resources like land, capital or skills, dominance of money lenders, inadequate access to bank credit, corruption, gender discrimination of wages, patrilineal inheritance, male dominated policies are some of the main sources of women disempowerment. The Scheduled Caste women were required to perform all the menial and impure duties for the upper class women during menstruation, child birth etc. and therefore they were considered all the more impure and defiling.[17] Dalit women have waged a long, arduous and bitter struggle against oppressive caste discrimination, economic exploitation, an unjust social order and marginalised political participation for the last sixty years. Dalit women are often raped and sexually assaulted as a form of retaliation by the upper caste people. Dalit means a person completely broken, destroyed and down trodden because of public persecution, group of human beings that are completely neglected and down trodden.[18] Indeed a congruence of class deprivation and gender discrimination can blight the lives of poorer women very severely indeed. It is the interactive presence of these two, features of deprivation – being low class and being female – that can massively impoverish women from the less privileged classes.[19] The blighting of the lives of Dalits or people from other disadvantaged castes, or of members of the Scheduled Tribes, is particularly severe according to Amartya Sen, when the Caste or Tribal adversities are further magnified by abject penury. Marginalisation and racial exclusion of Dalits find its manifestation in physical segregation of communities, restriction on resources like water and land, social prohibitions and even restrictions on entry to certain religious places. After independence, things are gradually changing but Dalit women still need empowerment. The Constitution of India, which came into force on 26th January 1950 provides fundamental rights to every citizen. Article 46 of the Constitution specifically provides that "The state shall promote with special care the educational economic interests of the weaker sections of the people and in particular of the Scheduled Castes and Scheduled Tribes and shall protect them from social injustice and all forms of exploitation." The Government of India has chosen compensatory discrimination as a means of achieving greater equality by adopting compensatory discrimination by deliberately overcoming some of those historically accumulated disabilities from which Dalits have suffered for many decades. The Constitution of India provides the following:

1. Right to equality (Article 14, 15 and 16),
2. Right against exploitation (Article 23),

3. Directive Principles of State Policy (Article 38, 39 (a) and (d) 42 and 44),
4. Elections (Article 325).

The Preamble of the Constitution of India incorporates the chief goals enshrined in the Constitution reflecting the spirit of equality, justice, liberty, fraternity and assuring the dignity of the individual. Article 14 of the Constitution of India says, "The state shall not deny to any person equality before law or equal protection of laws within the territory of India." Article 14 prevents any arbitrary discrimination. Article 15 of the Constitution ensures prohibition of discrimination on grounds of religion, race, caste, sex or place of birth or any of them. According to Article 15 (2) – No citizen shall, on grounds only of religion, race, caste, sex, place of birth or any one of them be subject to any disability, liability restriction or condition with regard to:

(a) Access to shops, public restaurant, hotels or places of public entertainment, or

(b) The use of wells, tanks, bathing ghats, roads and places of public resort, maintained wholly or partly out of state fund or dedicated to the use of general public;

(c) Nothing in this article shall prevent the state from making any provision for women;

(d) Nothing in this article or in clause (2) of Article 29 shall prevent the state from making any special provision for the advancement of any socially or economically backward classes of citizens or for the Scheduled Castes and Scheduled Tribes. Article 15 guarantees non-discrimination on special grounds, that is religion, race, caste, sex, place of birth or any of them. Article 46 provides for the promotion of educational and economic interests of the Scheduled Castes, Scheduled Tribes and other weaker sections. Article 23 of the Constitution provides prohibition of traffic in human beings and forced labour." Article 32 provides for the Right to Constitutional remedies in the forms of *Habeas Corpus*, *Mandamus*, prohibition, *certiorari* and *Qua Warrantee*. Article 338 provides for National Commission for Scheduled Castes and Scheduled Tribes. Article 340 provides for the appointment of a Commission to investigate the conditions of backward classes.

The activists and intellectuals assembled at the Bhopal conference on 12-13 January 2002 adopted unanimously the Bhopal Declaration on Dalit Rights.[20] The National Commission for Women (NCW) was set up on 31 January 1992 as per the National Commission for Women Act, 1990. Govt. of India enacted the Scheduled Castes and Tribes (Prevention of Atrocities) Act 1989. The Central Government made the Scheduled Castes and Scheduled Tribes (Prevention of Atrocities) Rules 1995 to enforce and facilitate the enforcement of the Act.

Hierarchies of caste and class interlock prevent many Dalit women from contesting elections.[21] When women refuse to bend down, under pressures and patriarchal bargains, they are even subject to physical violence. Chinna Poornu, a cobbler from Chellimedu in Dharmapuri district, in Karnataka, withdrew her nomination at the last moment out of fear of class backlash and physical violence. This illustration brings out the socio-political context in which Dalit women live in their homes. Of course, for empowerment there is still a long way to go. There have been instances of Dalit women abandoning their fight half-way due to lack of support from their husbands and their own community members. From their time of birth, women are culturally conditioned and ideologically indoctrinated into different roles in the institution of household – as housewives, mothers and daughters. In social terms, all Dalits particularly women suffer social oppression and economic poverty. The Dalit women are mainly employed in unorganised sector and work as labourers in agriculture, construction work, landless labourers, factory workers and other household and marginal works, as daily wage workers.[22] The plight of the Dalit women is poor because of lack of adequate employment, limited skills, illiteracy, restricted mobility and lack of any autonomous status in cities and towns. Dalit women suffer due to heinous socio-economic inequality and economic deprivation. As per Human Development Report 1996, there are 229 million 'income poor' but more than twice as many 554 million are 'capability poor'. No statistics can adequately capture the acute and heinous socio-cultural inequality and economic exploitation of the poor Dalit women of India. As regards Constitutional safeguards including reservation in services and scholarships in education, its advantages are generally captured by the creamy layer of the Dalits.

Despite several kinds of state assistance, Dalits are plagued with alarming rates of school drop outs. My personal conversation with one Dalit women brought out these hard facts of life. "My daughter was going to primary school. But I could not purchase text books, could not afford to arrange the private tuition for her. How could she be educated? She has to look after the house when I am at work and to look after the infants of the house. Getting education is not possible for the children of poor people like us." The relatively young Dalit women with young children are usually burdened with more domestic responsibilities. Poverty and lack of proper education and shelter, take its toll on the health of women who often do not get the nutrition sufficient to compensate for the heavy physical labour done by them.

During the last few decades, there has been an increase in the number of women joining the agricultural work force as labourers. This feminisation of agriculture indicates both an increasing proportion of women in agricultural labour and the deteriorating conditions of women labour due to casualisation of work and distress migration in the context where farming is itself becoming unprofitable. Dalit women, if educated, are fully capable of making a difference in their everyday lives temporally and spatially, however, they remain constrained by an overarching social system which renders uncollected and scattered resistance to everyday life incapable of unsetting existing unequal gender role and relations. Mass Media like TV, cinema and other ICT can help these Dalit women in empowering themselves. ICT can empower women by providing them knowledge about health, diseases and infirmities. According to World Health Organisation "health is a state of complete physical, mental, spiritual and social well-being and not merely the absence of disease or infirmities. Due to various socio-economic causes and unsanitary living and working conditions, majority of Dalit women do not enjoy good health and suffer from many diseases. Unsafe water sanitations, indoor smoke, unsafe sex, iron deficiency, zinc deficiency and overall under nutrition are reasons for the ill-health of Dalit women particularly those living in slums – these are the outcomes of poverty. Dalit women are generally the victims of this phenomenon. Low female wage rates and women's social inferiority result in their being increasingly concentrated in low-paid casual agriculture labour. The share of non-workers among women has declined from 73.32 to 68.97 per cent. Women became the disposable factor of production in agriculture.[23] According to the 2001 census, the share of cultivators among rural women has decreased from 42.74 per cent in 1991 to 32.32 per cent in 2001.

Empowerment is an active, multi-dimensional process, a process of awareness and capacity building to greater participation and decision-making power, the unleashing of the capacity of the individuals to be more self-reliant. It consists of greater autonomy in decision-making, greater ability to plan their lives, have greater control over the circumstances that influence their lives, free them from the shackles imposed by custom, belief and practice.[24] The Government of India designated the year 2001 as the year of Women Empowerment. The Ninth Five Year Plan Period (1997-2001) aimed at looking at women as empowered partners in the political and decision-making process. Education is seen as a key input in bringing about this change.[25] Literacy rate of women has been very low as compared to men of the same community/caste. The literacy rate among various religions communities and Dalits (SC/ST) are shown below in the table 1.

Table 1: Literacy Rate among Religious Communities, Scheduled Castes and Scheduled Tribes

(in per cent)

Community/Caste	*Male*	*Female*	*Total*
India	75.3	53.7	64.8
Hindu	76.2	53.2	65.1
Muslim	67.6	50.1	59.1
Christian	84.4	76.2	80.3
Sikh	75.2	63.1	69.4
Buddhist	83.1	61.7	72.7
Jain	97.4	90.6	94.1
Others	60.8	33.2	47.0
Scheduled Caste	66.64	41.9	54.7
Scheduled Tribes	59.17	34.76	47.1

Source: Census 2001.

Table 1 clearly indicates that the female literacy rate of both Scheduled Castes and Scheduled Tribes are the lowest among all other religious communities.

The extension work done by Agarwal (1994), has shown that ownership and control over land is the single most important economic factor in the women's being and empowerment.[26] Land ownership is critical in facilitating access to farm credit and other inputs. More recent work shows that women's ownership of land has a positive impact on reducing domestic violence.[27] Following sustained campaigns by the women's movement, the law on the inheritance of property – the Hindu Succession (Amendment) Act 2005, removes gender inequality in the inheritance of agricultural land. The 2005 Amendment to the Hindu Succession Act provides for daughters (including married daughters) to be treated as partners in joint family property. What this means is that Hindu women in all states now have a "birth-right" in joint family property which cannot be willed away by their fathers. According to the Hindu Succession Amendment Act 2005, recognising that sons and daughters are equal members of their natal family, laws now provide

Table 2: Women's Participation in Decision-making

Household Decisions	*Women alone*		*Husband alone*		*Wives and Husbands in consultation*		*Others in the household*	
	Rural	*Urban*	*Rural*	*Urban*	*Rural*	*Urban*	*Rural*	*Urban*
What to cook	85.4	0.3	3.5	3.8	1.1	1.8	8.4	7.1
Health care of herself	21.7	32.9	45.5	38.0	22.0	19.7	8.6	6.4
Purchase of jewellery	10.0	13.6	43.6	37.1	29.2	36.7	12.9	8.6
Visits to Parents	13.0	17.8	47.4	41.8	24.5	29.7	11.4	7.5
Spending Money she earned	35.9	54.4	36.9	19.1	19.3	22.3	5.5	2.5

for legal equality with respect to land rights in joint family properly for Hindu women and men across all states. The 73rd and 74th Constitutional Amendments are a landmark in the efforts of providing women an opportunity to enter the decision-making process at the local and district levels. The National Family Health Survey 1998-99 reveals that women's participation is restricted only to daily decision about what to cook. Decision about obtaining personal health care, spending the money that she earns, purchase of jewellery and so on, are taken in the majority of the cases. The Table 2 summarises women's participation in decision-making.

There is need for women empowerment. Self-help will be one of the best methods for empowerment of women.[28] Women have hidden potentialities which should be energized and then only the planned programme of self-help and empowerment will sustain. To make their thinking more effective, PRA (Participative Rapid Appraisal) is a useful method. Some of the key features of PRA are – it is participatory, edifying, flexible, adaptable, explanatory, inventive, representative and authorising.[29] PRA has led the women from a dependency syndrome to independent and collective action for development and empowerment with a self-help approach with the help of NGO and the Government. Experience of last few years suggest that Self-Help Groups (SHGs) are sustainable, have explicability, stimulate savings, and in the process help borrowers to come out of vicious circle of poverty.[30] The multi-dimensional process of empowerment requires awareness, access to education, and training, participation in decision-making and politics and the mobilisation of women for economic self-reliance. For empowering Dalit women, they need to change their outlook, thinking attitudes, beliefs and even behaviour. Dalit women living in various slums of India need intensive training for building their capacities and the contract of training varies from group to group, state to state and even location to location but primarily focuses on:

1. Violence against women and violence in general (both public and private);
2. The value of house work and childcare;
3. Health (nutrition, reproductive health, transmittable diseases);
4. The status of girl child (child-abuse, child labour and child marriage);

5. Legal literacy (para-legal training, filing police complaints, and cases etc.);
6. Fundamental and human rights;
7. Development schemes and programmes;
8. Workers' rights (fair wages, sexual harassment, unionisation);
9. Strategies for organising (within the slums, household and at work).

The training methodology usually consists of group exercises, role of plays, games, and songs, scrolls, charts, and audio-visual aids are also an integral part of training.[31] The Micro-credit movement in India is gathering momentum as women at the grass-roots organise themselves into SHGs. Dalit women need empowerment and the following qualitative indicators can be used for evaluating empowerment:

1. Increase in self-esteem and self-confidence.
2. Increase in knowledge and awareness levels on issues affecting the community, such as women's health, nutrition, reproductive rights, legal rights, literacy, etc to enable them to have informed choices in areas like employment, education and health.
3. Change in the women's role and responsibility in the family and community by enhancing access to legal literacy and information.
4. Visible increase or decrease and other forms of violence perpetrated on the women and girl child.
5. Change in social and other customs e.g. child marriage, dowry, discrimination against widows, reproduction cycle and family planning.
6. Visible changes in women participation in attending public meetings, training programmes and ensures equal participation in the economic process.
7. Increase in bargaining/negotiating power of the women as an individual as well as in collectives.
8. Formation of cohesive women's group/collective at village district and state levels.
9. Positive changes in social attitudes amongst the community members and recognising their contribution to the society, polity and economy.

10. Recognition of women's economic contribution within and outside the household.
11. Development of their ability to think critically and foster their decision-making ability.
12. Provide information, knowledge and skill for economic independence.
13. Women's decision-making over her choice of work, income and expenditure in her control or is she still subservient to male members in the family.[32]

According to Prof. Upender Baxi, Empowerment is one word; but it signifies myriad of processes of creation of agency, organisation and social consciousness. It remains problematic in patriarchal society when it aspires to empower women. It seeks to foster a kind of attitudinal change from old to new, enlarging social order from traditional to the rational, from folk society to modern society, from simplicity of illiterate, primitive to a conscientised organised society.[33] During the last ten years, there is perceptible change towards women empowerment in India due to various socio-political development and increasing role of Self Help Groups (SHGs). The SHGs are providing a support base to women from marginalised communities by mobilising community level participation and can enhance women's participation in Panchayati Raj Institution in the following ways:

1. Ensuring accountability of the Gram Panchayat;
2. Mobilising the Gram Panchayat;
3. Support to elected representatives;
4. Creating social capital.[34]

Such SHGs are also proving their usefulness by getting Micro-credits and assisting in micro-enterprise development. From 1985 onwards there are many government and foreign funded programmes for women's development in which NGOs and women activists have participated and gradually women empowerment is being achieved slowly. For the first time, the National Rural Employment Guarantee Act 2005 has specifically targeted women. We were also overwhelmed by the cynicism of the responses, particularly against the background of the films on Dalit women that we had used to stimulate the discussion. The DDs film was made very crisply, presenting the story of 1,000 women who have been part of the campaign for autonomy over production over seeds, over markets.[35] Rural Employment Guarantee Act 2005 has been now extended to all the districts and states of the country and it will gradually ensure empowerment of Dalit women also if the scheme is properly implemented. "Reservation in the institutions and the financial assistance in the form of scholarships and freeships constitute perhaps the most important factor in the development scheme for Dalits. Despite several kinds of state assistance, Dalits are plagued with alarming rate of school drop-outs."[36] The job reservation policy broadly envisaged representation of Dalits in all public services but a cursory glance at the figures of this representation is enough to get a pathetic state of implementation. Dalit women have made some progress in the educational field but still they have to enter many more areas such as business, political sphere, professional, engineering and medicines. According to the Report of the National Commission for Religions and Linguistic Minorities, the *Sarva Shiksha Abhiyan* (SSA) has greatly benefitted SCs/STs.

There has been a visible impact of special programmes and incentives for SCs and STs. Consequently, number of Scheduled Caste children in schools has shown a steady increase. During 1980-81 to 2003-04, their enrollment has gone up from 11 million to 23 million in primary classes; from 2.2 million to 8 million at the middle stage and from 1.1 million to 4.8 million at the Secondary stage and girls forming 44.8 per cent, 41.4 per cent and 38.2 per cent at these levels respectively. As against this, though the number of Scheduled Tribe children have also progressed but at a slow pace on account of difficult topography, unfriendly terrain, and forests, among other. During 1980-81 to 2003-04, enrollment of Scheduled Tribe children has gone up from 4.6 million to 12.5 million in primary classes; from 0.74 million to 3.7 million at the middle stage and from 0.33 million to 1.95 million at the Secondary stage and girls forming 45.9 per cent, 41.7 per cent and 37.4 per cent at these three levels respectively. As part of the *Sarva Shiksha Abhiyan* (earlier the District Primary Education Project and Education for All Programmes), a strategic shift is noticed in educational planning to target hither to unreached geographic areas and the marginalised groups of our society. Two-pronged interventions were launched, namely, the National Programme for Education of Girls at the Elementary Stage (NPEGEL) and the Kasturba Balika Vidyalayas (KGBV). Both schemes are being implemented in Educationally Backward Blocks (EBBs) where rural female literacy is below national average of 46 per cent and where the gender gap is also above the national average of 22 per cent. In all 2656 Educationally Backward Blocks have been identified in 20 states on the basis of the 1991 census. The NPEGEL launched in 2003 as an integral yet separate gender component for education of underprivileged disadvantage girls at the elementary level.[37]

NSSO Survey brings out chasm between OBC and SCs and literacy and property. OBC satraps Lalu Prasad, Mayawati and Mulayam Singh Yadav may have overtaken their upper caste counterparts in political clout, but this has not translated into the economic uplift of their brethren. While exposing the upper cast-OBC chasm, an NSSO survey sheds light on the intra-backward classes gap with SCVs/STs continuing to languish at the bottom of this heap, with a very thin creamy layer.[38] 12 per cent rural household among upper castes figure among those who spends Rs. 1155 and above per month against 5 per cent among OBCs while the figure for the highest bracket in urban areas Rs. 2540 or more and 13 per cent for upper castes and 3 per cent for OBCs. SCs at the bottom with just one per cent in the top group in urban areas and three per cent in rural areas. The NSSO survey also revealed the social realities in its study of distribution of households of social groups vis-à-vis monthly per capita consumer expenditure (MPCE). Those in the top bracket of spending class are almost double among upper castes compared to OBCs. In sharp contrast, the proportion of OBCs in the five lower MPCE classes in rural areas-less than Rs. 410 is 20 per cent as against 20 per cent for others. The share of SCs is high at 40 per cent and STs at 49 per cent. The urban share of social groups in this lower class (less than Rs. 675) stands at 40 per cent for OBCs and 21 per cent for others. SCs have the highest persons spending less than Rs. 675 per month with 51 per cent. It explains that creamy layer exists among OBCs but is nowhere compared to upper castes while SC/ST have very thin creamy layer. The spending pattern is borne out by figures for land holdings and literacy, the prime vehicle of social mobility. However, it also brings out the chasm between OBCs and SCs vis-a-vis the clout of land literacy. A case in point is the survey of those possessing 4.01 hectares or more of land in rural India. It is the highest (six per cent) for others and four per cent among OBCs while SCS holdings are only one per cent. The lowest possible category of land holders – 0.001 hectares or less in highest for the underprivileged. Four per cent STs and three per cent SC households find themselves in this bracket while it is two per cent for OBCs and others. The attendance in educational institutions is the highest for others, followed by OBCs and the SC/STs. In the age-group of 20-24, in rural areas, 68 out of 1,000 persons among STs attend educational institutions and 65 among SCs. The figure is as high as 105 for others and 73 for OBCs for urban areas. The attendance rate in this category is 249 for others, 159 for OBCs and 139 for SCs.[39] The low social status of Dalit women from insignificant economic status ascribed to them may be due to continued economic dependence on men along with illiteracy, low levels of skills, lack of access to training, credit etc.[40] So, there is need for women empowerment. Self-help will be one of the best methods for empowerment of women. Participatory Rapid Appraisal (PRA) is an approach and method for learning about rural life and conditions from with and by rural people. Women should identify their basic needs and hidden potential should be organised and then planned programme should sustain it. The PRA approach has been used successfully in Ranga Reddy District of Andhra Pradesh. During 1999 the NGO conducted PRA exercises in its ten villages in Parigi Mandal in Ranga Reddy District of Andhra Pradesh for the welfare of weaker sections especially Dalits. A total of 764 hoseholds were identified as people below poverty line in 10 villages out of which 714 (93) were SCs, 27 (four per cent) were BCs and 23 (three per cent) OCs. PRA has thus led the Dalit women from a dependency syndrome to independent and collective action for development and empowerment with a self-help approach.

Although the Government has started a number of welfare schemes namely *Janani Suraksha Yojna* (JSY), Integrated Child Development Scheme, National Maternity Benefit Scheme, *Antyodaya Anna Yojna* and National Family Benefit Scheme, the red tape and indifference of the concerned medical authorities led to the denial of medical care to two poor pregnant ladies. Justice S. Murlidhar in a verdict passed on 4th June 2010, directed the Government to plug loopholes in its much-touted welfare schemes. Both women victims namely Shanti Devi and Fatima (both belonging to the below poverty line) were denied child delivery care for not first furnishing a below poverty line card or cough out huge sums of money for availing child delivery card. Shanti Devi died while Fatima gave birth to a baby without any access to skilled medical health care in full public view under a tree. High Court of Delhi has awarded a compensation of Rs. 2,40,000 to Shanti Devi's family and Rs. 50,000 to Fatima. The High Court has also directed the Government to aid Fatima's daughter Alisha's education till the time she completed high school.[41] The Ministry of Women and Child Develolpment came into existence with effect from 01.01.2006 with Smt. Renuka Chowdhury taking over as Minister of State with Independent Charge. The Tenth Five Year Plan (2002-2007) called for a three-pronged strategy of social empowerment, economic empowerment and gender justice through creating an environment of positive economic and social policies for the women, allowing *de-jure* and *de-factor* enjoyment of all human rights, providing equal access to women to health care, quality education/strengthening the legal system aimed at elimination of all forms of discrimination and violence and building and mainstreaming gender perspectives into the Indian society. However, there are a number of constraints still faced by women and children especially those belonging to economically and socially disadvantages sections.

As a result of the various measures, during the period 2001-2005 the status of SC/ST women has registered quantifiable improvements. However, the government has a lot more to do to fulfill the Constitutional commitment of raising the status of SC/ST to that of the rest of the population. Towards the economic betterment of SC/ST, the Government commits to make all efforts not only to allow every landless SC/ST family with a minimum piece of land with ownership rights but also to maximise their productive capacities through upgradion of their skills, modernisation of methods and equipment and supply of seeds and pesticides. Special legislative measures are also being taken to ensure payment of minimum wages and equal wages for women, with no gender discrimination, especially in the informal/unorganised sector to make more concerted efforts for bringing SC/ST above the poverty line. The government also commits to organise landless and agricultural labourers on the pattern of *swarozgaris* of the SGSY with special focus on women for bringing the SC/ST women above the poverty line. As the practice of carrying night soil manually continues to be a matter of national concern, the government embarked upon a nation-wide programme for total eradication of manual scavenging on a time-bound basis by 2007. To this effect, the Tenth Plan commits to prepare State-specific Plans of Action to initiate time-bound programmes in respect of conversion of dry latrines into wet ones; identification of scavengers; weaning them away from this profession; rehabilitating them with training and alternative jobs; keeping a follow-up of the rehabilitated persons and bringing forth effective coordination between the Welfare Departments of the States and local bodies. In these national endeavours, the National Commission for *Safai Karamcharis* will play a lead role. Taking note of the urgent need for upholding the Civil Rights, on the one hand and preventing/curbing the persistent problems of social discrimination, exploitation, untouchability and atrocities against the SC/ST women, Government has initiated collaborative efforts with all concerned for effective implementation of the Indian Penal Code, 1860 and the other two Special Legislations the PCR Act, 1955 and the SC and ST (Prevention of Atrocities) Act, 1989. To this effect, efforts have been made to prepare state/district-specific programmes of Action ensuring preventive, investigative and rehabilitative measures in those districts/areas where the incidence of crime/atrocities/ violence against these weaker sections is high. Measures are also being undertaken to ensure that adequate number of Special/Mobile

Courts are set up with adequate staff in each district to provide both speedy and on-the-spot settlement/redressal of grievances.

Swayamsiddha is an integrated scheme for women's empowerment through promotion of self-help groups. The scheme was launched in February 2001, across the various states with a total budget outlay of Rs. 116.30 crore. The long-term objective of the programme is holistic empowerment of women through a sustained process of mobilisation and convergence of all the on going sectoral programmes by improving access of women to micro-credit economic resources. During 2005, 29 participants attended exposure-cum review meetings on 24th and 25th May 2005 at Delhi and later 26 participants attended it on 22nd and 23rd August 2005 at Delhi. *Swa-Shakti* Project was started by Government of India jointly funded by IFAD, World Bank in October 1999 and the Project Culminated on 30th June 2005. The overall objective of the programme was to bring out socio-economic development and empowerment of women through promotion of women's self-help groups, micro-credit and income-generating schemes.[42] By and large the programmes have benefited the most disadvantaged groups viz. Scheduled Castes (27.0 per cent) Scheduled Tribes (18.0 per cent), women headed households (11.0 per cent), marginal farmers (43.0 per cent) and the landless households.

Micro-credit is an important requirement for empowerment. The *Swarnjayanti Gram Swarozgar Yojna* (SGSY) a new credit linked poverty alleviation programme has covered one million rural poor families by linking about 50,000 SHGs with banks by 2000 A.D. The basic strategy adopted to promote empowerment of women through SHGs comprises the following activities:[43]

(1) Organising Women SHGs at the village level around savings and rotational credit programmes using their own resources;

(2) Facilitating regular interaction, exchange of information and exposure within and across these groups to increase their mobility and awareness;

(3) Linking the SHGs at the hamlet level with external credit sources such as banks, *Rashtriya Mahila Kosh*, International Fund for Agricultural Development (IFAD) and enabling women members to manage their credit, take decisions and transact business as managers not only as beneficiaries;

(4) Linking the SHGs with Government programmes like *Swarna Jayanti Gram Swarozgar Yojna*, thus enabling the members to expand their investment capital to carry on income generating activities after undergoing training in respective trades.

Information Technology (IT) has great potential in speeding up the development process and empowering Dalit women. For instance, the mobile phones, acquired through Dalit women by offering cell phone services in their neighbourhood. The poor require host of information including market prices, local weather conditions, pest alerts and medical advise to the patients. 98 per cent of the five thousand cell phones providers are women members of Grameen Bank in Bangladesh.[44] It would be fair to conclude that Dalit women have a long way to go before empowerment becomes an integral part of their existence in society. Empowerment of women is a process rather than a state to be achieved by which the status of women in society is continuously upgraded by systematic policies and progammes and the disparities between men and women are gradually reduced.[45] The broad categories to assess empowerment of women are literacy and education, employment, wealth and income, nutrition health and longivity; autonomy and decision-making within family and outside and share of political and managerial power in policy and programme framing for social and national development. For empowerment women's various capacities and capabilities have to be built up and developed by some of the following measures:

1. Enhancing women's access to an control over productive endowments (both private and held in common);
2. Increasing the productivity of women's labour and productive resources through expanding their access to extension services, credit, education;

3. Increasing women's returns to their labour and produce through expanding their access to commodity and labour markets and their ability to effectively bargain in the market place;
4. Increasing women's ability to use it for their own survival and security and for that of other family members;
5. Increasing the ability of women to gain complete control over their bodies; fertility, sexuality and their identities;
6. Increasing women's ability to exercise political power and claim their rights vis-à-vis the state and other bodies operating in the public interest.[46]

There are many challenges for those interested in capacity building of women. There is a new air of confidence among the women and it encourages their mobility.

Acceptance of women's empowerment as the societal need presupposes male domination in the society where every home is a male bastion. It appears as a protest against subjugation of women against their will, or ignorance and patriarchal system of families. As empowerment of any sort is a gradual and stabilising function spanning over several generations based on the realisation within the society. Addressing a meeting of the Chief Ministers in January 2003, the then Prime Minister Atal Behari Vajpayee said: "Make women's empowerment central to your strategy. Patriarchal attitude, dowry system and violence against women have to be dealt with firmly."[47]

According to Prasad and Madhavi (2001), Mass Media have an undeniable role in formation of social attitudes. Media are not only formed by but also transform societies. The gender and development approach uses the range of communications channels from big to small media, indigenous media and local to international media systems.[48] The National Sample Survey Organisation (NSSO) report released in the last week of May 2008, revealed that disparity in wages between 2004-05 when there was no national rural employment scheme and 2007-08 when the scheme was introduced by UPAI. In 2007-2008 rural women working in NREGA areas

Table 3: Representation of SCs, STs and OBCs in the All-India and Central Services (Group A and B) through Civil Services Examination (per cent)

Year	*IAS*			*IPS*			*IFS*			*Central Services Group A*			*Central Services Group B*		
	SC	*ST*	*OBC*	*SC*	*ST*	*OBC*	*SC*	*ST*	*OBC*	*SC*	*ST*	*OBC*	*SC*	*ST*	*OBC*
2004	13.1	6.6	28.6	12.5	9.0	23.9	5.0	10.0	25.0	19.0	9.3	27.0	-	89.0	-

Source: Ministry of Personnel, Public Grievances & Pension, Annual Report, 2005-06.

Table 4: Representation of SCs, STs and OBCs in 211 Public Enterprises as on 01.01.2005

Category	*Total No. of Employees*	*Representation of SCs, STs and OBCs*					
		SCs		*STs*		*OBCs*	
		Number	*Percentage*	*Number*	*Percentage*	*Number*	*Percentage*
Group A	1,65,405	20,864	12.61	6,607	3.99	10,410	6.29
Group B	1,54,174	20,335	13.18	9,444	6.12	13,001	8.43
Group C	6,64,501	1,31,204	19.74	64,957	9.77	1,13,407	17.06
Group D (Excluding Safai Karamcharies)	2,42,973	53,027	21.82	34,594	14.23	54,845	22.57
Total	12,27,053	2,25,430	18.37	1,15,602	9.42	1,91,663	15.61

Source: Annual Report of Department of Public Enterprises, 2005-2006.

were getting 54 per cent higher wages than casual women workers in urban areas. The Report pointed out that compared to an average daily wage of Rs. 48.50 for a woman in urban areas, women enrolled under the NREGA scheme got Rs. 79 every day in rural areas.[49] Employment generation coupled with skill-oriented education and training is one of the successful strategies for empowering Dalit women in India. The need of the hour is to motivate and help the Dalit women for developing their education, skill-related capabilities and modern outlook.

The representation of Scheduled Castes in India Railways and Public Sector Enterprises has been increasing over the years. Representation of SCs and STs in All India and Central Services are gradually increasing and the position can be judged by Table 3 as follows:

Representation of Dalits in 211 Public Enterprises has been as given in Table 4.

Increasing representation of Dalits as on 01.01.2005 is a positive indicator of their empowerment as it will make them economically independent. Once a member of Dalit family gets job, the whole family is directly benefitted and leads to empowerment. During the last ten years, changes at the global and national level have compelled the state to create new initiatives for women's empowerment in ways that would address the criticism of the earlier "clientelistic" approach adopted and at the same time initiate multi-faceted policies to empower Dalit women. "Increasing opportunities for education-based on reservation and entry into formal politics made Dalit women visible. Educated Dalit women also became visible in the new knowledge-making processes as writers and poets. Conferences like the Dalit Women's Solidarity Conference in Bangalore in 2001 brought together writers to share experiences specifically about violence against Dalits."[50] The increasing visibility of caste in public discourses and recognition of the relations of power along the caste lines were results of various independent and autonomous Dalit women organisations such as the National Federation of Dalit Women (in 1995), the All India Dalit Women Forum (in 1996) and the National Federation of Dalit Women (NFDW), launched in 1995. These organisations became champions of Dalit Women's cause and demanded immediate empowerment of Dalit women. The shift in state gender policy has been accompanied by the demands for political power, privilege and dignity for the Dalit women. Economic-oriented strategies for women's empowerment have been the mainstay of the state. Understanding the social context and social basis of inequality is central to examine power relations and therefore approached to empowerment. The process of empowerment is slow, and it may take several years before long-term impacts of various socio-economic programmes of empowerment can be realised or even felt. The macro-micro linkages of various programmes can prove useful for understanding the dynamics of empowerment and capacity building. Basic education, good health, quality of life and human attainments are directly valuable as constituent elements of basic capacity building for empowerment. Prema Gopalan has given an insight from her unique experiments in women's empowerment through net-working self-education and collective action – "the *Swayam Shikshan Prayog*" (SSP) and various lessons learnt from her experience on capacity building for women's empowerment.[51] Dalit women can learn through a variety of ways by *Sakhi Shibirs* (mini exchanges at the cluster level and visits to mandies (weekly markets) in group can provide women confidence gained by travelling and visiting administrative office at block and district level. It provides opportunities for dialogue with officials. Melavas or information fairs are restive occasions at which women disseminate and celebrate their achievements. Innovations in watershed development, use of new technologies by communities, federation building processes and training of women in masonry, embroidery, toy making, etc. are few examples. Self-education is geared towards enabling women to learn from each other how to identify survival needs, and strengthen their skills and mobilise community resources.

The life expectancy at birth among females has been steadily improving over the years from 55.7 in 1981-85 and 59.7 in 1989-93 to 65.3 in 2001. The life expectancy indicator highlights that number of older women will be on the rise. Special initiatives for the well-being of women during the Eight Five Year Plan (1992-1997) were as under:

1. Setting up of National Commission for Women in 1992 to safeguard the interests of women.

2. Setting up of *Rashtriya Mahila Kosh* in 1993 to meet the credit needs of poor and assetless.
3. Adoption of the National Nutritional Policy in 1993 to fulfill the Constitutional Commitment of improving the nutritional status of children, adolescent girls, expectant and nursing mothers.
4. Launching of the schemes of *Mahila Samriddhi Yojana* in 1993 to empower women by institutionalising their savings.
5. Launching of *Indira Mahila Yojana* in 1995 for women's empowerment through Self-Help Groups.
6. Proposal for setting up of National Resource Centre for Women.
7. Formulation of Draft National Policy for Empowerment of women.[52]

Chart – Empowering Dalit Women

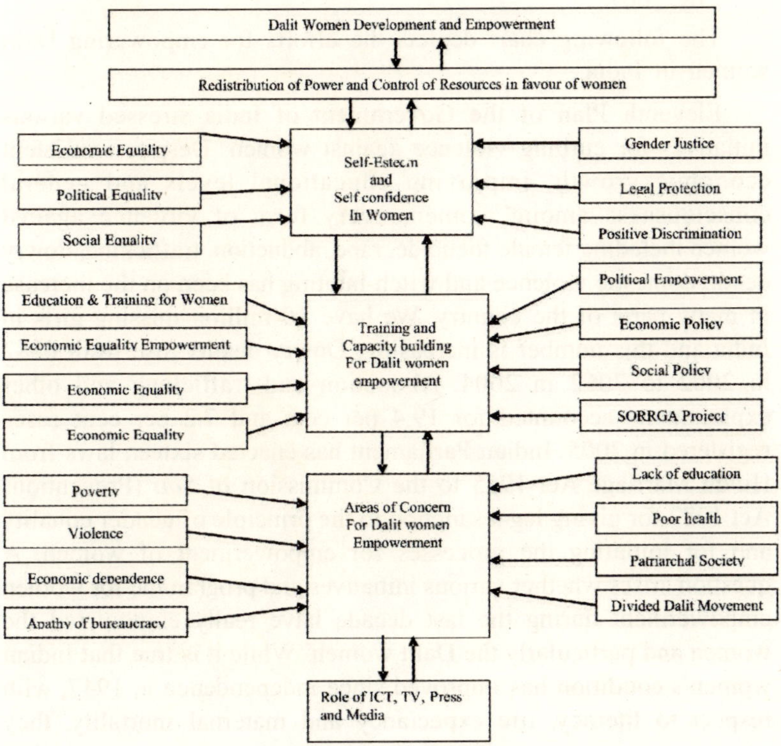

The Tenth Five Year Plan (2007-2012) adopted the National Policy for Empowerment of Women (2001) into action by a large number of initiatives and adopted the following Action Plans:

1. Reduction of poverty ratio by five percentage points by 2007 and by 15 percentage point by 2012;
2. Providing gainful (high-quality) employment;
3. All children in school by 2003;
4. Reduction of gender gaps in literacy and wage rates by at least 50 per cent by 2007;
5. Reduction in the decadal rate of population growth between 2001 and 2011 by 16.2 per cent;
6. Increase in literacy rate to 75 per cent within the Plan period;
7. Reduction of IMR (Infant Mortality Rate) to two per 100 live birth by 2007 and one by 2012; and
8. All villages to have sustained access to potable drinking water by 2007.[53]

The following chart depicts the efforts for empowering Dalit women in India.

Eleventh Plan of the Government of India stressed various initiatives for curbing violence against women. Despite consistent economic growth, improving educational levels and general consciousness among women, every form of violence against women including female foeticide, rape, abduction, trafficking, dowry death, domestic violence and witch-hunting has been on the increase in many parts of the country. We have 10 million missing girls in India and this number is increasing. Dowry deaths rose from 6882 in 2002 to 7062 in 2004. Abduction and trafficking and other exploitations accounted for 19.4 per cent and 7.2 per cent cases registered in 2005. Indian Parliament has enacted sixteen laws from Hindu Marriage Act 1955 to the Commission of *Sati* (Prevention) Act 1987 for giving legal sanction to the principle of gender equality and for initiating the processes for empowerment of women. A question arises whether various initiatives and programme for women empowerment during the last decade have really empowered the women and particularly the Dalit women. While it is true that Indian women's condition has improved since independence in 1947, with respect to literacy, life expectancy and maternal mortality, they continue to occupy a subordinate positions vis-à-vis Indian men in all spheres of life – economic, social and political.[54] Women landless labourers, Dalit and tribal women have seen only marginal improvement in their day-to-day conditions. Their low productive endowment base, as well as their lower access to credit, extension services, inputs and market information have excluded the marginalised sections, particularly the Dalit women from the gains of globalisation in terms of employment and increase in real wages combined with a rise in price of essential commodities, the consumption level and the well-being of the Dalits and tribals have in fact come down. A simple answer in 'yes' or 'no' will not be adequate to depict the realities of India society. Dalit women in India have very different conditions of life which are influenced by their earning capacity, employment, rural, urban set up, educational level, family background, political affiliations and so on. While within Dalit women, majority of them subsist below the poverty line, others enjoy a higher standard of living and social status. Ms. Mayawati has been Chief Minister of Uttar Pradesh many times during the last fifteen years, Meira Kumar is the present Speaker of the Lok Sabha and has been Union Minister earlier. However, localisation or decentralisation of political processes along with reservation opened up new opportunities for Dalits to take part in political processes, influence the allocation of government and community resources in their favour and protect and promote their human rights. However, harsh economic realities of women's lives, male resistance to women exercising political power, upper caste resistance to Dalits occupying public positions, women's lack of knowledge of working of public institutions like Panchayats are main barriers to their political empowerment. That is why wierings refers to empowerment as a process of exposing the oppressive power of the existing gender and social relations, critically challenging them and creatively trying to shape different social relations.[55] This requires capacity-building strategies for Dalit women which will strengthen their understanding of the complex existing realities.

In Andhra Pradesh, the President of the Coastal Andhra Madigas Mahila Samakhya (Federation of the Madga Women) Mrs. May Madigas has forcefully said, "Madiga women constitute half of the Madiga population of the total reservation benefits received by our men, we do not get even one per cent of these benefits. As women we face triple discrimination against us… we demand categorisation of reservation on the basis of gender."[56] If we study the overall situation of Dalit women all over India, there is no homogeneity as regards their socio-economic status. Women belonging to Dalit classes might have very different conditions in different states. *Mahars* in Maharashtra, the *Male* in Andhra, the *Pariars* in Tamil Nadu and the *Chamars* in Uttar Pradesh are relatively better off than other competing communities within the Scheduled Castes.[57] Mayawati belongs to the Jatavs (*Chamar*) Caste and Ram Vilas Paswan of Bihar to *Pasi*. *Chamars* and *Jatavs* (*Chamars)* of Uttar Pradesh joined the Bahujan Samaj Movement of Kanshi Ram in a big way and shifted completely towards Bahujan Samaj Party (BSP) by 1990.

Social empowerment encompasses women's educational, health and nutritional requirements as also their housing, sanitation and general amenities (like drinking water facility). Empowerment puts emphasis on the right of the Dalit women to organise in order to assert their rights through collective action as well as the self confidence, which comes from awareness that she has rights and is not depending on charity or compassion. Dalit women, who attempt to reform and democratise the process of their development from the inside of the society by resistance against alcoholism, upper caste atrocities and even bureaucratic structure often find that alliance of politicians, male members of the patriarchal social system and the vested interests have an almost impregnable strong hold on the central institutions of the society. Thus, the empowerment of Dalit women is multi-dimensional and is a long drawn process. Dalit women empowerment entails a process of struggle at both personal and collective levels. A key component of the struggle at the personal level is understanding oneself and one's relationship with others and the dynamics between oneself and the society at large. Self-learning is the main strategy to develop such understanding. [58] This will be the first step. As a Zen Master said, "The Journey of thousand miles begins with a single step." In Tamil Nadu, Dawn came into being in 1989 to work with the poorest women and girl children of the backward castes and Dalit communities of Virudhunagar district. It formulated a project called "SORRGA" in 1998 which stands for:

1. S– Shelter and solidarity to women victims of domestic violence.
2. O– Option for women other than attempting suicide other anti-victim area.
3. R– Rehabilitation of women and children who are affected by violence.
4. R– Reshaping the values that oppress women, in order to initiate action.
5. G– Gender sensitisation programme for women and men in all sectors of life.
6. A– Alliance building with others who work on the same issues.

SORRGA project encompasses both proactive strategies such as gender sensitisation, alliance building, and reshaping of social values, as well as reactive strategies such as providing an alternative ideology and material space in the form of short-stay homes, feminist counselling, alternative life-styles and employment options.[59] A feature film "*Pudia Padai* (meaning new path) – a great success in Tamil Nadu is about women called "*Sita*", got President's award and can be used for gender sensitisation programme. During the period 2001-2005, many schemes and programmes were implemented which have positively helped in the empowerment of Dalit Women. There is however no homogeneity as regards Dalit women's status. While in some states and cities they enjoy many privileges due to their socio-economic or political status, in other states or regions Dalit women have not yet been able to enjoy the benefits of empowerment and are still suffering from poverty, illiteracy, social backwardness and subsistence living below the poverty lines. The challenges to Dalit empowerment are many and very difficult to overcome. The journey to Dalit women empowerment is very arduous and long and India has only travelled a few files. The refreshing new face of India with increasing participation of Dalit women in the work force during the last ten years augurs well for the country's economy, in general and the much needed Dalit women's empowerment, in particular. It is at once the empowerment and betterment of the Dalit women and a boost to the national economy.

ICT building cinema, TV etc. have brought about awareness towards legal age of marriage of girls, antenatal check up, use of contraceptives, limited size of family, utilisation of health services for reproductive health problems and ability to keep money aside for the rainy-day by saving some money. ICT have brought tremendous attitudinal change in Dalit women in particular. ICT and particularly mass media are not only successful in changing the attitude towards immunisation but are also successful in changing false views regarding those diseases which were previously considered incurable, infectious or caused by divine curse e.g., measles, small pox, leprosy etc. ICT has also been trying to awaken the Dalit women regarding prevention and control of local and endemic diseases such as malaria, AIDS, tuberculosis etc., and making them aware about prevention and cure of such diseases. Thus, ICT has played an effective role in empowering Dalit women's health. Empowerment is not a point of destination but a space/ strategy to explore for each women, it is an evolving process and demands involvement, commitment and self-confidence.

References

1. Thorat, Sukh Deo, Chairman University Grants Commission, Quoted by Kumar Avinash, Sub-classification off SC Reservation, in Yagati, Chinnar Rao (Ed.) *Dividings*, Rawat Publications, Jaipur, 2009, p. 276.
2. Arun, C Joe, *Construction Dalit Identity*, Rawat Publications, Jaipur, 2007, p. 1.
3. Chalam, K.S., The Fragmented Assertion: Emergence of India – Caste Differentiation Among Dalits in *India in Dividing Dalits*, Edited by Yagati Chinna Rao, Rawat Publications, Jaipur, 2009, p. 91.
4. Jaffsclot, C., *India's Silent Revolution*, London, 2003, Shah, Ghanshyam, *Dalit Movement and the Search for Identity*, 2001, Dr. Souza, P.R., *Contemporary India: Transitions*, New Delhi, Sage Publications, 2000, Quoted by Arun, C. Joe, in *Constructing Dalit Identity*, Rawat Publications, Jaipur, 2007, p. 287.
5. Aloysius, G., Dalit Empowerment: Ten lessons from History in *Religions and Society*, Vol. 45, No. 4, 1998, p. 87.
6. Introduction to Dividing Dalits – *Writings on Sub-categorisation of Scheduled Castes* edited by Yagati Chinna Rao, Rawat Publications, Jaipur, 2009, p. 1.
7. Rahman, Zinab, *Empowerment of Rural Indian Women – Study of Uttarakhand*, Kalpaz Publication, Delhi, 2007, pp. 50-57.

8. Rao, Yagati Chinna, *Introduction to Dividing Dalits – Writings on Sub-Categorisation of Scheduled Castes*, Rawat Publications, Jaipur, 2009, pp. 2-3.
9. Thorat, Sukhdeo and Newman, Katherine S., Caste and Economic Discrimination, Causes, Consequences and Remedies, *Economic and Political Weekly*, Oct. 13, 2007.
10. Indian Institute of Dalit Studies (IIDS), National Conference on *Social Exclusion and Inclusive Policies*, 26-27, October, 2007, IIDS, New Delhi.
11. Sen, Amartya, Social Exclusion Application and Scrutiny–Social Development Papers – I, Asian Development Bank, 2000.
12. Sen, Amartya, *The Argumentative Indian – Writings on Indian History, Culture and Identity*, Penguin Books, 2005, p. 36.
13. Anand, Meena, *Dalit Women Fear and Discrimination*, Isha Books, Delhi, 2005, p. 13.
14. Jogdand, P.G., *Dalit Women Issues and Perspective*, Gyan Publishing House, 1995, p. 93.
15. Puhazhendlu, U and Gayaraman, B, Increasing Women's Particiaption and Employment Generation among Rural Poor : An Approach through informal Groups, *Indian Journal of Agricultural Economics*, Vol. 54, No. 3, July-Sept. 1999, pp. 287-295.
16. Kumar, H. and Vergese, J, *Women's Empowerment*, Regency Publishers, 2005, p. 110.
17. Anand Meena, *Dalit Women – Fear Discrimination*, Isha Books, Delhi, 2005, p. 12.
18. Jogodand P.G., (Ed.) Dalit Women – Issues and Perspective, Gyan Publishing, House, New Delhi, 1995, Also Nirmala Bhai P, *Harijan Women in Independent India*, B.R. Publishers, New Delhi, 1986.
19. Sen Amartya, *The Argumentative Indian–Writings on Indian Culture, History and Identity*, Penguin Books, 2005.
20. For details of Bhopal Declaration on Dalit Rights – Consult Chapter 4 from page 190-196 of Meena Anand's book *Dalit Women—Fear and Discrimination*, Isha Books, Delhi, 2005.
21. Stephen, F., Empowering Women in Gram Panchayats through Training in *"Building Women Capacities – Interventions in Gender Formation*, edited by Ranjani K. Murthy, Sage Publications, New Delhi, 2001, p.135.
22. Jain P.C., Jain Shashi and Bhatnagar Shudha (Edts) *Scheduled Caste Women*, Rawat Publication, Jaipur and Delhi, 1997, p. 96.
23. Muller, R.A. and Patel, R., *Shining India? Economic Liberalisation and Rural Poverty in the 1990s*, 2005.
24. Devi, Laxmi, *Women Employment and Societal Improvement*, Anmol Publications Pvt. Ltd., New Delhi, 1998.

25. Reddy, M.S.N. and Shobha, I, *Women Education in India – An Overview in Empowerment of People Grassroots strategies and issues*, R. Venkat Ravi and others, Kanishka Publishers, New Delhi, 2004, p. 63.
26. Agarwal, Bina, *A field of one's own : Gender and Land Rights in South Asia*, Cambridge, Cambridge University Press.
27. Panda, Pradeep and Agarwal, Bina, *Marital Violence, Human Development and Women's Property Status in India*, World Development 33 (5) 2005, pp. 823-50.
28. Venkataramana, M., *Participatory Development of S.C. Women – A Micro Perspective – in Empowerment of People – Grassroots Strategies and Issues*, Kanishka Publishers, New Delhi, 2004, p. 35.
29. Bheemappa , *Participatory Rural Appraisal : Learning with Farming Community*, Kurukshetra Vol. KLIV – No. 11, August 1996, pp. 558-59.
30. Rao V.M., *Women Self-Help Groups – Profiles from Andhra Pradesh and Karnataka*, Kurukshetra Vol. 50 No. 6, April 2004.
31. Asmita, Windows to the outside world – Experiences in Gender Training in Hyderabad Slums, in Building Women Capacities – Interventions in *Gender Transformation*, Edited by Ranjani K. Murthy, Sage Publications, New Delhi, 2001, pp. 180-81.
32. Raj, D. Sunder, Women Empowerment and Self-Help Groups – A Participatory Approach in Empowerment of People – *Grassroots Strategies and Issues* (Eds.) Ravi R. Ventakata and Others, Kanishka, New Delhi, 2004.
33. Baxi, Upendra, Forward to Lealamma Devasia and V.V. Devasia, *Empowering Women for Sustainable Development*, Ashish Publishing House, New Delhi, 1994, p. VIII.
34. Pant, Mandakini, *SHGs as Change Agent in Enhancing the Political Participation of Women in Local Self-governance – in Women Livelihood Rights – Recasting Citizenship for Development*, Edited by Shri Krishna Sage Publication, 2007.
35. Datar, Chhaya, Restructuring the Employment Guarantee Scheme – in *Shri Krishna – Women's Livelihood Rights*, Sage Publications, New Delhi, 2007, p. 159.
36. Anand, Meena, *Dalit Women Fear and Discrimination*, Isha Books, Delhi, 2005, pp. 51-52.
37. Mishra, Justice Ranganath, Report of the National Commission for Religious and Linguistic Groups, Government of India, p. 88.
38. Ghildyal, Subodh, Empowerment only on Paper? *The Times of India*, New Delhi, Nov. 2, 2006.
39. Ghildyal, Subodh, Empowerment only on Paper? NSSO Survey Brings out the Chasm Between OBC and SC in Literacy, Property, *The Times of India*, New Delhi, Nov. 2, 2006.

40. Puhazhendi U. and Jayaraman B., Increasing Participation and Employment Generation among Rural Poor, *Indian Journal of Agriculture Economics*, Vol. 54, No. 3, July 1990, pp. 287-95.
41. Garg, Abhinav, Pregnancy Care Denied, HC Orders Compensation, *Time of India*, New Delhi, 6 June, 2010.
42. Annual Report 2005-2006, Ministry of Women and Child Development, Government of India. p. 27.
43. Lalitha, N. and Nagarajan B.S., *Empowerment of Rural Women through Self-Help Groups – A Study in Tamil Nadu.*
44. Purushotham P., Empowering Rural Poor through Information Technology – in *Empowerment of People,* Edited by R. Venkate Ravi and others, Kanishka Publishers, New Delhi, 2004, p. 124.
45. Mukerji, Tilak and Somayajulu U.V., Empowerment of Women – Issues Relating to Methodology and Measurement, paper presented at the Annual Conference held at IIPS, Mumbai, Quoted in *Communication and Empowerment of Women-strategies and Policy Insights from India,* Edited by Kiran Prasad, Vol. II, The Women Press, Delhi, 2004, p. 478.
46. Murthy Fanjani K., *Introduction to Building Women's Capacities – Interventions in Gender Transformation*, Sage Publications, New Delhi, 2001, pp. 19-20.
47. Sunderarajan P., Pull Your Socks Up, Say PM, *The Hindu*, January 17, 2003.
48. Quoted by Manisha Joshi, Communication and Women Empowerment in Uttaranchal in Communication and Empowerment of women – *Strategies and Policy* Insights from India, Edited by Kiran Prasad, The Women Press, Delhi, 2004, p. 386.
49. Times News Network – Disparity in Wages between male, female workers in rural India reduced, *Time of India*, New Delhi, 28 May, 2010.
50. Subramaniam Mangla, *The Power of Women's Organising – Gender, Caste and Class in India*, Rawat Publications, Jaipur, 2007, p. 103.
51. Gopalan Prema, *Empowerment from Below: Self-Education and Empowerment of Grassroots Women's Collectives – in Building Women Capacities – Interventions in Gender Transformation,* Edited by Ranjani K. Murthy, Sage Publications, New Delhi, 2001, pp. 273-287.
52. Government of India, Planning Commission Ninth Five Year Plan, p. 336.
53. Goel Arun, *Women Empowerment – Myth or Reality*, Deep and Deep Publications, New Delhi, 2009, p. 23.
54. Murthy Ranjani K., *Introduction to Building Women Capacities – Intervention in Gender Transformation*, Edited by Rjani K. Murthy, Sage Publications, New Delhi, 2001, p. 17.
55. Wierings, S., *Women's interests and Empowerment: Gender Planning Reconsidered – Development and Chang,* 1994, 25, p. 833 (Article 829-48).

56. Smbaiali Guindimeda, *Madiga Dandora –A Social Movement for Rationalisation of Dalit Reservations in Dividing Dalits*, Writings on Sub-categorisation of Scheduled Castes, edited by Yagati Chinna Rao, Rawat Publications, Jaipur, 2009, p. 133.
57. Rao, Yagati Chinna, *Dividing Dalits*, Writings on Sub-categorisation of Scheduled Castes, Rawat Publications, Jaipur, 2009, p. 9.
58. Moharaj R. and Raman Lakshmi, Enhancing the Negotiating Power of Women with Families through Processwork, In *Building Women's Capacities, Interventions in Gender Formation*, edited by Ranjani K. Murthy, Sage Publication, New Delhi, 2001, p. 210
59. A Gandimathi – under the Guise of a Tatoring programme DAWN's Experience in Gender Sensitisation of Adolescent Girld – In *Building Women's Capacities - Interventions in Gender Formation*, edited by Ranjani K. Murthy, Sage Publication, New Delhi, 2001, p. 215.

6

The Embroidery Sector in the National Capital Region:

With Special Reference to Dalits and Muslim Women

Reality is what we take to be true. What we take to be true is what we believe. What we believe is based upon our perceptions. What we perceive depends upon what we look for. What we look for depends upon what we think. What we think depends upon what we perceive. What we peceive determines what we believe. What we believe determines what we take to be true. What we take to be true is our reality. (Zukav, – 1979: 328).[1]

Recall the face of the poorest and the weakest man/woman whom you may have seen and ask yourself, if the step you contemplate is going to be of any use to him.

There can be few societies in which embroidery has played such a prominent role as it has in India. Whether in the rural tradition in which embroidery featured strongly as dowry goods, wedding paraphernalia or group identifier; at the Courts of the Mughals and other ruling elites, in which embroidered textile adorned the carved stone halls as well as the persons of the nobility; or in the thriving export market that has made India's textile products famous for two millennia, embroidery has always been to the fore in India's uniquely rich textile tradition.[2] European Traveller Marco Polo, travelling in the late thirteenth century has commented on the high quality of embroidery from India. We learn from *Ain-I'Akbari*, the record of Akbar's reign, that special *Karkhanas* (workshops) for all types of textiles and other crafts were set up in the royal compounds.[3] Francois Bernier in 1663 has described how one of these workshops was given over exclusively to embroidery.[4] Embroidery has a very long history in the Indian sub-continent and even the earliest Indian needles were excavated at Mohenjodaro and Harappa civilisation which dates back to about 2000 B.C. Their existence naturally indicates a rich tradition of sieving and so also the possibility of embroidery.[5] Captain Alexander Hamilton who spent his time in East India Company from 1688 to 1723, target Combay (present day Khambat Fort of Gujarat) quilts as lucrative export good and declared that "the people of Combay (present day Khambat) are the best embroiderer in India and perhaps in the world.[6] Bengali embroideries were certainly on sale in England during the early seventeenth century; a record of a sale in Februaly 1618 describes a Bengali quilt embroidered all over with pictures of men and crafts (ships) in yellow silk, fetched the notably high price of £20.[7] The oldest surviving examples of Indian embroidery to have come to light so far as two pieces made for Jain nuns in the fifteenth or sixteenth century.[8] Kashmir has been famous for Kashmiri shawls which are decorated with intricate scenes involving human figures and animals. There is mention of a "embroidered map shawl" which depicts the whole city of Srinagar, complete with Dal Lake and the main bridges, mosques and gardens of the city, all worked out on a woollen gown which was gifted to the then Prince of Wales (later Edward VII) on his visit to India in 1875-76.[9] The finest and earliest patterned shawls had woven floral designs in their borders, but they later developed elaborate woven patterns all over in response to European and particularly French demand. Embroidery is an ancient variety of artistic, decorative and creative needlework in which designs and pictures are imaginatively created by stitching strands of some material on a layer of another material. Most embroidery uses thread or wool stitched onto a woven fabric, but stitches could be executed in for example, wire or leather strands and embroidery can be worked on to many materials. Embroidery has traditionally been used to decorate clothes. In ancient India, under the patronage of the rulers of Bhuj, exquisite wall-hanging and door decorations in silk were produced in the mochi style of embroidery.[10] Gujarat particularly the Kutch region, has a rich tradition of folk embroidery. The art passed down from one generation to another and embroidered garments with heavy mirror work became popular. Women are very skillful at this craft and embroidered garments with mirror-work form an important part of a Kutchi bridal trousseau. Indian embroidered Varanasi silk sarees, and Kanchipuram sarees are well-known all over the world. Today India is the largest producer of silk next to China and is renowned the world over for the beauty and excellence of hand prepared embroidered silk sarees. India is an old civilization but a new developing nation which has rich heritage in the field of arts. Embroidery is the art of decorating textiles with needle and thread with the most popular basic techniques of cross-stitch, crewel work and quilting. From times immemorial, Indian women have been passing on the art of embroidery to the new generations in various parts of the country. Other nations also have some records of embroidery work. "The Persian and Greeks wore quilted garments as armour. The earliest surviving examples of embroidery are Scythian (c. 5th–3rd century BC). The most notable extant Chinese examples are the imperial silk roles of the Qing dynasty (1644-1911/12). Islamic embroideries (16th–17th century) show stylised geometric patterns based on animal and plant shapes.

In India, there are many known varieties of hand embroidery and machine embroidery products known in different parts of the country. Hand embroidery is used by traditional artists, who are skilled by training in their craftsmanship and have inherited the art of embroidery from their ancestors, senior artists and traditional embroidery teachers. Machine embroidery has now replaced hand embroidery as machine saves a lot of time and hard artistic work. It is more convenient for mass production. India had attracted migrations from pre-historic times and people came with their cultural and household traditions which were absorbed and formed the rich cultural household traditions. Embroidery has been an important part of the household tradition. The best embroidery pieces, some of the richest embroidery in the world, are made by both Muslim and Hindu women who live in relative or even dire poverty and some of these pieces take months or even five to six years. Gold and silver, either gap threads or lurex, are used by some group of embroiderers to add sparkle while some use mirror glass known as *shisha* or *abla*. A talismanic role is also played by cowrie shells, red seeds, old zips, white buttons, silver trinkets, sequins, bits of watch chain and dangling triangular amulets, as well as tassels and pompoms.[11]

There are many Indian styles of embroidery and most popular among them are Phulkari, Kantha, Kashmiri, Chikankari, Zardosi and Kutch embroidery. Punjab and Haryana are famous for the Phulkari and Bagh embroidery. The Kasauti embroidery of Karnataka has three different stitches - the *negi*. The *gavanti* and the *menthi*. *Negi* is the long running stitch imitating the weaving technique; *gavanti* is a double running stitch which creates a pattern on both sides, and *menthi* is the cross-stitch. The Kasauti embroidery patterns are geometrical and show the influence of local beliefs, stylised *rathas*, Lord Hanuman, lotus flowers and various patterns of the conch shell, mingled with flowering bushes, birds and animals.

The traditional Phulkari embroidery of Punjab are sometimes traced back to Vedic ages. The famous Punjabi poet Waris Shah has mentioned Phulkari in the famous love story *Heer-Ranjha*. Its present popularity goes back to 15th century, during the reign of Maharaja Ranjit Singh. Phulkari is considered auspicious and is included in the bridal trousseaus. This art was learnt by the daughters from their mothers just as she learnt other household chores and customs of various festivals along with their songs and dances. Phulkari embroidery has a variety of styles for different occasions and purposes, although they differ by the use of horizontal, vertical and diagonal stitches apart from shading and variations in the design. The Chope, a red coloured cloth with embroidered borders, is presented to the bride by her grandmother during a ceremony before the married and considered very auspicious religious ceremony. Ghunghat Bagh or *sari-pallau* (covering for the head) has a small border on all four sides, in the center of each side which covers the head, a large triangular motif is embroidered. Suber is phulkari worn by a bride during marriage rites and comprises of five motifs, one in the centre and one each in the four corners. Varida Bagh (bag of the trousseau) is on red cloth with golden yellow embroidery symbolising happiness and fertility. This entire cloth is intricately worked in different colours showing patterns of small flowers.

Bawan Bagh (Fifty two gardens) has many geometrical patterns and very artistic, attractive and decorative. Chamba is a hybrid Phulkari having a series of wary creepers, stylised leaves and flowers, depicting the artistic styles of embroidery. Intricate floral patterns of embroidery called Bagh are primarily used on the *odhanis* and *dupattas* and are considered auspicious for the new born and the bride. Phulkari is now-a-days popularly used in home furnishings especially wall hangings, sofa throws and other soft furnishings. The researcher had the personal experience of visiting some friends in Faridabad, Ferozepur, Ludhinana and Chandigarh and could find these home furnishings in many houses. Now, some of these Phulkari embroidery work are very costly in the market though the women artists get very little part of the total selling cost.

Kantha Embroidery, according to one legend, relates to Lord Buddha and his disciples, who used to cover themselves with the thrown away rags patched and stitched together. The oldest reference to Kantha is in *Sri Chaitanya Charitamrita* by Krishna Das Kaviraj which was written some 500 years back. Kantha in Sanskrit language means rags and is called the recycling art evolved out of necessity to drape or protect against cold. The precious silks and Muslins, which became worn-out, instead of throwing them away, were piled in layers and stitched involving a simple running stitch. Kantha for the Bengali folk means embroidered quilt, using multiple layers kept together by the stitches generally used for sleeping on or as a light blanket. Kantha is also regarded to be *dorukha* meaning turning the worn out and old textiles and fabrics to things of beauty. It is a very creative art for the housewives. There are various motifs of Kantha like gods and goddesses, flowers, or geometrical patterns involving the process of laying the worn clothes in layers and stitching them together with variations of running stitch. There are generally seven different types of Kantha: the rectangular wraps heavily padded to make warm quilts and the whole piece is generally stitched in a wavy pattern and then simple embroidery is done on the finished quilt to make it more attractive and artistic. Secondly, Oaar Kantha are pillow covers in simple designs and thereafter a decorative border is sewn to make it more attractive and colourful. Thirdly, Durjan/thalia are quilted wallets made out of rectangular Kantha pieces and used by women folk to keep their money and valuables. Fourthly, Baiton Kantha are generally square wraps used for covering books and other valuables. They have collaborated borders. Fifthly, Sujani Kantha was started in 18th century in Bihar and are decorative quilted Kantha used as blankets or spreads during religious rituals and other special occasions like marriages, festivals and social gatherings. Sixthly, archilata Kantha are small covers for mirrors and toilet accessories with wide colourful borders generally kept near change rooms, bathrooms and children rooms. Seventhly, Rumal Kantha is used as absorbent wipes or plates coverings. They generally feature a central lotus with ornamental borders. The various patterns used in Kantha embroidery are locally called *goal*, *jhōd*, *jhinga*, *phool*, *dhan chori*, *golak dhaga* and are basically different patterns of the running stitch. This creative embroidery is the self-expression of women folk and sometimes these Kantha narrate a story, the emotions and various moods of the life of the embroidered.

Gujarat and particular Kutch Bhuj belt patronised the Kathi embroidery and the pattern includes animal motifs, flowers and peacocks adopted from the Kathi art. The base cloth is preferred to be silk or satin and the thread is cotton or silk floss. Generally, the base is black, embroidery is done in crimson, violet, golden, yellow and white with greens and blues sparingly used. The main stitch is herringbone, as it is faster to fill, other stitches used are an elongated darn or chain-cum interlacing done with an artistic taste. The mirror work is used to make the center of flowers, eyes of the birds or flower representations while the intervening spaces are generally filled with buds and leaves.

Chikankari Embroidery has a very interesting folk history in Uttar Pradesh. It is generally believed that the origin of Chikankari embroidery goes back to the time of the Prophet. It is believed that sometimes between 672-674 AD. while he was passing through a village in Awadh now Uttar Pradesh, he requested a villager for water. On being offered that, he gave the art of Chikankari to the poor villager as and art that will nevere let him go hungry and will enable him to spend his free time in creative work giving satisfaction to the soul. According to Megasthenes, the Chikan originated in East Bengal and he mentions chikan as the florals embroidery on fine Muslin in the 3rd century B.C. The word chikan comes from the Persian word chakeen meaning making delicate patterns on the fabric. Traditionally, chikankari is the white thread embroidery done on the white muslin or *mulmul* but now-a-days chikankari embroidery is quite popular in various colour shades. Chikankari *sarees*, *kurtas* and other garments are quite popular now-a-days. According to certain folk tales, Noorjehan, the beautiful queen of Emperor Jahangir introduced the art of chikankari, being herself an expert in embroidery and was inspired by the Turkish embroidery. In Chikankari the most common motif used is that of creepers. Floral motifs generally enrich the entire garment or just some parts of the same. Among the floral motifs embroidered lotus, rose, jasmine flowering stems and the paisley motifs are the most popular and in great demand in urban cities and metropolitan towns. There is simply no match for the shadow work in which herringbone stitch or Bakhiya is worked out on the wrong side of the cloth. There are various variations of shadow work. Mainly buttonhole stitch (hook), running stitch and chain stitch (Zanzeer) are used to give the fillers and tiny raised flowers are made with stitch resembling French knot. Various effects are created using a variety of stitches and combinations chikankari embroidery has been nurtured in Uttar Pradesh and the work is done on very fine muslin, georgette, chiffon and other fine fabrics. Chikan embroidery is generally suited for outer wear but these days exclusive creations are being done in cushion, covers, pillow covers and table linen.

Applique or Pipli work is an integral part of the decorative needle embroidery work of Pipli Village in Orissa and some part of Gujarat. It is based on patch work in which pieces of coloured and patterned fabric is finely cut in different sizes and shapes and then sewn together on a plain background to form a composite piece. Originally, parasols, canopies and pillows were made for the Rath Yatra but now many objects of daily use like lamp shades, garden umbrella and bed covers have been introduced and are in great market demand.

Aribharat is very unique embroidery of Kutch which is very picturesque and has the quality of jewellery. The best known is Aribharat which is named after *ari*, a hook, plied from the top but fed by silk thread from below, with the material spread out on a frame. This movement creates loops, which is repeated to form a line of chain stitches.

Kashmiri embroidery always draws inspiration from the beautiful nature around. The colours, the motifs of flowers, creepers and chinar leaves, apple, mango, etc., the most common one and the beauty of Kashmir is captured in the Kashida embroidery. The colours of the threads are inspired from the flowers of the Kashmir valley. Pastel colours are often used and Kashmiri embroidery is known for the skilled execution of a single stitch, chain stitch, satin stitch, the slanted dam stitch, stem, herringbone and sometimes *doori* or knot stitches are used but not more than one or two at a time. The base cloth whether wool or cotton is generally white or cream or other similar shades. Sozui embroidery or *dorukha* is often done so skillfully that the motif appears on both sides of the shawl each side having a different colour. The same design is also produced in different colours on both sides paper-made embroidery is another type of needle embroidery in which flowers and leaves are worked in Satin stitch in bright colours which are generally outlined in Black. Another type of embroidery is *ari* or hook embroidery; motifs here are the well-known flower design finally worked in concentric rings of chain stitch resembling coloured *zari* or *ari* embroidery.

Bagh is an offshoot of phulkari and almost always follows a geometric pattern with green as the basic colour. The embroidery is worked into Khaddar (coarse cotton cloth) with silk thread. Sometimes two or three baghs will be stitched together to form a Phulkari. The Banjara is the well-known embroidery of the Lambada gypsy tribes of Andhra Pradesh which is generally a mix of appliqué with mirror and beadwork. Bright red, yellow, black and white coloured cloth is laid in bands and joined with a white criss-cross stitch. Kashmir crewel is known for *Phirans* (woolen *Kurtas*) and *namdahs* (woolen rugs) with big floral embroidery in cheerful colours. Crewel embroidery is the same as chain stitch and is usually done with an awl (a small pointed tool for making holes) and is worked from underneath the fabric rather than above.

Kasuti is a typical delicate single thread embroidery done on handloom *saris* and is a unique creation of Dharwar region of

Karnataka. It is done in two styles called *gavanti* and *murgi* and has a wide range of motifs consisting of temples, peacocks, elephants, flowering trees and geometric forms spread across the *sari*.

Rabari embroidery is a pictographic representation of their mythology, beliefs, culture and traditional life. Rabaris are the nomadic people who came to Gujarat via Sindh, Rajasthan and Baluchistan. There is use of glass mirrors in various shapes; round, thomboid, rectangular, square, triangular and beak shaped and Rabari women embroider textiles as an expression of aesthetics, creativity and identity for ever. Rabaris embroider camel trappings, long adam jackets, chorani pants ludi (veil) the groom Kediyan and so many other ceremonial or daily utility things. Besides intensive use of shaped mirrors, the stitches are square chain interlaced with buttonhole for mirror work, single chain, knot, Romanian, blanket interlaced with herringbone, running or double running. The style is constantly evolving, due to the creativity of Rabari women and their extraordinary capacity for adaptation or keep the tradition vital. Hindu Rabari women make shawls of black wool tie-dyed in yellow, orange or red dots, which they embroider in floral motifs in yellow open chain stitch and decorate profusely with shisha (mirror), cowries and tassels.[12]

The gold embroidery known as *gota* work, is an intricate form of appliqué with patterns of amazing richness, worked out in minute detail in fine gold threat. Small pieces of zari ribbon are applied onto the fabric with the edges sewn down to create elaborate patterns.

Karchobi is a form of raised *zari* metallic thread embroidery created by sewing flat stitches on cotton padding. The technique is commonly used for bridal and formal costumes as well as for velvet coverings, tent hangings, curtains and the coverings of animal cart and temple chariots.

In Rajasthan Pichwai are well-known colourful embroidered cloth hangings typical of Nathdwara. The women of Rajasthan and Gujarat traditionally carry embroidered torans (frieze), dowry bags, shawls, *cholis* and *dupattas* as part of their dowry and these are the best pieces of mirror work done by the ladies.[13]

Zardozi embroidery or Kalabattis is an embroidery work done in metal wires. Varanasi, Lucknow, Surat, Ajmer, Bhopal and

Hyderabad are important centers for *Zari* work. *Zardozi*, a more elaborate version of *zari*, involves the use of gold threads, spangles, beads, seed pearls, wire, gota and *kinari Sardozi*, the imperial metal embroidery adorned the costumes of the royalty wall hanging, scabbards, walls of the regal tents and the rich trappings of elephants and horses. Intricate patterns in gold and silver studded with pearls and precious stones enhanced the beauty of rich and glowing silk, velvet and brocade. Zardozi is an ancient Persian Embroidery form (Zar in Persian means gold and Dozi is embroidery that has been passed down for generations and reached its peak under the patronage of Mughal Emperor Akbar. It was revived, the Muslim craftsmen of Hyderabad and Lucknow to cater to the tastes and demands of Nawabs and rich landlords of Awadh. They became popular for ceremonial occasions. The tribal groups of North-East India have relatively rich traditions of weaving, Embroidery in these regions is scarce and often imitates local patterns in women or other techniques. The embroidered shawls made in Manipur for warriers of the Angami Naga tribes are clearly in the tribal tradition of textiles. The splendid silk shawls worn by men of the Meitai (Vaishnavite Hindu) Community in Manipur echo designs from mainstream North Indian textile.[14] Shamilami is a combination of weaving and embroidery and was once a high status symbol in Manipur.

Embroidery artists are both Hindu and Muslim but over the years they have intermingled and adopted many of each others customs and embroidery patterns. However, one significant difference everywhere, relating to religion, is that Hindu women will often have greater freedom of movement than many Muslim women, who never leave their small village and its immediate environs.[15] Most women embroiderers embroider in the winter months when there is less outdoor work to do.

With the modernisation, exposure to mass media and information technology, education of girls is becoming an essential part of progress and embroidery is threatened because it takes lot of time, patience and hard work with needle and thread. Horses, whose regalia for marriage ceremonies were so lavishly embroidered, have been replaced by cars and scooters. The bridegroom now likes to dress in a cheap western suit, and prefers the bride to bring a transistor radio and cash rather than embroideries as her dowry.[16]

As India moves forward into a modern economy with emphasis on women education, its inspired tradition of folk embroidery is under threat. The Crafts Council of India has initiated training projects, thus reviving old traditional embroidery of Indian craftsman. After the economic reforms of 1991, there has been an economic boom in the country. Fashion designing and luxurious purchases are now the symbols of prosperity.

Fashion industry is getting corporatised as big houses are getting large orders from abroad after "Indian Fashion Weeks" are organised in the Capital. According to Sangeeta Singh and Samyukta Bhowmick, the weights of fashion can be summed up as follows: (i) The organised market for designer apparel is over Rs. 250 crore. (ii) The global market for designer wear is five per cent of the total apparel market. (iii) The global market for designer wear industry is largely dependent on the small-scale sector and in unorganised informal sector of home-based workers. (iv) Consumers for designer wear have an annual household income of Rs. 10 Lakh plus. There are three Lakh such households growing at 40-45 per cent. (v) Designer wear industry is expected to grow to Rs. 1000 crore by 2015. (vi) More than 81 per cent of the population is below 45 years, who is the fashion-conscious. The fashion industry is now becoming a part of retail. The size of the shopping middle class are estimated to the tune or 30 crore. Over 2.2 crore people form the super-rich class who want to be always well-dressed with latest fashion design items. Embroidery work, *Zari* work and other types are therefore likely to get a new market and future with corporatisation of garment and fashion industry. NOIDA, Ghaziabad and Gurgaon are going to be hub of these retails.

Indian Embroidery is again in great demand and big malls are exhibiting many embroidered clothes and house decoratives, and the affluent neo-rich are purchasing them. Thus, there is a revival of embroidery work. Kutir, for example is taking the Indian embroidery industry to new levels but not at the expense of ethnicity or culture. At the heart of the fashion designer, it is the interest of the Indian craftsman. There are 50,000 creative and inspiring embroidery designs now available on web-site. Most well to do women of Delhi recognise tiny boutique (*Kutir*) in South Delhi for its fresh style, unique embroidery at affordable prices and utterly

Indian originally creative work. In big Indian hotels of major cities, boutiques are offering embroidery items. Products and information about embroidery is now available in Bay and patronised by the Ministry of Tourism, Govt. of India. Kantha of Bengal, Zardozi of Delhi, Kasuti of Karnataka, Phulkari of Punjab, the gold thread embroidery and gota work of Rajasthan, the *zari* work of Hyderabad are now recognised as some of the brilliant specimen of Indian embroidery and are in great demand by the affluent group of Indians and NRIs.[17]

Women's contribution in terms of economic contribution to family resources is not given due status in society. Many husbands say my wife does not work, she stays at home. Dr. Amrita Pritham, a known Punjabi poetess expressed her views on Women's Day celebrations as under:

- My wife does not work says husband.
- Who does the cooking, the cleaning and the washing?
- Who fetches water, looks after children, nurses the sick?
- Whose work provides the daily energy for a man to earn a wage, for children to go to school?
- Whose labour unseen, unheard and unrecognised?

In was only on Women's Year (1975) that government recognised the economic contribution of women to the family, society and the nation. In India particularly in Northern India, embroidery is an art passed by generations to generations and it is a creative work which can also be made a part of economic resource. The present study aims at analysing the embroidery sector in National Capital Region of Delhi. Delhi became a state in December 1991 with an area of 1,483 sq. km with Capital at New Delhi. The total population of Delhi is 13,850,507 with 7,607,344 males and 6,243,273 female. The urban population is 93.01 per cent and density of population is 9340. The number of SC is 2343000 (16.92 per cent) with negligible ST population. Delhi has nine districts, 158 villages and 62 small townships. In the last decade the direction of economic change has been vastly more affected by private capital flows, privatisation and pressure to adopt open markets and export-oriented growth. Cuts in social spending have increased the burden of women's labour. Inequalities are increasing; and the number of persons living in poverty, a category disproportionately occupied by women and children has been growing.

Embroidery workers form part of the home workers and the informal sector. The informal sector covers workers who work part-time in their own homes and can be categorised as household sector. Household sectors are contributing to the national economy and are sources of income to the families but they are not separate legal entities and need not maintain complete set of accounts (including balance sheets of assets and liabilities). The informalisation of non-agricultural labour force in developing countries are characterised by feminisation.[18] Women make more than one half of the labour force in developing Asian Countries[19]. Women embroidery workers learn their art of embroidery from family elderly women and now there are training centres. Women, working from home save travel time and get the possibility of adding to family income while still doing their own household work. Most of the embroidery workers take up work on a sub-contractual basis. The pull factor from the informal sector in South East Asia has gradually created an expansion of household workers doing creative embroidery work and adding to their family income from per piece payment system.

Most of the embroidery workers are migrant labourers, who belong to Dalit sections of the society or Muslim community, who have migrated to Delhi in search of better wages and better opportunities for making a living. The poor migrant people generally live in urban slums of Delhi. The total population in urban slums of Delhi, according to Census of India 2001 was 2,025,890 which constitute 18.45 per cent of slum population and they are reported to have 56.46 per cent literacy rate. Urban Delhi alone contains 11.2 per cent slum dweller. The majority of slum dwellers earn their livelihood from informal sector activities located either within or outside slum areas and many informal sector entrepreneurs whose operations are located within the slums have also clientele extending to the rest of the city. Most slum dwellers are in low-paying occupations, such as informal jobs in the garment industry.[20]

The Researcher visited the ladies from Kutch, Bhuj (Gujarat) who sell mirror work and Kutch work in Janpath. They are selling their embroidery pieces for the last 35 years. They have been given cubicles of 6 × 4 feet on Janpath where they display such colourful sheets, cushions, bags and wall hangings with beautiful and most attractive patterns. It is done by women folk in the interiors of Kutch and Bhuj. These women folk of Gujarat become intermediaries and the sellers. Those who have connections/resources are doing well. They are able to get stalls in Delhi Haat (market) and Suraj Kund exhibition-cum-mela ground. There are 10 families here. Six have Kholis while others use the footpath. Each seller has 50 people behind her to do the embroidery work. However, since embroidery is a part of informal unorganised sector, they are not able to get good price for their products. Big business houses and their agents now directly reach their villages and order for exports. There is hardly any voice of these women folk of Gujarat, who sell their products for very low and inadequate price. Now, in Delhi there are more than 130 embroidery garments houses who get embroidered pieces directly from the village women through their intermediaries and agents. Many fashion designers have their website and launch their own creations through them.

Urban slum dwellers which include embroidery workers share common problems such as living in cramped, over-crowded and unsanitary conditions, face poor access to jobs and training, irregularity of wages/labour, highly dependent on public bodies to provide water, health-care, solid waste, hygienic sanitation system, violence against women, youth under employment/unemployment, alcoholism drug abuse and mal-nutrition. These slum dwellers suffer multi-dimensional problems like environmental complications.[21] According to 2001 census, Delhi's population is 1.378 crore. At present half of this population lives in sub-standard areas which have features similar to slums. These include 14 lakh people living in unauthorised colonies, about 13 lakh in JJ Clusters, about 12 lakh in resettled colonies, about 1.5 lakh in rural areas.[22] The majority of new migrants from different states arrive on continuous basis as a constant flow exerts a tremendous pressure. In addition to the shelter problems, high pollution, unsanitary conditions, inadequate health, educations and recreational facilities are complicating the urban life in the Capital city of India.[23] According to the National Institute of Communicable Diseases, about 50 per cent of the water supplied to 92,933 clusters is not potable or fit for drinking purpose.[24]

Poor sanitary conditions, the most common problem for all slum dwellers in Delhi. Delhi has a number of agri-enterprises, non-agri-enterprises and enterprises without premises which includes informal sectors like embroidery. District-wise number of enterprises with selected principal characteristics under 5th Economic Consensus 2005 is shown in Table 1 as follows:

Table 1: Enterprises in Delhi

Name of Districts	*Agri-enterprises*	*Non-agri-enterprises*	*Without premises*
1. North West	792	129842	21806
2. North	338	79322	5928
3. North East	707	89970	15929
4. East	1454	90702	11142
5. New Delhi	53	12991	344
6. Central	72	77538	4017
7. West	246	100724	16106
8. South West	1146	61129	7488
9. South	520	106249	13478
Total	5328	748467	96238

Source: 5th Economic Census of Delhi – Directorate of Economics and Statistics (2005).

Globalisation has brought about greater feminisation of the labour force. An estimated 12.39 crore women work in the unorganised informal sector. The female work participation rate is reported to have increased from 19.7 per cent in 1981 to 25.7 per cent in 2000. In Delhi living conditions of women embroidery workers are the most deplorable.

Kalyanpuri, Himmatpuri, Khichripur colonies have deplorable hygienic conditions and acute scarcity of water. The residents of these slum colonies are predominantly economically weaker sections migrants from the Scheduled Castes (SCs) with little education and no education. About 25 parks have already been encroached by *jhuggis*.[25] The majority of squatters living in Sanjay Camp (Trilokpuri) and Ambedkar Camp (Himmatpuri) are Muslims while in the Indira camp (Kalyanpuri) the people are predominantly from other Hindu Backward Castes. According to a sample study, two thirds of the squatters are illiterate. Less than one-tenth have education upto higher secondary level. Most of the squatter children are born at home attended either by *dais* or female relatives.

Muslim and Dalit embroidery workers are generally poor. Poverty has four dimensions viz., social equity, economic prosperity, ecological security and responsible and responsive governance.[26] Poverty is associated with poor resources, large expenses on poor quality health-care, social functions associated with death and marriage and high interest loans taken from private sources to meet unaffordable and crippling expenses. Generally, low caste status and daily wage labourer who live in unorganised sector are associated with long-term poverty. Strategy for poverty reduction articulated by the World Development Report 2000-2001, focusses on promoting opportunities, facilitating empowerment and enhancing security opportunity promotion involves making markets work for poor people, and build their assets by encouraging effective private investment, expansion into international markets, and addressing asset inequalities across gender, ethnic, racial and social divides and getting infrastructure and knowledge into poor areas. Empowerment involves laying the political legal basis for more inclusive development, creation of public administration that promote growth and equity, promoting inclusive decentralisation and community development and gender equity, besides tackling social barriers and supporting poor people's social capital. The security dimension involves formulating an approach to help poor people manage risk, developing national programmes to prevent, prepare for, and respond to financial and cultural shocks, designing national systems of social risk management which are also pro-growth and addressing civil conflicts.[27] In spite of all theoretical formulations, poverty reduction remains a most difficult challenge for India. What is required is to make a dent on poverty is to provide proper health-care, information about markets and connections with the world outside, besides provision of credit on affordable terms.[28]

Many women embroiderers of Delhi do not earn even Rs. 17 daily. Literacy rate of Indian women is alarmingly low, due to sex linked inequality and heavy physical work under unpleasant and harsh working conditions. Women comprise nearly 70 per cent of the total population, living below the poverty line. Table showing trends in combined poverty in Delhi.

Table 2: Number of persons living below poverty line in Delhi.

	Persons in lakhs	*Percentage*
1983	18.39	26.22
1993-94	15.51	14.69
1999-2000	11.49	8.23

(*Source:* Planning Commission, Govt. of India).

However, ICT can be of great help if the embroidery workers of Delhi come together and form an association to take the benefits of various poverty eradication programmes. In order to link poor urban/rural producers with international markets, the International Trade Centre (ITC) of the UNCTAD/WTO has launched an Export-led Poverty Reduction Programme (EPRP) aimed at empowering poor people to genrate higher income by establishing links between market-oriented production and overseas buyers.[29]

This programme is based on 10 building blocks of analysis, operations, support environment, and social concerns which include identifying products and markets, identifying producers and matching products, market and producers under analysis, developing the products and human resources under operations, providing micro-finance and other support services under support environment and finally incorporating gender and environment as important social concerns.[30] Important lessons from poverty alleviation programmes in South Asia include treating poverty in a comprehensive way by incorporating health-care, education and nutrition, giving adequate attention to the preservation and enhancement of natural resources and environmental hygiene to make poverty eradication programme sustainable and appropriate targeting of programme. [31]

Kutir is well recognised not only in Delhi but almost all over the world for its fresh style, unique embroidery, affordable prices and utterly Indian original products. What began for Mamta Kheror as a thesis project on Kanjeevaram fabric is hitting the fashion world as *Kutir*, the epitome of elegance and ethnicity in Indian wear for women. *Kutir* is now getting orders from abroad—Vancouver, London, New York and Middle East. *Kutir* is a boutique in South Delhi, where you can meet Mamta and can be immediately comforted by her warm presence and sincerity. He has to its credit 50,000 creative and inspiring embroidery designs both hand-made and machinery made designs. *Kutir* was established in 1985 with the idea that designer wear should be accessible to every Indian and a very real desire to keep the age-old culture and traditions alive by supporting the authenticity of local Indian craftsman. The literal meaning of *Kutir* is home and it has been a welcome home for many unemployed women in the lower strata of society, who find Mamta as a guide, mentor and employer. Kutir's most popular clientele are the Indian working women and women executives. At present Mamta employs about 100 women and men with the aim to provide them opportunity to earn livelihood with a sense of self-respect and pride as crafts persons currently, Kutir workers are primarily embroiderers. It is necessary to work (embroidery workers) under some NGO like SEWA in order to build people's trust, bring in more transparency for local monitoring and control, go for projects of longer duration and involving groups and NGOs. Poverty itself becomes a barrier to economic growth in terms of limited markets for the private sector products and services like embroidery work. There is need to explore alternative market outlets for embroidery. Cooperatives can be made to procure raw material requirements for embroidery work. There are already instances of cooperative and corporate alignment in procurement and processing in India. Another important role it can play is in the field of provisions of market information for the producers through the use of information technology for which it has resources and capacity.[32]

Sharan (Society for Serving the Urban Poor) was established in 1979. It is a progressive working organisation operating in slums and resettlement colonies of New Delhi. It has evolved a sustainable and participatory programme to help women become financially self-sufficient. Loans over $150,000 have been disbursed with a complete return rate. These loans are utilised for income generating activities such as woolen cardigans, embroidery, bindi-making etc. Sharan promotes over 80 small thrift groups comprising 15 to 20 members and has disbursed over 100,000 over the last 15 years.

Role of ICT

ICT can play a very decisive role in empowerment of embroidery workers. The knowledge about various dimensions of empowerment is generally imparted through T.V., education or internet which generally include the following:

(i) Economic Empowerment;
(ii) Social Empowerment;
(iii) Political Empowerment;
(iv) Empowerment through education;
(v) Empowerment through preservation of indigenous knowledge traditions;
(vi) Empowerment through values, new consciousness about democracy, right to vote, fundamental rights and national policy for women empowerment.

The use of ICT becomes very useful for attainment of the ultimate goal of women's empowerment. Access to information is the key for economic social and political empowerment of women.[33] Empowerment is basically exercising control over ones' lives. This has two aspects. The first is control over resources (financial, physical and human). The second is control over ideology (beliefs, values and attitudes. Empowerment starts with changes in consciousness and in self-perception.[34] According to Karen Oppenheim Mason, women's empowerment in the domestic sphere is mainly a property of social and cultural systems rather than individual traits and preferences. In the context of domestic empowerment, the variations across communities are due to variations in community values and norms about gender roles.

Micro-credit self-help group and cooperative credit societies can help empowerment of women. ICT has its role to play in bringing gender awareness of cooperative leaders, prepare women for leadership role and promote women's groups to organise themselves through cooperative credit societies. Gangamma is an illiterate Indian woman of Scheduled Caste and used to make beautiful embroidery pieces, getting Rs. 10 per piece which took her two or three days to embroider. Her entire family was bonded to Dhannamal because she once borrowed Rs. 1000 from Dhannamal for treatment of her husband and she was not able to repay the loan and its interest. Later she took a loan from the Seva Mahila Cooperative bank to pay off her debt of Dhannamal. This is an example of empowerment of the poor by timely assistance of cooperative credit society. If women's potential is fully utilised, women empowerment will gradually emerge and alleviate the poverty of the women folk.

Using IT, women can have access to government information such as rules and regulations, provisions available for women, policies, administrative and on-line services. For example, in the case of Gyandoot Project (Dhar, M.P.) through *Soochanalayas* (Information Kiosks) women can send their complaints with assurance of reply within a maximum period of seven days. Once educated and empowered, women can send complaints regarding drinking water, functioning of school, public distributions system, beneficiary-oriented schemes and expect a reply within seven days. Information technology can be used in codification and dissemination of women's indigenous knowledge of local medicines used for ages by mothers and administered to their children.

IT can also be effectively exploited for technological empowerment, improving health, nutrition, reproductive health, maternity and child care etc. Women's use of IT can abolish their geographical, social and cultural isolation and enable them to become well informed citizens and empowered members of the society.

The following four recommendations have been made for empowerment of embroidery women:[35]

1. Make education, formal and informed a priority in particular for the development of ICT and take measures to promote girls' education so as to enable girls and women's access to ICT;
2. Take concrete steps to increase the number of female students at all educational levels in Media and ICT-related subjects, including in science, mathematics and technology including through methods such as distance and *e*-learning;
3. Establish or where they already exist, expand skill training, vocational and employment training and capacity building programmes for women and girls and women's non-governmental organisations on the use, design and production of ICT;
4. Enable equal access for women to ICT based economic activities, such as small business and home-based employment, to information systems and improved technologies and to new employment opportunities in this area and consider developing telecentres, information centers, community access points and business incubators;

The common wealth of learning has found that women in Asia used distance education to:

1. Improve income generation;
2. Find a career that would enable them to support their families and send their children to university;
3. Improve work performance;
4. Increase self-confidence;
5. Develop interest in learning new things;
6. Most had to overcome strong opposition from family members which often dissipated when the benefits to the family as a whole were demonstrated;
7. Women enthusiastically and successfully take advantage of *e*-learning opportunities;
8. ICT can be a very positive educational approach for women for both formal and informal education.

Plan of Action suggested by the World Summit on Information Society:

(i) Work on removing the gender barriers to ICT education and training and promoting equal training opportunities in ICT related fields for women and girls;

(ii) Promote teleworking to allow citizens, particularly in the developing countries, LDCs and small economies, to live in their societies to increase employment opportunities for women;

(iii) Target young girls to increase the number of women in ICT career;

(iv) Encourage *e*-learning opportunities;

(v) Encourage distance learning with the help of radio, TV, internet, CD-ROM, audio and video cassettes;

(vi) Women can avail flexibility of time and appreciate the use of computer conferencing with course directors;

(vii) IT sector should ensure that women receive opportunities to gain flexible skills for complex and specialised jobs;

(viii) Embroidery workers can be greatly benefitted if women bring embroidery designs and pattern to the ICT centre for getting them standardised using computerised scanners and digital cameras;

(ix) Women should get micro-credit to acquire GSM cellular phones and resell telephone calls and phone services within their locality or villages; Recently, Union Minister, P. Chidambuaram, launched the UTI Mutual Fund's "micro-pension scheme for the unorganised informal sector women workers. He said "Micro-pension is a very laudable step."[36] He noted that micro-pension scheme would ensure financial protection to the women of the informal, unorganised sector. He said workers in the unorganised sector accounted for 20 per cent more than those employed in the organised sector in the country. Among the workers of unorganised sector a vast majority of them were women. Embroidery women workers should take advantage of this Micro-pension scheme. In India UTI Mutual Fund intends to bring 30 crore low-income group workers under its Micro-pension arrangement as this segment constitutes almost 90 per cent of the country's workforce and is not covered under any pension or Provident Fund Scheme. This is part of the UTI AMCs strategy to promote "inclusive growth in the country".

A Case Study of the Self-employed Women Associations (SEWA)

SEWA literally means "service". There is a book written by Daniel W. Crowell titled "*The Sewa Movement and Rural Development*", which given detailed account of the origin, development and various activities of this non-government organisation. Kalima Rose has written a full chapter "*SEWA-Movement*" which elaborately cover the various details of SEWA. It is a women's support network of unions, cooperatives, bank, services which increases employment options and raises wages, besided bringing a sense of unity and strength. Briefly, its various activities can be categorised into five parts:

1. Unions – It has trade groups of garment tailors, bidi-rollers, head loaders, and cart-pullers, used garment dealers, vendors, domestic workers, Income workers, scrap collectors, construction workers, Papad wafer rollers, carpenters, smiths, agricultural labourers, tobacco processors, fuel traders, embroidery workers etc. Unions help in getting formulated policy support, protective legislation, implementation and enforcement and social security.

It provides help in court cases, issuing identity cards, negotiations, group rallies lobbying, protests and establishing employer employee nexus.

2. Cooperatives – These take care of vendor cooperatives, kerosene vendors, vegetable suppliers, fish vendors and artisan cooperatives of weavers, bamboo workers, block printers, patch workers, embroiderers. It also takes care of service cooperatives of child care providers, industrial cleaners, waste paper collectors, community health workers. Cooperatives help them in various other activities like marketing, raw material skills and management, training and contacts with others.

3. Bank – This branch takes care of savings, credits, life insurance, mortgaging and asset titles. This is a great help to the workers in times of emergencies.

4. Services – Video *seva* is a great achievement and is often utilised by unions and cooperatives for proper projection of their achievements and future programmes. Other services include child-care, training, communication, legal-aid, community health service sewa polytechnique, maternity protection scheme.

The SEWA successfully integrates a complex myriad of lives, occupations and issues into a union and provides women guidance and security against incredible odds of vulnerability, invisibility and poverty. SEWA grew, organically, slowly absorbing more and more trade, rooting itself in the reality of poor working women. Experience of SEWA shows that women's empowerment has to be linked up with the struggle of other marginalised group, if it is to be sustainable.[37] SEWA aims to (i) protect the interest of women workers; (ii) encourage their participation at all levels of organisation; (iii) initiate action to change policies and laws in India.

The SEWA movement, started in Ahmedabad in 1972 by Ela Bhatt has now taken an all India character. SEWA organises women who work in their homes, in the streets of the cities, in the fields and villages of rural India, with no fixed employer caring for their small riches in the economy, day by day with only their wits to guide them against incredible odds of vulnerability, invisibility and poverty."[38] SEWA has a large following of Muslim and Dalit movements in its fold and has been expanding its area of operations to new places. SEWA in India was instrumental in gaining recognition by the ILO and Indian Government for home women workers. Yet all of these women workers need protection and as more women in the north were beginning to work at home with computers, home-based work took on a different connotation, SEWA helped organise Home Net International, a network of group supporting home-based work. Together, these women convinced the trade unionists that organising women in their communities, as SEWA and other development organisations do, provides an alternative to the way traditional unions organise women workers.[39] The 1996 convention recognises that home workers can be independent or produce for an employer. Governments, who ratify it are expected to pass laws that treat home workers the same as other wage earners.[40] SEWA has become firmly rooted all over the country where its work has begun to make inroads, some common pictures of how women are dealing with their problems emerge. First, women are better fighters than men of the day-to-day poverty which paces them, by exercising incredible ingenuity in making ends mat. Second, women spend almost all their earnings on food, clothing and shelter. Third, women want their children's lives to be better than their own, and make sacrifices in order to ensure that they reveal an exceptional ecological consciousness. They have the ability to be flexible to combine domestic work and income-earning activities and to shift occupational skills as the season or market demands.[41] SEWA, Delhi was started in 1999 in Jahangirpuri and has now expanded the operations to include Raghuvir Nagar, Sunder Nagri, Rajiv Nagar and Anand Vihar areas. It has membership of 13570. The membership profile is as under:

1.	Nand Nagri	–	2574
2.	Raghuvir Nagar	–	7189
3.	Jahangir Puri	–	992
4.	Rajiv Nagar	-	1556
5.	Anand Vihar	-	989
6.	Book Bazar	–	270
	Total:		13,570

SEWA Delhi is registered under Delhi Trust Act. It has following main activities:

(i) Organising women members;

(ii) Development activities like micro-finance and micro-insurance;

(iii) Employment generation activities are promoted like embroidery work.

(iv) Working with the Government Department to ensure successful delivery of services and Government Schemes to households in operational areas.

(v) Conducting non-formal education.

SEWA, Delhi Cooperatives have 541 women members. Sewa Delhi workers are informed about Pension Scheme of Delhi for senior women citizens/old age women at the rate of Rs. 350 per month. Embroidery centre of Delhi, SEWA has been established in Sunder Nagri in October 2005. It has established linkages with six export houses. SEWA, Delhi can be contracted at the following address:

Delhi SEWA Centre
7/5 First Floor, South Patel Nagar,
Delhi—110 008.
Ph.: 011-25840937/25841369/45009369.

A Case Study of Hasinaben – A Muslim Women

Hasinaben is today the master craftswoman. Hasinaben comes from an illiterate family of traditional block – printers of Gujarat. Earlier, she used to work at home but the earnings were not sufficient. After coming in touch with SEWA (Self Employed Women's Association) a trade union registered in 1972, and founded by Smt Elaben Bhatt, in spite of opposition by her-in-laws, she joined Sewa at Abodana Mandali and was trained as master-craftswomen. Besides block printing, embroidery, stitching, puppet-making and other handicrafts making skills are taught to Mandali Members in accordance with their aptitude. SEWA helped Hasinaben and other Mandali members to open a saving bank account and purchase insurance policies from SEWA itself. Over the years, Hasinaben began to earn well and the opposition from her in-laws ceased. She has now become an expert master-craftswoman with block printing and began to make her own dyes. Thanks to SEWA, she got an opportunity to go abroad to display her skills. Now, she is the master craftswoman for Abodana Mandali Cooperative and if someone visits the Abodana to see how women do different kinds of work – embroidery, designing, stitching, dyeing and block printing, one is always greeted by Hasinaben. She now goes to big cities like Delhi, Chennai, Bangalore and other capitals to exhibit and sell the products of Abodana Mandali under the banner of SEWA. Hasina is today an empowered, confident and self-sufficient women who is able to send her children to school.

The Indian tradition has always idolised the woman as a source of *Shakti*, Inherent Power. It is only a matter of time before tools like ICT help the women, whether Muslim, Dalit or any other, to rediscover their potential. In the times to come, we will see the re-emergence of women as valuable members of society that compelled them to rediscover their inherent strength and become empowered.

The communication initiative network brought communication and media to the centre for social and economic development. Datamation foundation undertook a project of "putting ICT in the hands of women of Kanpur and Chiken Embroidery workers of Lucknow". They established the centres in several poor communities in Lucknow/Kanpur area. Extensive outreach and strategic partnerships were made with local opinion leaders to target women in informal sector and involved in the informal sector and significant proportion of Muslim women.

Centre provided training in the target skill areas:

1. Computer skills,
2. Handicraft skills,
3. Health knowledge.

The project aimed to address three key questions:

(1) Can ICT improve the capacity of women engaged in informal sector to increase their income and enter the formal sector to generate sustainable livelihood?

(2) Can ICT improve capacity of women engaged in handwork trades as Chiken embroidery to increase their income?

(3) Can ICT improve capacity of chiken workers to engage in alternative sources of livelihood given over saturation in chiken industry and the associated returns.

Field observation suggests that this project tuned out to be a watershed in the following ways:

1. The projects success created new opportunities to move beyond the original objective and provide a very powerful and innovative model for creating a significant shift in the market potential of chiken workers.
2. The project requires technical assistance in the form of industry specific international marketing expertise.

Project evaluators used several instruments to obtain quantitative and qualitative evaluation monitoring and evaluation data (M and E). Education development centre use an abbreviated Critical Success Factor (CSF) method to address the applied research question which appeared to work effectively.

1. This project attracted women from both Muslim and Hindu community.
2. In case of Muslim women, the obstacles are many and level of participation and response to an ICT centre provided a valuable model for other activities directed towards these women as their communities severely restricts their physical movement and revenue generating opportunities. As the numbers coming to such centres grow there is greater self-confidence among these women who inspire and encourage others to enable them to achieve sustainable livelihood.
3. Initially they depend on the project staff for additional support in developing management skills so as to become self-sufficient in conducting their business activities.
4. Women in chiken industry faced over production and declining demands so they needed to explore new markets through SEWA, FABINDIA, Khadi Gramudyog and other such programes.
5. Project worked with IIT to develop software with an engraver which enables workers to develop low cost moulds, so that women can create more modern patterns quickly and tailor them. IIT software developed for project could help women

enter key market areas that require fast turn around and design modifications.

6. In order to maximise benefits of this project, industry specific international expertise *waqf* enabled that would establish specific links with international buyers and formulate formal well-devised sustainable business plans.

Such a project can be a powerful and innovative model for creating significant shift in market patented of Chiken workers.

References

1. Zukav, G., *The Dancing Wuli Masters* : Fontana Collins, Glasgow, 1979.
2. Rosemary Crill, *Indian Embroidery,* V and A Publications, London-1999. p. 7.
3. Abul Fazl Allami, *The A'in'i' Akbari* tr. H. Blochmann 1873 (3rd edition, New Delhi 1977) A'in 31, pp. 93-6.
4. E. Bernier, *Trends in the Mughal Empire AD 1656-1668* ed. A constable London 1891. p. 259.
5. Rosemary Crill, *Indian Embroidery,* Vand A Publications London 199. p. 7
6. A Hamilton, *A New Account of East Indies*, Volume 2, Edinburgh ,1727, rpr. 1930, Vol I p. 86.
7. India Office Library, Court Book IV, F 135 quoted in Irwin and Hall, 1973 – p. 35.
8. K. Riboud (ed*.). In Quest of Themes and Skills*, Textiles, Bombay, 1989 pp. 2-3.
9. Rosemary Crill, *Indian Embroidery*, 10 Plate on p. 32–C. 1860.
10. Swarn Khandpur, *tell me more about India*, India Book House Ltd., Mumbai, 2000. p. 55.
11. Paine Sheila, *Embroidery from India and Pakistan*, The British Museum Press, London, 2001.
12. Sheila Paine, *Embroidery from India and Pakistan*, The British Museum Press, London., 2001, p. 14.
13. *Indian Embriodery, Arts and Crafts – The soul of India* http/www/ culturapedia.com/craftsembroidery/htm pp. 1-4.
14. Nilima Roy, *Art of Manipur*, New Delhi, 1997, p. 29.
15. Sheila Paine, *Embroidery from India and Pakistan*, The British Museum Press, London, 2001 p. 9.
16. *Ibid.* pp. 19-20.
17. Ref. http/www.culturopedia.com/crafts/embroidery/html – Arts and Crafts of India.

18. Charmes J., *Informal Sector, Poverty and Gender – A Review of Empirical Evidence*, Background Paper for the World Development Report 2001. St. Auentin en Yvelmes – University of Versaities.

19. Gammage R. and Mehra S., *Trends, Counter-trends and Gaps in Women's Employment* – World Development, 1999, Vol. 27. No. 23. UNICEF – Florence Italy – Working Paper 97.

20. Sabir Ali, *Globalisation and the Urban Poor in Sociology of Globalisation – Perspectives from India,* Edited by Sakarama Somayaji and Ganesha Somayaji. Rawat Publications Jaipur, p. 289.

21. Sabir Ali, *Environmental Situation of Slumms in India*, Uppal Publishing House, New Delhi, 2003..

22. Bartr K.G , *Squatter Resettlement Programme,* Department of Housing, SPA, 1992.

23. Sabir Ali, *Slums within Slums*, Vikas Publication, New Delhi, 1991..

24. Sabir Ali, *Evaluation of Environmental Schemes with Particular Reference to Low Cost Sanitation Programme in Slums and Resettlement Colonies of Delhi*, Council for Social Development, 1996.

25. Sabir Ali, *Major Problems of Delhi Slums: New Delhi*, Uppal Publishing House.1998, p. 6.

26. Cousart E.A., *Poverty Alleviation in the Phillipines: The Social Reform Agenda and Role of the Private Sector*, Regional Development Dialogue 20(1), 1999, Spring 79-95.

27. World Bank, *World Development Report 2000-2001 – Attacking Poverty*, OUP, London, 2001.

28. Jaya Raman, R and Lanjou W.P. , The Evolution of Poverty and Inequality in Indian Villages, *The World Bank Research Observer*, 14(1) Februay, 1999, pp. 1-30

29. Sukhpal Singh – *Reaching the Poor Under Globalisation and Structural Adjustment Regions in India – The Institutional Dimension in Sociology of Globalisation – Perspectives from India* , 2006, edtited by S. Somayaji and G. Somayaji, p. 228.

30. ITC (International Trade Centre), *Export-led Poverty Reduction Programme: Linking Poor Producers to International. Markets*, 2002, http:/www/intracen.org/eprp.

31. Vyas, V.S., Poverty Alleviation and Nutritional Enhancement in South Asia: The Missing Links, *Asian Journal of Agricultural Economics* 2(2), 1997, Pp 101-108.

32. Sukhpal Singh, Globalisation and Structural Adjustment Required in India – in *Sociology of Globalisation – Perspectives from India*, Edited by Sakarama Somayaji and Gandsha Somayaji – 2006, p. 230.

33. Shaik, N. Meera and Rao, D.V.M., IT for Empowerment of Women, in the book *Information Technology and Management*, 2002, p. 110.

34. Dubhashi, Medha, Empowerment of Women through cooperatives, *The Administrator*, Lal Bahdur Shastri National Academy of Administrators, Mussoorie, December 2001, Vol. XLIV No. 2, p. 120.
35. Sophia Hyer, New Technologies Creating New Opportunities for Women – An International Perspective, *Women in Global Science and Technology*, March 7, 2005.
36. Mistry Khurshid, *Micro Pension Schem*, Swift Post, July-Septemebr 2008, Vol. III, Issue 3, p. 17.
37. Naila Kabeer, *Reversed Realities – Kali for Women*, New Delhi.
38. Kalima Rose, *SEWA: Women in Movement in the Women, Gender and Development Reader,* edited by Nalini Visvanathan, Lyin Duggan, Laurie Nisonoff, Van Wiegessma p. 1997.
39. Irene Tinker, Empowerment Just Happened : The unexpected Expansion of Women's Organisations in *Women and Gender Equity in Development Theory and Practice – Institutions, Resources and Mobilisation*, Kuke University Press. Durban and London 2006. p. 289.
40. Prugl, Elizabeth, The Global Construction of Gender : Home based work in the Political Economy in the 20th Century, 1999, Also Prugl, Elizabeth and Irene Tinker, Micro-entrepreneurs and Home Workers : Convergence Categories – *World Development* 25 (9), 1997, 1471-82.
41. Kalima Rose, *SEWA: Women in Movement in The Women, Gender and Development Reader,* edited by Nalini Visvanathsan.

7

The Embroidery Sector in NCR: Overview and Recommendations

> "I do not want my house to be walled on all sides and my windows to be stuffed. I want the culture of all the lands to be blown about my house as freely as possible. But I refuse to be blown off my feet by any." *–Mahatma Gandhi*

> "Do not ask the Iron Smith how the iron tastes, ask the horse who holds the bit in his mouth." *–Dhoomil*

The technology driven new information order is dominated by social monopolies therefore it is not representative of the views and perspectives of large social groups. Women though they are 48 per cent of population are marginalised including Dalit women whose members are nowhere clearly found in any census. The 2001 census showed the number of Muslim to be 13.4 of the population i.e., 138 million out of the total of 1029 million.

Therefore, there is an apparent need to eliminate the imbalances and inequities faced by Muslim and Dalit women. It will come from respect for each others cultural identity and right of these marginalised groups to participate to exchange ideas, information and communication process. With the onset of information revolution there is growing marginalisation of 'knowledge poor' due to increasing imbalances in access to information technology. This adversely affects the life and future of Muslim and Dalit women, who have to be included in the global information order. We have to correct the present imbalances and lack of pluralism in information centres, content and sources of information.

If ICT is a gender neutral medium, then it should be harnessed to provide equal opportunity for everyone. But it seems to have created new poverty lines of both haves and have nots. Instead of being a democratic medium to provide level playing field, it has led to limiting the information to smaller spaces of privileged few, thereby creating social monopolies. Diffusion of information gets limited by income, infrastructure institution and skills.[1] Therefore, if an embroidery worker learns computer, she can improve her income, acquire new skills as well as become a part of a cooperative or export group. Her life will undergo a betterment thereby empowering here in many ways. Empowerment is the beginning of liberation, formulation and realisation of human potential. In case of Muslim and Dalit women, it is a process of becoming aware of suppression, exploitation and victimisation. Only then the sense of personal dignity, self respect and self-esteem will dawn for improvement in their quality of life. This awareness will instill change in attitude and enable them to become equal partners in community development.

Social movements around the world have used the internet to build support for their cause. Women's issues have also been flagged through *e*-mail petitions networking and women's dedicated portals and websites e.g. womenasia.com, sitagita.com. a profile of netizens indicates 66 per cent are working 75 per cent are over the age of 25, 42 per cent have purchasing power, 87 per cent use internet to download information and 98 per cent use it for *e*-mails though not many Muslim women are among them.[2] The World Conference at Beijing heralds the era of online activism thereby creating space for women's political activity and opportunity. Most Muslim and Dalit women acknowledge never visiting cyber café and feeling inadequate and helpless in technology-savvy internet driven world. But they would like their daughters to be learning computer since it will bring them a better job with a well-paid and comfortable future. It is important to explore social and cultural dynamics which enable women to take over intellectual resources and material assets so as to place their experiences, needs and requirements in the forefront. They can put their concerns on the net and explore distinctive potential of women organising themselves to find solutions of their problems of exclusion and marginalisation. By networking and joining together for their education, employment and empowerment, life of the Muslim and Dalit women can change. Different encounters can bring relevant, context specific and gender-sensitive participatory and pluralistic process to address their fundamental human needs. Vocational, technical and long distance education are effective for women as it builds skills enhances possibilities of opportunities in work market.

A survey done by Ranjana Agarwal on 252 respondents working in different IT companies in Jamshedpur and Delhi in 1999, showed access of IT limited to upper caste and higher class of people having command on English. Muslim women were 1.6 per cent while eight per cent OBC were there and while no SC and ST were present all belonged to younger age group. Fewer women reached higher grades when compared to men.[3]

A basic problem which holds true for women in general in the case study of embroidery workers mainly from Muslim and minority groups in particular is their invisibility which leaves them unaccounted, unattended and inaccessible literally and figuratively. The battle against invisibility of women's work has began as the government of India has made it, amply, the focus of interest with its national policy on women and all pervasive drive towards their development and thereby empowerment. Systematic information about women's activity at home and outside would enable estimation of welfare levels and intensification of structural adjustment policies and programmes to bring ICT to their doorstep, thereby opening new vistas of progress.

The research work titled "Information and Communication Technology (ICT) and Women Empowerment: A study of Embroidery Sector in the National Capital Region (NCR) with special reference to Dalits and Muslim women – 2000-2005 (Chapter 6) has been carried out as a part of Ph.D. programme from Dr. K.R. Narayanan Centre for Dalit and Minorities Studies, University of Jamia Millia Islamia, New Delhi, under the supervision of Professor M. Mujtaba Khan. The research thesis contains total seven chapters. The first chapter briefly introduces the concepts of Information and Communication Technology (ICT), women empowerment, the embroidery sector and their inter-relationship. It presents a picture of glaring inequalities – social, economic and political that consistently defines and circumscribes women's lives in India. Trends in overall economic development and social well-being reveal that amidst all the cultural diversity, economic reforms and political awakening that has taken place in the country, women continue to suffer from gender inequalities, exploitation, violence and lack of adequate education. Embroidery workers from unorganised informal sector of Indian economy suffer from exploitation, low wages, difficult working conditions and poverty. Although Indian Constitution provides fundamental rights, special safeguards to minorities and special protection to Dalits, the overall condition of embroidery workers continues to be exploitative, oppressive and unjust due to poor wages and difficult working and living conditions. One of the most understudied areas in informal sector activities in developing countries is that of home-based manufacturing activities.[4] Embroidery workers as home work is undertaken largely by poor, married women with children, who could thus supplement the family income. The scarcity of good data is both a cause and consequence of this invisible status and such activities are not covered in conventional labour force survey methods.[5] This researcher has therefore undertaken this study to examine the role of ICT in empowering women with special reference to Dalits and women workers in the National Capital Region for the period 2000-2005.

Role of ICT in Empowering Embroidery Sector Women

Information and Communication Technologies (ICT) has been playing a very important role in the economic development of the country. The essence of IT is included in the dictum which states that information about any event or phenomenon taking place anywhere in the universe at any time is made available to any person anywhere at any time through communication and transport system built in by ICT. Computer Technology, Communication Technology, multi-media, animation and virtual reality technology through internet, telephone, cellular phones, T.V., radio, wireless technology are all parts of the ICT today. Cyberspace is a metamorphic, conceptual or virtual area, where files, data, images, text, motion video clips, music etc. All fly back and forth, computer to computer, user to user. Cellular cell has by now reached 16 crore hands in India and has greatly facilitated social empowerment, economic empowerment and communication empowerment. Delhi and NCR areas top all the other states in use of cellular phone. Internet is international network of computers – it is also known as world wide web (WWW) because its configuration is similar to a web woven by a spider. The total number of internet subscribers in India, by the end of June 2006 was 80 lakh. Internet has given boost to *E*-governance, *E*-commerce and *E*-finance. The ICT with computers and communication as the main ingredient has brought a new age called "the information GE". India has been doing extremely well in IT software, ITES and BPOs and has brought employment to thousands of young educated people. As evident in all works of life, information and communication technology have facilitated new dynamics across globally national and local levels. It has facilitated changes in the life of women and enabled linkages between formal and informal networks such as women NGOs and other autonomous groups as well as the organised and unorganised sector and government and the people. ICT has enabled an interactive link between the micro and macro levels. Involving women at all levels of development thinking, planning and implementation will make a world of difference not merely to women but to the capacity of society. This will envisage and carry out planned social change which will permit human kind to live in harmony with native and itself.[6] In order to bring women to the centre stage it will require drastic changes in the way societies conceive of relations between man and woman and the dismantling of countries old structures of thought and practice. Women's status is dependent on relations in the family, class and the social group to which they belong. It is inherited through historical institutions and culture-based on social relations between the genders as well as class relations.[7] ICT has enabled political mobilisation which has resulted in the emergence powerful middle and low caste groups through India. The expanding powerbase of low caste political parties, appointment of Dalit as President of India in July, 1997 signaled increasing prominence of Dalits in terms of social change. However, there was little systematic inclusion of Dalit women who remained at the periphery and continue to witness the enlarging digital divide. They continue to do menial jobs and remain unorganised invisible and voiceless even in this age of communication technology. Therefore, it is imperative to educate them and train them in computers so that they can change their lives and more so educate their daughters whose life promises to be better in these new times of ICT revolution. ICT has provided easier access to information leading to sharing of experiences and organisations which have emerged in form of Self-Help Groups or association like SEWA or non-government organisations have enabled many embroidery workers to come to the fore. At the National Master Craftsman Workshop at Delhi Haat, the researcher could meet many such master craftswomen who were felicitated and encouraged to come to the fore to sell their creations and feel proud of their achievements.

Various Dimensions of Women's Empowerment in Indian Context

Women are all not a homogeneous group; it is critical to recognise and encompass differences among them. Women are embedded in social group and marginalised in multifarious ways both as individuals and groups. The question is not just including the women in policies and programmes but of unravelling the gendered structure of patriarchal institutions that are notoriously resistant to change.[8] In a country like India, nearly 72 per cent of the Scheduled Castes and 59 per cent of the Scheduled Tribes depend upon wage labour. A person can be employed and still be poor; the issue is not of exclusion but the nature and terms of inclusion.[9] Women's right to livelihood is an economic right which cannot be bracketed separately from practical and social empowerment.[10] Economic-oriented strategies for women empowerment have been the mainstay. Of the state and organisations associated with development and capacity building of women. Access to ICT is based on social dimensions. Many societal and institutional barriers exist like *purdah*, caste prejudices and discrimination, lack of self-confidence and inferiority complex which prevents them from availing facilities like computer education, vocational training and employment opportunities that are available around them. Efforts to address issues of empowerment, if addressed only on economic dimension will overlook complex social dialectics. Organising women is seen as a successful empowerment experiment as in SEWA model which brought them together to share, articulate and assert their needs for capacity building. It enabled them to negotiate the conditions of their life within the male dominated institution of family as well as caste to reduce their sense of subordination. It involves a process of "transformation of consciousness". Reformulation of identity enables women to perceive herself as worthy entity which translates into action that challenge norms which reinforce her subordination.[11]

Embroidery Sector Women Workers and Need for Social Protection in the Informal Economy

Embroidery work is basically home-based work. Home-based work has a dual and contradictory character: on the one hand, as a source of income diversification for poor women workers and the emergence of micro-enterprises, the on the other hand, it is source of exploitation of vulnerable women workers as intermediaries/middle men attempt to contain cost. There is need for social security/protection of these embroidery women workers. There is great need for public action to promote such artistic embroidery work as a possible new labour intensive growth strategy in developing countries like India. According to National Sample Survey Organisation there are 30 million home-based workers in India and they are concentrated (around 70 to 80 per cent) in three sectors: bidi; insense stick (agarbathi) and garments (which include embroidery) manufacturing. Government of India, Ministry of Labour should engage itself in the formulation of a National Policy on home-based workers. Representatives of Self-employed Women's Association (SEWA) should be associated in formulating a comprehensive social security scheme for home-based workers (which include embroidery workers also). There is a need to prepare profile of embroidery sector workers of the state and national level. For embroidery workers, a Welfare Fund should be built up by the Government and embroidery workers should be given the following benefits at a minimum:

1. Specific health benefits, related to the nature of home-based work, including maternity benefits.
2. Scholarships for children to go to schools, college and vocational training institutes.
3. Old age pension,

4. Life Insurance,
5. Child Care Facilities.[12]

The story behind the stitches of the embroidery work is both a parable and a paradox; embroidery traditions are a unique mechanism for display of artistic work and creativity, it is also a new experience for a rural women entering the economic mainstream for the first time, but these embroidery doing women carry the stigma of inferiority and backwardness as India enters a period of hi-tech industrialisation, globalisation and privatisation.

Ramba Ben, a mirror embroidery women, who migrated to Delhi from Banaskantha (Gujarat) told the researcher that, "The lives of my family hang by the thread, I embroider." Some of her embroidery pieces are truly representing the beauty, authenticity, original creativity and spontaneity of the products. But what prices/ wage the embroidery workers get when they sell such pieces out of economic necessity. It is really an irony that embroidery as an industry and profession is done under primitive conditions without the support of pension, insurance, a fixed salary, medical care and even proper recognition in society.

Data from the National Sample Survey (61st Round) reveals that while women's employment has increased in urban areas, the new opportunities are of low quality and unremunerative, being primarily self-employment, home-based work at piece rate (applicable to embroidery work) or part time work in the informal sector.[13] Globalisation and economic reforms have adverse impact on real wages and a decline in the average daily real earnings of regular workers in both rural and urban areas, as well as a decline in the real wages of casual workers in urban areas. Data from the NSS (61st Round) point to the high level of income insecurity of women informal sector workers. An income of less than Rs. 2000/- per month is considered to be "remunerative" by as many as 30 per cent of women informal sector workers in urban areas, revealing the levels of unemployment and low expectations of women workers.[14] For all intents and purposes; informal sector workers are workers without rights. There is no legislation and no effective mechanisms to ensure minimum wages, working conditions, social security or occupational health and safety of women workers of embroidery sector which forms a part of the informal sector.

Embroidery workers are mainly in the informal sector and earn about 30 INR per day. Wages being determined-based on the type of stitches and therefore can vary enormously. Women get work through middle-men on piece rate basis for this arduous and time consuming work and this arrangement reduces their bargaining power and they receive far below the prescribed minimum wage. Since there are too many embroidery workers, who are migrants from Rajasthan, Haryana, Gujarat, Bengal, Orissa, U.P. Bihar and even from Bangladesh, they are generally exploited and given very low wages for their work. The vulnerability of women workers is clearly noticeable in the feminisation of poverty and the exploitations of women in low paid, hazardous and insecure jobs in the unorganised sector and in the export processing or special economic zones.[15]

Main Findings of the Survey and Research Conclusions

India is undergoing a phase of socio-economic change which has created a turmoil and "thousand mutinies" together in both rural and urban areas. Due to widespread urbanisation and migration of labour towards cities, they are becoming a conglomerate of cultures, with people from all neighbouring rural areas staying in the cities to find work and means of livelihood. First, one or two members of the family come and gradually all the others to facilitate their living as well as additional hands to be able to earn more to as to meet the expenses of a city life. The local population owns the houses and migrant workers live as tenants. Gender, caste, religion provides basis for social prejudices, creating structural barriers in percolation of development benefits. The problem of inequality and exclusion emerge as important problems into the provision of basic amenities like drinking water, sanitation facilities, housing and employment. The manifestation of inequality can be noticed in terms of access to education, employment, health facilities and social interaction. For bringing empowerment of women, following recommendations can be useful:

"(i) Establish specific mechanisms to promote and protect gender equity in recruitment and promotion of women in all levels and fields of expertise at the workplace, disseminate those policies and monitor their performance.

(ii) Recognise differential needs of female employees compared to those of men and establish women's entitlement to adequate material support without a cost to their consideration for recruitment and promotion."[16]

(iii) Ensure gender training up to the highest levels of authority and underline the importance of gender equity policies in the overall development policies of the country.

(iv) Establish affirmative action to encourage and support education of female students from Dalit communities and Muslim communities to ensure their fullest development.

(v) Various recommendations and suggestions as enumerated in the National Policy for the Empowerment of Women (2001) should be implemented by the State and Central Governments and the Judiciary of the state.

(vi) Education upto 12th class should be made compulsory for all girls with provisions for free books, free tuition fees and some monetary allowances to the girls from Dalit and Muslim communities-based on their individual cases.

(vii) All embroidery workers should become members of non-government organisations like SEWA which are taking care of their individual and group problems and challenges.

(viii) Training in embroidery for women/girls at least for a six month programme be made available so that they can learn the embroidery craft and get a diploma/certificate for attending the same.

(ix) Each embroidery worker should be able to indicate her name on her creation like a painter or a designer. They should not remain nameless and unrecognised.

(x) Embroidery is a rich traditional heritage of India in all its variety and design patterns. It needs to be conserved, preserved protected and encouraged.

Due to increase in machination and technology induction, hand embroidery is a dying or declining tradition which needs to be revived and master crafts women be encouraged by the government as well as exporters and designers. The researcher got an opportunity to visit Delhi Haat where two great embroidery traditions of Soof of Gujarat and Kantha of Bengal were represented. The crafts women said that since they could not get educated and learn computer they faced a major handicap in selling their masterpieces. Many markets and exhibitions were missed by them. The entire sales through *e*-commerce was denied to them. The rates of their work was not commen state with the effort and expertise they had mastered. Mostly their sales were sold with marginal profits which were often reduced by bargaining purchasers. There were no regular sales forums where their creations could be continuously displayed and sold.

The Delhi Haat, Suraj Kund Festival in Faridabad and exhibitions and trade fair at Pragati Maidan were successful experiments in this direction. Only limited crafts women could make entry into these coveted forums, largely denied to many embroidererers in far-flung areas of the country.

(xi) Each state capital must have similar market forums where traditional embroidery, handloom and handicrafts could be displayed and sold.

(xii) *E*-commerce sites should be created for selling these rich traditions of the country.

(xiii) At vantage tourist places and points embroidery of that state should be sold through cooperatives or self-help groups which should be networked and organised to work like an interest group. Group interaction and opportunities to form networks will enable shaking off old foundations of subordination powerlessness in embroidery workers. This will help in sowing seeds of much less talked about "preservation and encouragement" of embroidery.

Since embroidery is done by many home-based workers, they work in very sorry and severe conditions. There is lack of lighting, neat and clean environs and healthy and hygienic working conditions. In general, the overall situation of a woman of poor family on lower middle class in India has to change. Grassroots women organisations can play a significant role in process of empowering women specially with the help of information and communication technology. They can involve the local community in the processes of decision-making through the creation of a social space for sharing experiences that can be particularly empowering for participants. With ICT, they can work beyond their local and national territories to mobilise and lobby at national and international forums. ICT can involve action vertical and lateral action has that facilitate diffusion of information and strategies for action. The local self-help groups and cooperatives can have control and authority through which relationship between embroidery workers, intermediate organisations and markets can be channelised. The use of telephone is very basic in enabling first hand communication between participants and fastening connection with many more. Internet and T.V. and radio can often convert passive members into active participants and mobilise them to not only attend meeting and training programmes but also take interest to bring more and more participants in the fray, set group priorities and goals. As women become more familiar with other members, they can have collective interests which need to be protected. They have to negotiate for benefits, question the undesirable and protest and challenged unfavourable conditions designed at the top and thrust up on them.

Main Findings of the Research

1. Information and Communication Technology is a powerful tool for empowerment of women both as individual and collective entity. It fastens connection and communication between diverse women who recognise their self worth through association with similar others. The familial identity of Indian women inhibits her from responding to questions on personal welfare and identity. ICT enables them to develop a self-identity by merely possessing a telephone number which initiates a process of transformation of consciousness. Once a woman relates to a group and internalises that there is reformulation of identity. She sees herself as a worthy entity. This translates into action challenging norms that reinforce women's subordination.[17] It was reiterated by respondents that IT can be major agent of change. It has affected their lives directly by giving them an outlet for communication. The walls around them are no more impregnable as they can speak with any one with a phone. An old man in Khader village succinctly declared "My daughter is no more confined indoors even if I want. She can speak to a boy at the end of

road and plan to elope." Many women could not even read and write and had to be interviewed. They highlighted importance of mobile phone in speaking to their employer when in need of leave or emergency and contact their family members way back in the villages from where they migrated to Delhi to get a decent job for subsistence.

- There were mostly migrant labourers involved in embroidery mainly from Bangladesh, West Bengal, Bihar and U.P., Gujarat, mainly its Kutch region.
- These women have accompanied their husbands, who have migrated for jobs as drivers, watchmen, peon, salesmen and such lower jobs. They contribute an additional income to the family by taking work on piece rate depending on type of embroidery.
- They live mainly in rural part of the suburban townships like Khader to Sarita Vihar, Okhla and Shahpura Jat to Friends Colony, Kotla to South Extension in South Delhi.
- The big fashion houses were located on MG Road in South Delhi.

Recommendations and Suggestions

1. State-wise and nation-wide surveys need to be carried out to assess the status of women after the communication and information technology expansions in the last decade and how ICT can be used more effectively to enable women gain "control over material assets, intellectual resources and ideology"[18] thereby challenging existing power relations to strengthen their organisational capacity and crystallise visions and perspectives that will move them beyond their present situation.
2. Empowerment studies need to be conducted to know whether there is growth in women's self-confidence, in their knowledge of their rights, their willingness to participate in public action.
3. Information and Communication Technology is an important agent of change as it enables linkage and networking to an organisation or group. It is with the help of Self-Help Groups or Associations that empowerment of women can take place. Grassroots movements and women's organisations also play

an important part in the process. Using this empirical empowerment occurs most definitely when women mobilise themselves and take leadership positions in work settings, thereby become conscious of their power relations and decisions-making ability.

Like beauty, empowerment lies in the eyes of the beholder. Perceptions are very important. "This study of empowerment involves finding out what people think, and how they feel – or at any rate, what they say they think and how they say they feel. This kind of information is subjective. It involves feelings and impressions, rather then numbers" (Bellenger, Bernhardt and Goldstucker, *Qualitative Research in Marketing*, American Marketing Association). With this perspective in mind, the researcher focussed on the individuals rather than mere numbers. This study has limitations, like any other the researcher could focus on the NCR only and the sample of study was limited in scope. Due to practical difficulties and time constraints, the period of study had to be restricted to the period 2000 – 2005. However, the present opened the door to a new area of investigation and highlights the need for further research. The researcher has made an effort to understand the phenomenon of empowerment in the Indian context. The interaction of researcher with the subject (Dalit and Muslim women in the embroidery sector) brings a unique perspective to this study. It would be worthwhile for future researchers to make a comparative analysis with other countries/cultures, if there is scope for more indepth study from various perspectives.

Looking Ahead – Some New Proposed Laws

Empowering women by changing marriage laws and redefining sexual offences is the next big thing on the Legislative agenda of the Government of India. Some of the proposed new legal deals for women are as under:

1. The draft Bill on sexual harassment covers women in the unorganised sectors in educational institution, although there are no changes in Section 354 of IPC (Indian Penal Code) which defines assault to women with intent to outrage her modesty as sexual harassment, but the Bill enhances the punishment with reference to Section 509. The draft Bill

proposes to enhance punishment for the offence like eve teasing to seven years while leaving the larger offence of intentionally outraging the modesty of women unchanged.

2. The draft bill proposes to amend the Hindu Marriage Act 1955, and the Special Marriage Act 1954 by introducing "irretrievable breakdown of marriage" as enough ground for divorce and the six-month reconciliatory period is proposed to be waived. This proposed law will be detrimental for women as existing laws do not provide adequate financial security to those who are separated from their husbands.
3. The Ministry of Home Affairs is proposing amendment to the Indian Penal Code to widen the definition of rape to include sodomy and penetration with fingers or foreign object. This proposal is not enough as the proposal to raise the age of consensual sexual relationships from 16 to 18 years will make even consensually kissing a 17 years old girl a serious offence.
4. The Home Ministry is planning changes like death or life imprisonment under Section 300 of IPC to prevent honour killings, as also changes in the Indian Evidence Act. This proposal is not enough as complete overall cover for marriages across caste and religion.

Geeta Ramaseshan, Advocate Madras High Court has said "What is sought to be introduced has not taken note of the recommendations of women's groups over 20 years. This can lead to confusion, even in our understanding of a serious crime. Some women activists feel that the *Vishaka* vs *the State* landmark judgment gave clear guidelines in 1997, and recommended elaborate procedures against sexual harassment at the workplace. The proposed bill will cover sectors like the hospitality industry which includes catering services and restaurants, NGOs, health services, coaching centres, domestic workers, tailoring and beauty parlours and educational institutions bringing students and researchers into the ambit of protection. It will prove to be most beneficial to the poor women who work as domestic help or in factories and thus provide a platform for grievance redressal to the victim women.

Kirti Singh, Supreme Court Advocate says: "Easier divorce is fine but our laws of maintenance and alimony do not provide women and children the financial support they need. There is no law which gives a women any right in the assets acquired by the spouses during the time they lived together unless it has been acquired in her name." Some feminine activists point out that "divorce being achieved on irretrievable grounds means men may well continue to have the upper hand." B.S. Joon, Director Prosecution, Delhi Government has said: "The proposed amendments have their pit falls. The one dealing with divorce on irretrievable grounds weighs more towards men while that on sexual assault is harsh on them." Director and co-founder of NGO called "Kali for women" has said, "Legislations are always piece meal. Laws have to keep pace with the changing conditions. If we wait for the state to become gender sensitive in one go, we will be waiting for ever".

Political empowerment of women will come when the Lok Sabha passes the Women's Reservation Bill, which has already been passed by the Rajya Sabha, reserving 30 per cent of seats in State Legislatures and Lok Sabha to the Women. Government of India, U.P.A.-II, Government is waiting for a more conducive political atmosphere to pilot the bill. If the Women Reservation Bill is passed, a third of the available seats in national, state or local governments will be reserved for women. Let us see when the people of India change their mind-set and ignore their vested interests to bring this sweeping new legal deal to reality.

References

1. Sharma Kumund, Women and ICT: Communication Across Divides: A Key note address at International Conference on Empowering Women through information and Knowledge from Oral Tradition to ICT Vol. I, Pune, May 30 – June 8, 2003.
2. *Ibid*, p. 6.
3. Agarwal Ranjana, Women in Information Technology where do we stand: A case study, A paper presented at an International Conference "*Empowering Women through Information and Knowledge*", Vol. II, pp. 251-259.
4. United Nations Children's Fund, Florence, Italy – *Social Protection in the Informal Economy: Home-based women workers and outsourced manufacturing in India* – December, 2002.
5. Mehrotra, Santosh and Mario Biggeri (2002), Social Protection in the Informal Economy: Home-based women workers and outsourced manufacturing in Asia. Innocent Working, Paper No. 97 – Abstract.

6. Young, Kate, *Planning from a Gender perspective: Making a World of Difference. The Women, Gender and Development Reader,* Ed. Visvanathan Nalini, Zed Books Ltd, London and New Jersy.
7. Subramaniam Mangala, *The Power of Women Organising*, Rawat Publications, Jaipur.
8. Krishna Sume, *Women's Livelihood Rights, Recasting Citizenship for Development*, Sage Publications, New Delhi, 2007, pp. 32-33.
9. Jeyaranjan J. and Padmini Swaminathan, *Understanding Persistent Poverty in India*, 2005.
10. Mazumdar Mahalika, *Women's Right to Livelihood and its Positive Linkage with Human Developmen*t, 2005.
11. Subramainiam Mangala, *The Power of Women's Organising: Gender Caste and Class in India*, Rawat Publications, Jaipur, 2007.
12. Mehrotra, Santosh and Mario Biggeri, *Social Protection in the Informal Economy: Home Based Workers and Outsourced Manufacturing in Asia*". 2002, PTI.
13. Chandrashekar. CP and Jayanti Ghosh, *Women Workers in Urban India,* Macroscan, February, 2007 -<www.macroscan.org>
14. National Sample Survey 61st round 2004-05.
15. Government of India – Planning Commission – *The Mid Term Appraisal of the 10th Five Year Plan.*
16. Faranak Mraftab, *On Loan from Home, Women's Participation in Formulating Human Settlements Policies – in Women, and Gender Equity in Development Theory and Practice – Institutions, Resources and Mobilisation*, edited by James Jacquette and Gale Summerfield, London 2006.
17. Subramanian Mangla, *The Power of Women's Organisation, Gender Caste and Class in India*, Rawat Publications, Jaipur.
18. Batliwala, Srilatha, *The Meaning of Women's Empowerment: New Concepts for Action in Gita Sen et al*...eds. *Population Policies Reconsidered: Health Empowerment and Rights,* Cambridge: Harvard University Press, 1994.
19. Shah Natascha and Kallury Krutika, Nation – Women Bills, *India Today*, July 5, 2010, p. 21.

Index

A

B

C

D

F

G

H

I

J

K

L

M

N

O

P

R

S

T

Z